Nature's New Voices

Nature's New Voices

Edited by John A. Murray

Fulcrum Publishing
Golden, Colorado

Library of Congress Cataloging–in–Publication Data
Nature's new voices / edited by John A. Murray.
    p.   cm.
Includes bibliographical references.
ISBN 1-55591-117-X
    1. Natural history—United States.   I. Murray, John A., 1954– .
QH104.N27 1992
508.73—dc20   92-53030
                                                  CIP

Printed in the United States of America
0 9 8 7 6 5 4 3 2 1

Fulcrum Publishing
350 Indiana Street, Suite 350
Golden, CO 80401

To Tom and Marilyn Auer

Our village life would stagnate if it were not for the unexplored forests and meadows which surround it. We need the tonic of wildness,—to wade sometimes in marshes where the bittern and the meadow-hen lurk, and hear the booming of the snipe; to smell the whispering sedge where only some wilder and more solitary fowl builds her nest, and the mink crawls with its belly close to the ground. ... We can never have enough of nature. We must be refreshed by the sight of inexhaustible vigor, vast and titanic features, the sea-coast with its wrecks, the wilderness with its living and its decaying trees, the thunder-cloud, and the rain which lasts three weeks and produces freshets. We need to witness our own limits transgressed, and some life pasturing freely where we never wander.

—Henry David Thoreau
Walden (1854)

Table of Contents

II   West of the Continental Divide

Preface

Several years ago a man living in Delta Junction, Alaska, reported to state wildlife officials that there were some unusual tracks in the snow outside his cabin. A biologist was duly summoned from his computer station in the regional headquarters and sent out into the cold fresh air where all true scientists—like all true writers—belong. A day later the breathless explorer called his supervisor. These were not, he reported, the tracks of a moose, steppe bison, unicorn or any other indigenous, extinct or apocryphal ruminant of the subarctic. These were, he insisted, the tracks of a Rocky Mountain mule deer (*Odocoileus heimonus*). After further study and photographic confirmation, this amazing fact was unanimously agreed upon and announced to the incredulous public. A young mule deer buck was wintering on the Upper Tanana River about four hundred miles from the nearest polar bear. Previously the species had been verified only as far north as the Cassiar Mountains in the southern Yukon. Concerted efforts, involving a helicopter and rifle-fired anesthetic darts, were made to capture and radio-collar the intruder. The deer, however, would have nothing to do with this mischief. The last the defeated posse saw of their charge, he was headed west, bucking the snowdrifts up the Tanana River toward Siberia.

Good writers, like that now-legendary deer leading his species into a new country, take literature where it has not been before. They are happiest on the frontier, pushing the language over the boundary, exploring some new variation on an old theme, pioneering an approach that will confound tradition, seduce reviewers and delight readers. These writers pioneer the trails that later become highways, and their books are the maps we use to explore both human nature and wild nature. They create new rules by breaking old rules, knowing that only by taking risks—in form as well as content—can they create a work that will endure, for a work that lasts is never like any other work that came before. Edward Abbey's *Desert Solitaire,* for example, is strikingly different from Henry Beston's *The Outermost House,* which, in turn, bears little resemblance to Henry Thoreau's *Walden.* And yet all are classic works of nature writing, adapting the old Roman naturalist's calendars of Marcus Varro and Lucius Columella, which were derived from Greek prose forms, to the American experience. In keeping with these observations, each of the authors in *Nature's New Voices* shows us a new country. These writers also prove that we need not undertake an expedition to New Guinea in order to encounter nature and create a successful work of literature. Sometimes a new country is that old country waiting to be rediscovered and reclaimed outside our doorstep, whether we live in New York or New Mexico. Thoreau put it this way:

> We are wont to imagine rare and delectable places in some remote and more celestial corner of the system, behind the constellations of Cassiopeia's Chair, far from noise and disturbance. I discovered that my house actually had its site in such a withdrawn, but forever new and unprofaned, part of the universe.

When I began my undergraduate studies at the University of Colorado, Boulder, in August 1971—back then you could still ride your bicycle through the middle of campus—nature writing, as a literary genre, was not taught anywhere. Seminars could be found on Thoreau, the literature of the American frontier and the familiar essay, but the nature essay, like most of the nonfiction genres, had yet to be formally admitted to the academy. All that has changed. Today, as evidence of its increasing stature, nature writing is taught in one form or another, in English or Environmental Studies departments, at nearly every university and college. I've had the opportunity to teach nature writing, either as a literature course or as the module of a creative writing course, at three universities and have consistently found that the students were eager to learn more about the history of the genre and to write nature essays of their own. So popular are courses in this subject, which have become something of a cottage industry in higher education, that several years ago the twenty-thousand-member Modern Language Association, the professional organization of English professors, published a 191-page instructional book to assist teachers with syllabi and pedagogy in this burgeoning new academic discipline (*Teaching Environmental Literature: Materials, Methods, Resources*, edited by Frederick O. Waage [New York, 1985]).

Nature's New Voices, then, is designed not only for the general reader interested in learning more about the younger generation of nature writers, but also for teachers, students and practitioners of the nature essay. For teachers in particular, the anthology will be helpful in interdisciplinary environmental studies courses, field study courses, writing workshops, contemporary literature courses and literature seminars. Although several fine anthologies representing the better-known nature writers have been published in recent years,* *Nature's New Voices* is the first edited collection to feature exclusively the work of the younger nature writers; it will nicely complement the anthologies already in existence. *Nature's New Voices* presents readers with a diverse group in this respect, including nationally recognized writers such as Gretel Ehrlich, author of the critically acclaimed *The Solace of Open Spaces* (New York: Viking, 1985), and two winners of the

---

*See especially: Frank Bergon, *The Wilderness Reader* (New York: Signet, 1980); Daniel Halpern, *On Nature* (San Francisco: North Point, 1988); Stephen Trimble, *Words from the Land* (Layton, Utah: Gibbs Smith, 1988); Thomas J. Lyon, *This Incomparable Land: A Book of American Nature Writing* (Boston: Houghton Mifflin, 1989); Robert Finch and John Elder, *The Norton Book of Nature Writing* (New York: Norton, 1990).

John Burroughs Medal for Nature Writing, David Rains Wallace and Richard Nelson, as well as less well known authors who can expect such recognition to be forthcoming in the 1990s. *Nature's New Voices* has attempted to be as geographically inclusive as possible and includes writings from states not often represented in nature anthologies, such as Alabama, South Dakota, Michigan, Hawaii, North Carolina and Ohio. For the most part, entire essays have been used, so that readers can have maximum exposure to the various styles and rhetorical approaches. Also, this collection does not duplicate nature writers already found in other anthologies, whose excellent work would otherwise be represented here. These include Doug Peacock, Charles Bowden, Steve Trimble, Gary Nabhan and David Quammen, among others. Regrettably, I also did not have room to include the work of many other gifted young writers in this genre, and I would direct readers to the books of Debbie Miller, Harry Middleton, Alan S. Kesselheim, Bob Schacochis, Jeff Rennicke, Rick McIntyre and Linda Hasselstrom.

As with any edited collection, *Nature's New Voices* came into being as a result of the efforts and assistance of many individuals. I would like first to give special thanks to Annie Dillard, Ed Hoagland, Barry Lopez, John McPhee, Wendell Berry and Bill Kittredge for suggesting specific nature writers in their regions and elsewhere in the country. Their advice and counsel made *Nature's New Voices* a richer and more worthwhile anthology. The authors, their agents and their publishers have been exceptionally helpful at every juncture, and I thank them all; no anthology is possible without such enthusiastic support. I would particularly like to extend my gratitude to Bob Baron and the entire staff at Fulcrum Publishing, who immediately saw the value of this collection and gave the book their unqualified support. Whatever understanding of nature I have derives in large part from the courses in American literature I took from Robert D. Richardson, Jr., at the University of Denver a number of years ago, and I owe him, as do so many of his students, an enormous debt.

The dedication acknowledges the invaluable contribution to nature writing made by Tom and Marilyn Auer, editors and publishers of *The Bloomsbury Review*. For eleven years their review has helped direct readers toward valuable new books, particularly those published by smaller presses. In so doing, they have helped to nurture at least several careers. My heartfelt thanks to them. As always, I must express deep gratitude to my parents, for their constant encouragement and kind assistance over the years, and to my son, who is a continual source of happiness and inspiration. Finally, I thank Fen, whose heart has been a mountain.

J.A.M.
Fairbanks, Alaska, July 1992

Acknowledgments

Permission to reprint is gratefully acknowledged.

Gerard Gormley, "Orcas of the Gulf" from *Orcas of the Gulf*, copyright 1990 by Gerard Gormley. Reprinted by permission of Sierra Club Books.

Jan DeBlieu, "Loggerhead Rites" from *Hatteras Journal*, copyright 1987 by Fulcrum, Inc., reprinted by permission of Fulcrum, Inc.

David Rains Wallace, "The Softshell" from *Bulow Hammock*, copyright 1988 by David Rains Wallace. Reprinted by permission of Sierra Club Books. David Rains Wallace, "Ground Thaw" from *Idle Weeds: The Life of an Ohio Sandstone Ridge*, copyright 1980 by David Rains Wallace. Reprinted by permission of Ohio State University Press.

Rick Bass, "Sipsey in the Rain" from *Wild to the Heart*, copyright 1987 by Rick Bass, reprinted by permission of the author and Stackpole Books.

Conger Beasley, "The Return of Beaver to the Missouri River" reprinted by permission of the University of Arkansas Press from *Sundancers and River Demons: Essays on Landscape and Ritual* by Conger Beasley, Jr., copyright 1990.

Introduction

Although several important works of natural history were written before and during his time—from Griffith Hughes's *The Natural History of Barbados* (1750) to George Catlin's *Letters and Notes* (1841)—Henry David Thoreau (1817–1862) is traditionally credited with being the inventor of the nature essay. After a series of promising early essays, including "Natural History of Massachusetts" and "A Winter Walk," Thoreau produced the world's first unified collection of nature essays in *Walden: or, Life in the Woods* (1854). Thoreau lived at Walden Pond on some forested property owned by Ralph Waldo Emerson from July 4, 1845, to September 6, 1847. While at Walden Pond, Thoreau built a cabin with his own hands and maintained a large vegetable garden. The twenty-eight-year-old writer sought the seclusion of Walden in part to help process the death of his brother John, who had died of tetanus (lockjaw) after accidentally cutting his finger while shaving. *Walden*, which underwent six major revisions over a seven-year period, earned its author around fifty dollars in royalties. The only other book published during Thoreau's lifetime was the colossal failure *A Week on the Concord and Merrimack Rivers* (1849), which sold just a few hundred copies. When the publisher returned the unsold copies, Thoreau wrote, "I now have a library of 900 volumes, over 700 of which I wrote myself." Thoreau was not much more successful with the periodicals. One of the most famous letters in American literature is Thoreau's fiery epistle to James Russell Lowell, editor of the *Atlantic Monthly*, denouncing Lowell for changing a key sentence in one of Thoreau's articles:

> I have just noticed that that sentence was, in a very mean and cowardly manner, omitted. I hardly need to say that this is a liberty which I will not permit to be taken with my MS. The editor has, in this case, no more right to omit a sentiment than to insert one, or put words into my mouth. I do not ask anybody to adopt my opinions, but I do expect that when they ask for them to print, they will print them, or obtain my consent to their alteration or omission. I should not read many books if I thought that they had been thus *expurgated*. [July 22, 1858].

Thoreau is now considered one of the major American authors. There are currently twenty-five editions of *Walden* in print and dozens of doctoral dissertations have been devoted to his work. Almost as influential as *Walden* has been his seminal essay "Walking," which describes how once-powerful civilizations fell as a result of environmental abuse. Thoreau warned prophetically in 1862 that "the civilized nations—Greece, Rome, England" were sustained by "the primitive forests" and survived only as long as "the soil [was] not exhausted." Thoreau saw that wilderness was an integral part of civilization, and that as America diminished her stores of wilderness, so did she destroy the ultimate source of her power: freedom. In "Civil Disobedience" (1849) Thoreau argued that people have a moral obligation to oppose injustice through passive resistance, a philosophy he adopted from the teachings of Christ. Both Mahatma Gandhi and Martin Luther King cited the essay as a chief source in their writings, and the essay, together with *Walden* and his journals, have rightfully earned Thoreau a place among the world's authors. "He [was] as ugly as sin," wrote Nathaniel Hawthorne of Thoreau, "long-nosed, queer-mouthed, and with uncouth and somewhat rustic, although courteous manners." Ralph Waldo Emerson was a bit more kind: "It was a pleasure and privilege to walk with him. He knew the country like a fox or a bird, and passed through it as freely by paths of his own. He knew every track in the snow or on the ground, and what creature had taken this path before him." When Thoreau died of tuberculosis at the age of forty-four in 1862, Emerson observed that "the country knows not yet ... how great a person it has lost." Largely as a result of Thoreau's pioneering efforts in *Walden,* the nature essay is at the current time one of the most important nonfiction genres.

The three major themes of *Walden*—communion, renewal and liberation—continue to pervade the genre and are evident in the seventeen essays featured here. By far, the most prevalent theme is the first, communion, which involves the intimate sharing of the human spirit with the natural world. Naturalist Jan DeBlieu, for example, sojourns on a remote North Carolina beach for the opportunity to observe the miraculous birth of loggerhead turtles:

> The sand below was writhing with life. Tiny flippers appeared from all directions and sank beneath tumbling grains of sand, rising and squirming in a wild attempt to break through to the top. Heads gaped and stretched toward me as rivulets of sand poured down. I reached in and brought out four of the animals. Four or five more immediately filled in the gaps.

Similarly, Texas-born nature essayist and fiction writer Rick Bass, intrigued by tales of a small beautiful wilderness area in northern Alabama, joins a Sierra Club outing into the remote mountainous region. "Suddenly," Bass writes,

> we are in a canyon. I am beside myself with joy. Slick rock walls, sheer faces, wet with leaking springs; tall cliffs, like out West! There are dogwoods everywhere. The blossoms hang motionless over the canyon, and our boots fall silently on the thick carpet of fern and moss. There are huge leafy trees everywhere; it is like a drizzling rain forest. Thompson Creek sounds wild. There are felt-covered green

> boulders everywhere, the smallest ones as big as refrigerators, and we
> pick our way around them.
>
> The lure of the creek is irresistible. We will not stop until we get
> there.

In both cases, the authors vividly convey the excitement of encountering, and being transformed by, wild nature.

Elsewhere, novelist and poet Conger Beasley shows us a new side of the powerful Missouri River, which was once an open highway into the western wilderness, but has now been "dammed, diked, dredged, and drained to suit the needs of the dying barge traffic industry." Despite these unfortunate developments, the river is fighting back—while Beasley and a companion float from Atchinson, Kansas, to Parkville, Missouri, they see a beaver, long thought to be extinct in the area:

> The sensation was more than adequate, oddly compensatory for all
> the changes that time and human endeavor [have] wrought upon
> the region. ... As if in acknowledgment, more beaver boomed their
> warning signal. We laughed and called out to them. This time, I
> thought, we'll share the river together.

Like Conger Beasley, travel writer and English professor John Hildebrand notices much evidence of change on an outing through Hemingway's Big Two-Hearted River country, but still finds the moment of communion he is looking for: "With the one good brookie for breakfast, I waded back to the confluence. ... Scrambling over the trail, I heard a racheting song overflow the riverbanks as a kingfisher swooped upstream." Further west, in southwestern Colorado, forest ranger Ed Engle pursues the haunting song and favorite haunts of the elusive Western Nightjar with the same fervor that the Romantic poet John Keats once sought out and listened to the English Nightingale. After he leaves the mountains, "the poorwills [stay] with me, more like a fragrance that [floats] through my mind than any kind of exact image." Not far from Engle, nature writer Dave Petersen takes us into his beloved Colorado aspen groves, a realm he literally identifies with heaven:

"If heaven is to be found right here on earth, as I am inclined to believe it is, surely its throne room is the Rocky Mountain aspen grove." Here Petersen is treated to an epiphany—a mother black bear and her three spring cubs—which at once embodies and evokes the mystery and splendor of the high, quaking forests.

Both Frank Stewart and James Houston pay homage to the awesome beauty that is Hawaii, a group of tropical islands where exotic birds beckon from dark green forests and molten red rocks flow as if they are alive. Poet Frank Stewart's search for communion leads him to a "small grove of mamane trees," the habitat of the elusive 'elepaio bird:

> I knew the 'elepaio by its call before I ever saw one. I used to hear them whistling deep in the forest, often in the treetops. Later, after I'd seen the subspecies of neighboring islands—in certain places after searching a good deal, ... I still hadn't seen them in this grove. ... Then, one day my friend brought an inexpensive bird caller along on our hike and began to screech with it as we reached the grove. The 'elepaio came from all over; they swooped into the trees above us ... and finally landed, nearly close enough to touch. There are some mysteries you have to search for a long time, my friend said; others come to find you.

On a hike through Hawaii Volcanoes National Park, novelist and screen-writer James D. Houston learns to look at rocks, as the Roman Stoics did and as the Native Hawaiians do, as having life: "... they too have life ... each rock was once a moving thing, as red as blood and making eyes of fire in the night." Such is the power of nature to challenge belief and enrich life.

A second theme found in these essays is renewal, the rejuvenation of the fatigued spirit through contact with the regenerative forces of wild nature. Although present to a certain extent in all the essays, this theme is most evident in three selections. Gretel Ehrlich's essay comes to mind first, as, through the seasonal essays of *The Solace of Open Spaces*, she seeks to come to grips with the tragic death of a beloved companion. The Big Horn Mountains of northeastern Wyoming are a nurturing, healing presence in this book, quite literally holding and protecting the author from storms of the spirit as well as storms of the land:

> It's May and I've just awakened from a nap, curled against sagebrush
> the way my dog taught me to sleep—sheltered from wind. A front
> is pulling the huge sky over me, and from the dark a hailstone has hit
> me on the head.

One is reminded here of the essays of another American nature
writer, Theodore Roosevelt, who also traveled west—to the
Badlands of North Dakota—and started ranching after his wife
died during childbirth. "Space," Gretel Ehrlich writes, "has a
spiritual equivalent and can heal what is divided and burdensome
in us. ... Space represents sanity, not a life purified, dull, or 'spaced
out' but one that might accommodate intelligently any idea or
situation."

Naturalist David Rains Wallace seeks a different sort of
renewal as he reexplores the subtropical hammock near Daytona,
Florida, that he first visited with his parents as a child. Here the
author searches ostensibly for the lost innocence and wonder of
boyhood, but finds much more than that—an unexpected connec-
tion between himself and nature:

> I wondered if I might explore the hammock not only as a home of
> wild plants and animals but as a connection to my wayward brain.
> The brain is like forests in being diverse and multilayered. I'd even
> felt in the western mountains that the old-growth forests might have
> a kind of consciousness arising from complexity. Like my brain, the
> hammock was structured hierarchically, with newer, more complex
> things growing from older ones. Most mysteriously, brain and
> hammock shared a propensity for mimesis, for producing similarities
> between different things.

Bruce Berger's approach to the theme of renewal is also strikingly
innovative, as he meditates upon the deaths of cactuses, and
discovers a rebirth—the endless cycles of nature—even in their
annihilation:

> Cactus tell us nothing of what's ahead, any more than the death of
> a close friend: all they reveal is process, but process which retains,
> even in human terms, immeasurable beauty. Their odd green lives,

if nothing else, bring to consciousness our complicity in a mystery that becomes, even as we reject it, our own.

Berger sees death not as an ending, but as a reentering of nature, as a "kind of radiance."

The theme of liberation—which involves the sense of being disencumbered and quite literally freed from some internal or external burden—is particularly evident in the selections by Dan O'Brien and Richard Nelson. For rancher Dan O'Brien a trip across the West with his female peregrine falcon Dolly offers him the opportunity to escape troubling memories of the past:

> ... I pieced together the shotgun my father had given me. I ran my fingers over the chip in the stock and remembered the morning, twenty years before, when I had dropped it while trying to take it apart in the dark. The sharp pain in my left ear came back to me and I shook my head. It had been a terrible time; a time that would be nice to forget. But that was impossible because everything I was or did went back that far in my memory. It was really all that was left of my father, and in a way it had given me the *freedom* [emphasis added] to start moving. If I traced the genesis of this trip with Dolly back far enough, I would find the old shotgun.

Alaskan writer Richard Nelson seeks a wholly different kind of liberation when he takes to the stormy ocean waters of the North Pacific and begins surfing:

> I was thirty years old when I first encountered surfing, and I've pursued it intensely ever since, not only as a sport but as a way of engaging myself with a superbly beautiful part of the natural world.

Surfing enables Nelson to nearly leave his body behind as he races down a great swell:

> There is an electrifying sense of weightlessness and acceleration as I drop toward the bottom and twist the board into a hard turn that sets me skimming along parallel to the wave's crest. ... I strain forward to outrace the whitewater cascading at my heels, and feel like a molecule hitching a ride on a meteor.

In such moments, he feels "the immensity and power and fecundity of [the] ocean," and is, if only briefly, liberated from the constraints of gravity and mortality.

What will happen to the genre in the 1990s? Because nature writing is currently absorbed in its social responsibilities, it would appear the form is approaching its maturity. No evidence of senescence is yet manifest—it has not exhausted the idiom, become institutionalized, slipped into satiric self-parody, fallen into the hands of unskilled practitioners, been rejected by a younger generation of writers or lost its readership and hence the capital that supports it in the publishing world. If anything, the genre seems to be gaining in size and momentum; there are several thousand titles listed in *Books in Print* and more books are released each month. The sheer exuberance and optimism of nature writing have already gone a long way toward reversing the urban skepticism that has pervaded Western literature since the end of the Romantic Age; the resanctification of the Earth also reverses a trend of secularization that began with the Renaissance. Both forces reflect good and healthy changes in literature and society. Future literary historians may very well view nature writing as the major nonfiction genre of our time, and see it also as a vital force that helped to revivify lyric poetry, which had become increasingly antivernacular, and the social novel, which had become often antinarrative.

At its best, contemporary nature writing is capable of achieving the qualities of all literatures that endure: universality, a high level of craft, depth of feeling, stylistic innovation and personal revelation. Nature writers such as those gathered in this volume are more than interpreters and commentators, they are highly skilled artists creating with deceptive simplicity in a form that is not close to being exhausted. Since the times of Moses and Christ, the wilderness has been a place of vision, inspiration and insight, and these modern nature writers are descendants of the prophets of earlier eras. They are also political—in the tradition of Thoreau—and attempt to be critics of society in the best sense of the word. These writers are trying, above all, to transcend a cultural alienation from nature that goes back to the Doctrine of Dominion over Nature in Genesis 1:28, and to replace those homocentric traditions with the far saner biocentrism we have relearned from the original inhabitants of America. There are some themes, though, more important than issues of politics and government, and nature writing addresses these as well. Edward Abbey touched on these themes— faith, love, family, friendship, place—in one of the last interviews he gave before he died. "Writing is a form of piety or worship," Abbey observed. "I try to write prose psalms which praise the divine beauty of the natural world."

I

East of the Continental Divide

Nature was here something savage and awful, though beautiful, I looked with awe at the ground I trod on, to see what the Powers had made there. ... This was that Earth of which we have heard, made out of Chaos and Old night. Here was no man's garden, but the unhandselled globe. It was not lawn, nor pasture, nor mead, nor woodland, nor lea, nor arable, nor waste land. It was the fresh and natural surface of the planet Earth, as it was made forever and ever. ... It was Matter, vast, terrific ... the home, this, of Necessity and Fate. There was clearly felt the presence of a force not bound to be kind to man. It was a place for heathenism and superstitious rites. ... We walked over it with a certain awe. ...

—Henry David Thoreau
"Ktaadn" (1864)

Gerard Gormley

Gerard Gormley lives in Manchester-by-the-Sea, Massachusetts. He is the author of *Orcas of the Gulf* (Sierra Club, 1990), which relates the natural history of the killer whale in a manner similar to Victor B. Scheffer's *The Year of the Whale* (Scribner's, 1969), a book that won the John Burroughs Medal for Nature Writing in the year of its publication. Gormley proves himself very much Scheffer's equal in *Orcas of the Gulf*, as he produces a rich synthesis of impressionistic nature narrative and factual reportage. The book follows the day-to-day life of an orca pod as it migrates from continental slope waters near Nantucket Island into the Gulf of Maine. In this selection we are introduced to the family group as they swim south of Nantucket in the North Atlantic. Shortly we are led to a graphically portrayed "clash of the titans," as the orcas attack a herd of humpback whales. Gormley's description has all the power of a passage from *Moby Dick* as he skillfully relates the complicated, bloody battle of life and death that ensues.

Orcas of the Gulf
(circa 1990)

Mid-August. Over cobalt-blue water eighty miles south of Nantucket, Massachusetts, an albatross soared in the early morning light. Since sunrise the wind had been freshening out of the southwest, opposing the prevailing current and raising steep waves, but the weather was fair. Apart from a diagonal brushstroke of cirrus cloud far to the north, the sky was a flawless blue vault, the air so clear that the albatross could see waves crimping the horizon six miles away.

Pointing upwind when it wished to slow and examine the surface, swinging off the wind to speed up, the great bird followed a habitat interface marked by a change of sea color from cobalt to green. Now and again the bird swooped down to snatch food from a wave, then swung back into the wind and rose some fifty feet before resuming its zigzag course. Rarely did it need to beat its slender, ten-foot wings.

Twelve orcas came into view, swimming eastward over the continental shelf break. Like the albatross, they were following the habitat interface, but in the opposite direction. The pod's youngsters leapt from wave to wave. The adults maintained a more leisurely pace, boring through the eight-foot seas with fluid ease, their bodies straddling the troughs as they left one wave and penetrated the next.

The albatross turned and followed the orcas, but seeing no signs of feeding from which it might be able to scavenge, it soon swung back into the wind and moved out of sight.

The orca pod included two bulls, marked by their high dorsal fins and heavyset builds. Though not much longer than the cows, they were much stockier. One bull, a twenty-two-footer with scarcely a mark on his body, looked recently matured. The other was nearly thirty feet long and weighed eight tons. His back was laced with crisscross scars and pockmarks. Three bullet holes had perforated his dorsal fin, which was as tall as a man and came to a curly point. His sides bore puckered dents from tissue lost in accidents or fights. His teeth, the size and shape of half bananas, were darkened and worn. The gum tissue on the right side of his jaw was swollen as big as a seal's head. The two bulls seemed clearly related. Their dorsal fins were tipped with similar wavy hooks, and both bulls bore unusual gray chevrons on their left flippers.

Leading the pod was a twenty-four-foot cow at least as old as the ailing bull. She and he had identical gray patches behind their dorsal fins and similar white patterns on the undersides of their flukes. Her left flipper had a chevron similar to his, and her saddle patch and fluke patterns suggested kinship at least to the old bull, if not to both males. Her dorsal fin, a third as large as theirs, had no genetic tale to tell, but an old fisheries tag embedded in the base of her fin bore a 1919 date.

In addition to the old cow and two mature bulls, the pod included three other cows, two immature males, and four immature females, one of them a nine-foot suckling still showing the pointed snout and pink patches characteristic of first-year orcas. Soon her snout would round out and the pink would fade to ivory. By the time she was a year old, she would sport the same jet black and snowy white coloration as the adults.

Staying to one side of the pod, the old bull swam with his mouth partly open to cool his infected jaw. At one point he gnashed his teeth as if in pain, and the growth spewed bloody pus.

A cow drew alongside him and uttered a lengthy pulsed phrase that sounded like a creaking door hinge. As she sonared the bull's swollen jaw and tried to investigate it with her tongue, he patted her with his flipper, then gently pushed her away.

White bellies flashing, two young males corkscrewed underneath the bull, then together shot out of the water ahead of the pod and bellywhopped. They wriggled and rolled against each other, dove, and popped up on opposite sides of the pod. As they bobbed in the wave crests, whistling to each other, the younger bull slipped a six-foot flipper under one of them and upended him. Buzzing like a chain saw, the juvenile chased the bull and hurdled him. With amazing agility the bull did a snap roll and snatched the youngster out of the air with his great paddlelike flippers, then hugging him against his chest, completed the roll and pulled him under. Apparently in need of air, the young male struggled desperately to get free. The bull held him underwater a while longer, then released him, rolled, and spanked him hard with his five-foot dorsal fin. The youngster rejoined his playmate, and they resumed their antics.

As the pod entered an area where great currents were colliding, the waves became steeper and lost all semblance of rhythm. Rather than waste energy fighting the craggy seas, the orcas began swimming in a series of shallow dives, each lasting about seven minutes. As they swam, they simultaneously called to each other and probed the sea with sharp pulses of sound. Their sonar clicks picked up a school of hake far below, but they did not give chase. Orcas typically prefer not to dive much deeper than 15 fathoms, though if necessary they can plunge many times that depth.

From all directions came a commotion of natural and mechanical sounds, but the orcas' sharp sonar clicks and strident communication calls stood out sharply from the background noise, so they had no interference problems. Still, they often remained silent for extended periods, the better to take prey by surprise, or simply to assess various sounds for their survival value. Just now, for example, they heard slow cataracts of mud and sand hiss down along the shelf break 90 fathoms below and knew that the tide was ebbing from the Gulf of Maine. From 170 fathoms below and to their right came a *boing*, followed by heavy snapping sounds that told them sperm whales were down there, hunting squid. Deeper still and farther out, a submarine purred through the blackness. Listening through acoustic windows located in various parts of their bodies, orcas are able to monitor sounds from all directions without having to change course.

Overhead drifted a stray from the sapphire blue Gulf Stream, a Portuguese man-of-war, its body an iridescent bubble in the sunlight, its deadly purple tentacles trailing so deep that several orcas had to avoid them. As the pod surfaced for air, seventy saddleback dolphins came skipping along from the south, then sensed the orcas and swung back out to sea. Shortly afterward, fifty pilot whales rose out of the darkness, spotted the orcas, and went deep again without even taking air. When orcas are not hunting in earnest, many animals tolerate them to come close, even swim among them, but those included in the orcas' diet know when to stay clear. And this was one of those times.

The orcas had just returned to swimming depth when the old cow applied full drag with flippers and flukes, coasted to a stop, and hovered head down, listening. The others followed her example. The keenly alert old cow had detected a faint sizzle of turbulence as two large bodies sped through the darkness far below the pod. Judging by the bottom sounds that framed the racing whispers, the unseen animals were inside the shelf break. That meant they could be no more than 90 fathoms deep. A quick estimate of angular velocity, based on past experience, told the orcas that the creatures below them were reaching speeds of forty knots. Such speed suggested bluefin tuna or some other warm-blooded sprinter equally good to eat. Still silent, the orcas listened and waited.

The faint hiss of cavitation faded, suggesting that the animals had plunged over the shelf break, but soon the sound returned, growing louder and louder. Moments later a ten-foot swordfish flashed out of the depths ahead of the pod, with a large mako in pursuit some five fathoms below. The broadbill rocketed through the waves and soared twenty feet into the air, its purple-blue back and silver-gray undersides glistening in the sunlight. A second later the mako, twelve feet of driving muscle sheathed in iridescent blue and snowy white, burst through the surface and bared its long curved teeth. It seemed certain to intercept the broadbill in midair and rip out its belly, but just as the shark broke water, the swordfish executed a marvelous maneuver. Throwing off a great arch of sparkling spray, the fish jackknifed, pointed its sword downward, and plunged like a living harpoon. The three-foot sword rammed into the mako's open mouth and burst through the back of its skull. With a heavy slap the two fish struck the water, then rolled over and over, the mako snapping off teeth as it tried to bite through the sword. The combined strength of the combatants severed the sword two feet from the tip, leaving the mako permanently impaled and unable to use its jaws effectively. Massive volumes of blood billowed darkly from its head. It tried to escape, but brain damaged, could only swim in circles.

The orcas approached. Seemingly oblivious to them, the broadbill rammed the mako with its splintered remnant of sword. As the broadbill circled to make another charge, the young bull orca darted in and severed its tail, then the mako's. Neatly biting off thick steaks of firm flesh, the orcas consumed the broadbill and the mako, leaving only their heads to spiral into the depths, joined in death as they sank to the bottom. For all their great size, the mako and broadbill had yielded only a few hundred pounds of meat. Divided among eleven orcas (the suckling took little solid food as yet), that amounted to a mere snack for each.

A while later, again moving silently near the surface, the orcas surprised two eighty-foot blue whales that nearly swam right over them. Defecating in alarm, the whales took deep breaths, popped their nostrils shut, and sounded. By the time their flukes arched gracefully beneath the waves, the whales were making fifteen knots and were quickly working their way toward twenty. With scarcely a glance at the blue whales, the orcas continued on their way. Perhaps they were not quite hungry enough to take on such swift, powerful prey, for a well-fed blue whale that size weighs over a hundred tons.

The calf of that year, swimming safe and snug between her mother and the old bull, squealed and nuzzled her mother. The cow twisted her flippers, more winglike than the bull's broad paddles, and rolled onto her side. Still on the move, the calf pressed against her mother's belly and nursed. While the pod slowed to accommodate cow and calf, two juvenile females rubbed against the younger mature bull and excited him, then coquettishly avoided his advances. A juvenile male tried to nurse along with the calf and was rebuffed.

When the calf had drunk her fill, the pod resumed its original pace, about the speed of a brisk walk. The calf napped on the move, once again safely tucked between her mother and one of the bulls. For the better part of an hour the pod ambled along, staying generally over the shelf break.

From somewhere west of the pod came a cupped clap of sound. Still silent, the orcas spyhopped and scanned the area. They saw a minke clear the water and come down on its belly with a loud splash. The orcas headed that way.

Minutes later they came within sight of the minke, which was so busy feeding on mackerel stunned by its breaching that it did not sense the danger until too late. While most of the orcas spread out behind the whale, the younger bull circled wide ahead of it and doubled back. Frightened by approaching pod, the minke sped up and tried to go deep, but the bull was waiting. With a broadside body block that could be heard for a mile, he slammed into the minke and slowed it down, then seized its sharply pointed snout in his jaws and held the whale in place. Although the minke was twenty-five feet long, several feet longer than its attacker, it could not break the orca's grip. The minke went limp, then began to shudder and moan.

The rest of the orcas arrived, trailed by the senior bull, who merely looked on while one cow seized the minke's flukes and another sank her teeth into its genital slit and ripped open the skin. Then, while she gripped the flap of loose skin, the other cow and the young bull began to roll. They spun the minke like a piece of work being turned on a lathe, skinning it so neatly that it began to look like a freshly peeled fruit. As each long sheet of skin and subcutaneous fat was peeled away from the blubber, the orcas divided it among themselves, the senior bull getting first share. It took some twenty minutes to flay the minke, which through it all continued to shudder and moan. Surprisingly little blood was shed, but the surface all around became covered with a film of oil that formed rainbows and made water bead up on the orcas' backs. The youngest orcas watched the first part of the skinning process, then lost interest and began playing nearby.

The two adults who had been holding the minke shared the last sheet of skin between them, nibbled away the minke's lips, then forced open the whale's mouth and ripped out its tongue. Hemorrhaging massively, the minke went limp and appeared to lose consciousness. The orcas shared the tongue among themselves, leaving the rest of the minke, its blubber intact, to scavengers. Still bleeding heavily from the mouth, its flayed body glowing grotesquely orange against the dark depths, the minke sank slowly out of sight.

During the hour or so that the orcas fed on the minke, hundreds of sharks had been attracted to the scene. As some took exploratory bites on the sunken whale, the minke came to and made a feeble attempt to swim away, but then the sharks struck in force and brought its suffering to a bloody climax. Frothy pink bubbles rose and burst. Scraps of blubber floated to the surface. Scavenging jaegers mobbed the area, darting and swooping over the surface, fiercely contesting every morsel.

Slowly the sounds of ripping flesh became fainter and then inaudible as the orcas drifted back toward the shelf break. While the elders napped at the surface, the youngsters darted among them, chasing each other and anything else that came within range. The younger bull rolled belly-up and let the suckling calf ride on his belly. When he needed air, he rolled and gently dumped her to one side. She tried to swim atop his back and failing that, returned to her mother's flank. The bull moved close, affording the calf a snug space between himself and her mother.

When the shelf break was once again audible below them, the orcas resumed their eastward course, sonaring as they went. They soon began receiving strong echoes from a score of halibut that had ventured near the surface to feed. The orcas took air, went deep, and spread out. Without subjecting themselves to uncomfortable depths, they were able to dive below the halibut and herd them up against the surface, where the orcas easily outmaneuvered the frantic fish. The pod's two big bulls, despite their heavy builds and tall wobbly dorsal fins, staged an impressive show of speed and agility, turning tighter and tighter circles until their chosen halibut were caught.

Although the big bull had the look of a fading old scrapper who kept himself going on sheer grit, he was the first to catch a halibut. The catching proved easier than the eating, though. The hundred-pound flatfish was five feet long and half as wide, far too big to swallow whole, and the bull's infected jaw made it difficult for him to tear the flapping fish into pieces. The powerful halibut's struggles must have caused the bull great pain, for suddenly he flipped it over his back and struck it a mighty blow with his flukes. The halibut soared thirty feet into the air, hit the surface with a heavy slap, and lay there stunned. Four juvenile orcas shared it among themselves, then hurried to catch up with the others.

Moving sometimes in a cluster, other times in twos or threes, the orcas seemed to dislike doing anything the same way for very long. Now and then an adult surfaced and left a fish for a juvenile. All in all, though, pickings were lean for the next hour or so. As if swimming randomly until a meal presented itself, the orcas cast this way and that along the shelf break.

Outside the northeast shelf break lies a thirty-mile-wide belt of blue-green "slope" water, so called because it flows over the continental slope, where the bottom drops one mile in ten. Here cold currents from the Gulf of Maine and Nova Scotia are tempered by the Gulf Stream, keeping slope water temperatures near 50 degrees Fahrenheit year round and making the region a favorite wintering place for many species of fish and mammals.

North of the pod's present position lie Nantucket Shoals. Ahead, in sunlit shallows above vast submarine mesas, are some of the world's richest fisheries. Over Georges Bank, Browns Bank, and several smaller inshore banks, giant bluefin tuna and other

prime prey begin feeding in spring. By August of each year they
have fattened themselves into prime condition. It is then, between
July and September, that orcas are most frequently seen inside the
Gulf of Maine. They are not seen in the Gulf every year, though
they may be there and simply go unreported. ...

The orcas are about to enter an area of great mixing. Cold
tidal outflow from the Gulf of Maine, discharged through Great
South Channel between Cape Cod and Georges Bank, spills
southward over the edge of the continental shelf and collides with
prevailing deep-ocean currents and warm eddies from the Gulf
Stream. This meeting stirs the sea to great depths, mixing cold and
warm water with bottom nutrients and exposing the mixture to the
energizing effects of sunlight. The resulting vitalization supports
a tremendous abundance of life, while the diversity of habitats
along the shelf break fosters a great diversity of life. This general
rule—that habitat diversity seems to foster species diversity—is
particularly true of habitat interfaces such as the shelf break. Where
forest meets meadow, for example, you usually find a greater
diversity of species than in forest or meadow alone.

The air remained clear and bright, the sea spangled with light. For
miles around the sky was still cloudless, but far away a thunderhead
grew treelike on a dark trunk of rain.

As the orcas continued northeastward over the shelf break,
they felt the prevailing westward current joined by a colder flow
from the north. The upper waters began to swarm with sand lances,
short-finned squid, and many species of fish that had gathered to
prey on sand lances and each other. Picking off what squid and fish
they could without exerting themselves, for energy would be
wasted in pursuit of small prey, the orcas turned northward into
Great South Channel. Within minutes the water temperature
dropped from 65 to 55 degrees Fahrenheit.

The old bull opened his mouth wide and curled his tongue
to channel the cooler water against his abscessed jaw. He passed the
old cow, who had stopped and was facing northeast, listening to

something. The others doubled back and gathered around her. The old bull circled the pod and continued to cool his swollen jaw. The two immature males began butting each other and splashing noisily. With an outcry that sounded like the clang of a heavy iron gate, the old cow silenced them.

Several kittiwakes appeared out of the southwest and passed overhead, their wingbeats rapid, their flight path straight and purposeful. The old cow reared back with her head above the surface and watched the kittiwakes fly out of sight. Now a dozen greater shearwaters appeared over the southeast horizon, flying in the same general direction as the kittiwakes. From the south and not far behind the shearwaters came a flock of skuas. Three different species of birds seemed to be converging on a spot miles to the northeast. The old cow made a guttural sound akin to a gargle. The young bull repeated the sound, and together they led the pod northeastward. The ailing bull followed.

A five-mile swim brought them within sight of some thirty humpback whales, which were diving under schools of sand lances, then blowing great clouds of bubbles that drove the small fish to the surface and concealed the whales as they rose to swallow their prey. The roaring sound made as the whales released air underwater was similar to the old orca cow's guttural signal.

Kittiwakes, shearwaters, and skuas were feeding on fish spilled from whales' mouths at the surface. Just below the surface, a dozen giant bluefin tuna swam alongside the humpbacks to catch sand lances dribbling from the whales' mouths. Some of the humpbacks slapped the tuna away with their flippers.

One humpback detected the orcas and trumpeted a warning. The bluefin tuna fled the area at speeds approaching fifty knots. The humpbacks broke off their feeding and gathered in small groups at the surface. Nursing cows and their escorts protectively flanked calves that, though thirty feet long, were still nursing and quite dependent. The adult humpbacks' breathing became rapid and took on a wheezing sound.

The orcas dove and swam below the herd while the humpbacks remained at the surface, flippers and flukes curled inward to protect their underbellies. Shafts of sunlight, redirected by surface chop, probed the orcas' formation like flickering spotlights. Spiraling strings of bubbles formed by the sweep of humpback flippers and flukes sparkled in the light.

All at once the young orca bull sounded a chilling scream and flashed through the humpback herd, rushing one whale after another, passing so close to some that the tip of his dorsal fin grazed their bellies. As though swept up in the spirit of the hunt, most of the orcas followed the young bull's example. The water became clouded with the feces of frightened humpbacks.

Humpbacks are the slowest of the rorquals, toothless and seemingly defenseless, yet what promised to be a massive slaughter instead became a clash of titans. Bellowing and trumpeting like enraged elephants, the humpbacks lashed the sea white as they defended themselves against the streaking orcas. Flukes clapped like thunder. Flippers flashed like mammoth swords. And through this scene of awesome power the orcas—half the size of their prey—darted and weaved, screaming as they went, seeming to revel in the shrieking excitement as they whipped the humpbacks into a frenzy.

Meanwhile the old orca cow and bull, guarding the suckling calf, cruised well below the herd and gauged the humpbacks' reactions. It appeared that the orcas had hoped to stampede the humpbacks and pick off a straggler. If so, the strategy was failing, for the humpbacks were holding their positions.

Leaving the old bull to guard the calf, the senior cow recalled the attackers and signaled a change in tactics. Led by the old cow, the orcas began seizing humpbacks by the flukes, then darting clear as the various rorquals proved able to defend themselves. Moving in pairs through the herd, the orcas thus attacked one after another of the humpbacks. The rorquals suffered little more than deep scratches, for the orcas were merely testing their strength and mettle.

Then the orcas came upon six adult humpbacks gathered at the surface with heads together and bodies extended like the arms of a gigantic starfish. The circle enclosed by their heads sheltered three calves. In this formation the adults could breathe at will and avoid attack from above or ahead, while using flippers and flukes to protect their flanks and bellies. The orcas circled the formation and made feinting rushes, but the humpbacks lashed out with their flukes and repelled them.

Having completed one full circuit of the humpback herd, the old cow led her pod back about half a mile. There, at a signal from her, the orcas rushed a humpback calf flanked by its fifty-foot mother and her smaller male escort. The adult humpbacks began trumpeting and lashing the water white. It was remarkable how well the big whales maneuvered: they could swim forward or backward, wheel and turn within half their lengths, and whip their bodies into snap rolls that spun their fifteen-foot flippers like gigantic blades. Lashing out with their powerful flippers and flukes at any orcas that came within striking range, the two adult humpbacks kept the calf between them and defied their attackers.

Although the orcas outnumbered this humpback maternal group by ten to three (the ailing bull and suckling calf merely observed), five of the orcas were young and inexperienced. They tried to mob the calf, but with body blocks that sounded like big boats colliding, the adult humpbacks bumped them away and struck out at them. Colossal sheets of bubbles trailed from the humpbacks' one-ton flippers as they cut through the water in lethal edgewise chops. Even more dangerous were their flukes, which could strike above and below with crushing force or slash sideways with even greater speed and strength than the flippers. Although the orcas pressed the attack from all directions, they could not penetrate the humpbacks' defenses.

At a signal from the old cow, the orcas broke off the attack and left the area, but no sooner were they out of sight than they went deep and quietly circled back. When the humpbacks were once again visibly overhead, silhouetted against the surface glow, the orcas attacked silently out of the darkness.

The humpbacks sensed their approach, but too late. The young bull orca slammed into a calf and sank his teeth into its flank. An extraordinary clap of sound as the orca split open the young humpback's skin was followed by a gargantuan ripping noise as the bull spun and peeled away a foot-thick slab of blubber weighing at least a hundred pounds. The calf's blubber had separated from its underlying muscle tissue as cleanly as the peel from a thick-skinned orange.

Feces clouded the water, obscuring the orcas' vision as the humpback mother swung under her calf and lashed out at the attacking bull with flukes and flippers. The old orca cow sounded a loud danger call. Narrowly escaping injury, the young bull surfaced at a safe distance and settled down to eat. He was joined by the old bull and cow, with whom he readily shared his prize. The calf had been nursing for eight months and was in prime condition. Its blubber, which resembled stringy bacon, was apparently a great delicacy, for rather than wolfing it down, the orcas bit off ham-size chunks and seemed to savor each bite. While they ate, the rest of the pod attacked another trio of humpbacks.

Leaving the last portion of blubber for the ailing bull, the old cow and young bull went back for more.

Although not yet fully grown, the young bull was a formidable animal. He could streak through the sea at thirty knots, maneuver like a dolphin, and bite like a great white shark. As he matured, he would add another six feet and two or three tons and be a match for anything in the sea except perhaps a bull sperm whale. With maturity he would also acquire a bit more caution. Meanwhile, his cockiness sometimes got him into trouble, as was about to happen now.

Sounding a strident call, he darted ahead of the old cow and attacked an adult humpback that had become separated from the rest. The old cow and several others hurried over to help. While two cows seized the humpback's flippers and a third gripped its flukes, the young bull sank his teeth into the whale's genital slit and tried to rip open its belly. With a might born of desperation, the fifty-foot humpback freed its left flipper, which it swept downward in a vicious edgewise chop toward the young bull's back.

The old bull had finished the last of the blubber and was approaching the attack scene at the moment the humpback tore its flipper free. Seeing what was about to happen, the old bull accelerated from five to thirty knots within seconds and seized the humpback's flipper just before it struck the young bull. The old bull's momentum twisted the one-ton flipper safely clear, but the impact burst his abscess and dislodged two teeth already loosened by infection and bone damage. As he rolled clear and released his grip, sharp barnacles on the humpback's flipper lacerated his lips and tongue.

The big bull's charge threw the other orcas off balance, enabling the terrified humpback to break free and fight off its attackers long enough to reach a nearby group of other humpbacks. The orcas did not follow.

Bleeding heavily from his mouth, the old orca bull rested at the surface and gingerly flexed his jaw to make sure it was not broken. Then he used the tip of his tongue to probe his teeth. One was gone altogether. Another had been ripped halfway out of its socket and was sticking sideways into his mouth. Rolling and puffing in the swells, he prodded the loose tooth with his tongue and managed to push it out of his mouth. Blood now poured freely from both tooth sockets. Having no doubt put the worst of his pain behind him, after what may have been many months of suffering, he closed his eyes and rested. The young bull swam over and floated next to him.

The rest of the orcas made no further attempts to launch lethal attacks on the humpbacks. It may be more energy efficient to eat a fifty-ton whale than to chase down thousands of smaller animals, but even the most formidable predators must weigh efficiency against risk. Serious injury can mean death for any predator, and it appeared that the humpbacks in this herd were too strong and feisty for the orcas to make a kill.

Nonetheless, for an hour or more the orcas followed the herd, now and then separating some hapless humpback from a hundred or more pounds of its blubber. None of the rorquals was mortally injured, but many were left with wounds a foot deep and several feet across. The orcas fed primarily from the flanks, which the humpbacks had difficulty protecting. Little of the muscle tissue underlying the blubber was damaged. Some tried to force open the humpbacks' mouths to get at their tongues—which can weigh several tons apiece and are prized by orcas—but were unsuccessful.

At last the orcas left the humpbacks in peace and swam back to rejoin the bulls, who were now ten miles away, napping at the surface and calling occasionally to mark their position. The others gathered around them and went to sleep. Dozing in the current, they drifted back toward the shelf break.

Apparently too winded to dive, the humpbacks continued to wheeze and puff their way along the surface. Many left wakes greasy with oil and pink with blood. Some had lost hundreds of pounds of blubber. One would think that their suffering must be great, yet evidence indicates that a whale's blubber is fairly insensitive to pain. If so, the loss of a hundred-pound slab of blubber may be no worse an ordeal for a whale than is a badly skinned knee for a person.

After fifteen minutes or so, the humpbacks dove and headed northeastward.

A number of reliable observers have described orca attacks on minkes. In some cases, the orcas ate only the skin and subcutaneous fat layer. (This part of a seal, called *muk-tuk*, is relished by Inuit and polar bears.) Usually the orcas ate the tongue, as well. Sometimes all or most of the minke was eaten.

The minke attacked in this chapter suffered greatly, but this is not to suggest that orcas are particularly cruel. Lions often take hours to kill large prey, such as buffalo, and predation in general is a cruel business. As for orcas' habit of flaying whales, is it any more cruel than wild dogs eating the internal organs of a wildebeest while the hapless animal watches its own ordeal? And is either of these more cruel than a songbird dismembering a caterpillar and eating it alive? If we wince less at a caterpillar's demise, it is probably a matter of scale and whatever personal values we bring to these events.

The more sensitive among us may find comfort in the belief that prey animals go into shock and are spared the worst of their agony. We have no way of measuring another creature's pain, but the annals of surgery prior to the introduction of general anesthesia indicate that patients often screamed and struggled throughout lengthy operations. Many prey animals must suffer just as badly. For reasons unclear, nature has imposed cruel standards of suffering on its creatures. Imagine the pain wild animals like the old bull orca must endure when they develop severe infections or tumors.

Attacks like the preceding orca-humpback scene have been witnessed on three different occasions by Canadian biologist Hal Whitehead over Grand Banks, Newfoundland. The "starfish" defensive formation used by humpbacks was described to me by Douglas Beach, a biologist at the National Marine Fisheries Service in Gloucester, Massachusetts. About a third of the humpbacks seen in the Gulf of Maine bear parallel scars thought to be caused by the teeth of orcas.

By taking only a modicum of blubber from each whale, orcas are certainly conserving a resource, but it is unlikely that they do so purposely. More likely, they take what they can get with minimal risk. Orcas are not unique in their preference for tongue meat. Many terrestrial predators also regard the tongues of their prey as delicacies. Tongues and livers are often the first body parts eaten.

While resting on the move, orcas usually swim very slowly, covering only a few hundred yards on each long dive. Resting pods have been seen to enter tidal rips and be pushed backward for up to thirty minutes. Wild orcas appear to need only a few hours of sleep a day, most naps probably lasting ten to twenty minutes. Having no natural enemies, they may spend much of their waking time in a state of relaxed meditation, and thus need little in the way of sound sleep.

Assuming the narrative's events to be current, the 1919 fisheries tag (an artistic liberty) suggests that the old cow had lived for at least seventy years. Most reference books estimate life expectancy for *Orcinus orca* at thirty to thirty-five years, based on the counting of tooth layers and ovarian scars, but the validity and accuracy of these aging techniques have long been questioned.

Recent findings suggest that the life expectancy of *Orcinus orca* is equivalent to our own. In 1981 the International Whaling Commission's Scientific Committee concluded that the age of orca females at first pregnancy is at least seven to eight years, and that male orcas do not mature sexually until about sixteen years of age. It seems unlikely that males destined to live only thirty to thirty-five years would take half their lives to mature.

Michael A. Bigg, a research scientist with the Canadian Department of Fisheries and Oceans, who has closely studied the orcas of British Columbia since 1971, states that "the life span and ages of sexual maturity of the species are probably close to our own." Moclips (now known as the Whale Museum), a nonprofit research organization in Friday Harbor, Washington, has been studying the orcas of Puget Sound since 1976. From Moclips's studies and Dr. Biggs's research, it is estimated that female orcas in the wild can live up to one hundred years and that males can live from forty to sixty years.

All evidence considered, it appears that orca maturation and longevity correspond to our own. This, together with clannishness, may explain the species' low reproduction rate of four to five percent per year. In many parts of the world, men have been killing orcas faster than given communities can reproduce, and the animals may tend not to breed across community lines. In habitats where orcas have been heavily exploited, the species may be endangered. ...

Assuming that orcas of the western North Atlantic maintain extended families of the type found in British Columbia, the old cow in our story is probably the mother of both bulls, and most likely matriarch to the entire pod. In British Columbia, sixteen pods of orcas that live near shore year round have been studied by scientists since 1971. These "resident" pods number about ten to fifteen animals each and appear to be genetically isolated extended families with lifelong membership for all, including adolescent and mature males. While going their separate ways for the most part, various pods stay in touch acoustically over considerable distances, and occasionally get together to socialize or hunt.

Similar temporary amalgamations of pods may take place in the Gulf of Maine. Pods seen there typically number ten animals or less, but as many as one hundred orcas were seen in one group near Cape Ann, Massachusetts, within the past decade. The second-largest group reliably reported in the Gulf of Maine was forty to fifty strong. It is possible that the habitat hosts an unusually large pod of some one hundred orcas, which may periodically break up into smaller hunting groups. Still, groups larger than ten to fifteen are rarely sighted, so it seems more likely that smaller pods occasionally join forces to form larger ones.

Jan DeBlieu

Jan DeBlieu lives with her husband Jeffrey Smith on Roanoke Island, North Carolina. She grew up in Wilmington, Delaware, and has worked as a journalist for regional newspapers and national magazines. DeBlieu is the author of two books: *Hatteras Journal* (Fulcrum, 1987) and *Meant to Be Wild: The Struggle to Save Endangered Species Through Captive Breeding* (Fulcrum, 1991). In this passage from *Hatteras Journal*, which is a memoir of her life on the Outer Banks of North Carolina, Jan DeBlieu describes some of her experiences at the Pea Island National Wildlife Refuge. This refuge protects the nesting grounds of the loggerhead sea turtle. Following in the footsteps of such sea turtle aficionados as Rachel Carson and Archie Carr, Jan DeBlieu chronicles, through personal narrative and scientific explanation, the natural history of this fascinating relict from the Age of the Reptiles. At the end of the essay, DeBlieu focuses upon the young sea turtles hatching from their eggs on the beach. A few feet beyond, they face a gauntlet of ghost crabs, sea gulls and other predators. Once in the sea, the nets of fishing trawlers pose another threat. A week later, a major hurricane will further endanger them. Such are the enormous odds these long-enduring animals face in the late twentieth century.

Loggerhead Rites
(circa 1987)

One July evening just before dusk I stood on a narrow, gently sloping beach two hundred miles south of Cape Hatteras with the hope of catching a glimpse of prehistoric times. A southeasterly wind tousled the sea oats, and a calm surf with thin coils of foam rolled across a mosaic of footprints in the sand. Next to me Cindy Meekins yawned, touched her toes, and did a spurt of jumping jacks in an effort to wake up. Behind us were two pale blue, wood-frame houses with porches rimmed by short white railings, the kind of fusty, weatherbeaten retreats that tourist guides describe as charming.

The exclusive resort where I had settled in for the night could not have been farther removed from Hatteras and its gritty souls. An hour before, the yacht that serves as the ferry from Southport had taken me from a private parking lot to a private dock, where two suntanned porters in docksiders and tennis shirts relieved me of my baggage and escorted me up a gangway to a waiting tram. After four months without dependable water and lights, arriving on Bald Head Island was like being thrust into a foreign world where niceties can be taken for granted. But by the time I stood on the beach in the thickening darkness, I had forgotten the island's opulence and turned my thoughts to the activities of the night. At

9:30 I was to mount a three-wheeled, all-terrain cycle and embark on a search for loggerhead turtles, a species of giant sea turtle that once nested abundantly in the middle Atlantic and is now threatened throughout its range.

The sky was covered solidly with clouds, and occasional flickers of lightning appeared on the western horizon. Meekins, the island naturalist, yawned again, glanced at the sky, and frowned. "You may not have picked the best night to come," she said. "We generally run the patrol in any weather except thunderstorms, but if it gets rough it's less likely that the turtles will come in. You're almost guaranteed to see something this time of year, barring terrible weather. Let's hope this storm stays to the south."

Her words were disheartening. I had driven to Bald Head, the island that forms the tip of Cape Fear, in hopes of watching a loggerhead female dig a nest in the sand and lay a clutch of eggs. During the previous month I had helped the Pea Island National Wildlife Refuge run a daily patrol to check for loggerhead tracks on a thirteen-mile stretch of beach where only about a dozen sea turtles nest each summer. On several mornings I had found the tractorlike marks where a turtle had dragged herself across the sand. But I had yet to locate a nest. I knew I stood little chance of seeing a turtle on Pea Island, so I had decided to travel south to the most frequently used nesting ground in the state. Each year more than a hundred loggerheads lay their eggs on the beach at Bald Head between late May and late August. In mid-July it is not uncommon for ten or more two- to three-hundred-pound reptiles to lumber ashore in a single night. I had timed my trip to Bald Head for what Meekins predicted to be the busiest week of the season, and now a storm threatened to steal the show.

I dug my toe in the sand and tried to ward off a feeling of gloom. As the director of the island's turtle program, Meekins had given me permission to stay at her headquarters that night; I was not sure her schedule would allow me to stay longer. And if a front settled in, most of the turtles would probably remain in the surf until it passed.

Oh well, I told myself, I still might get lucky. If not, at least I had gotten to sample some new terrain. From the ferry an electric tram had taken me down a winding, washboard road past two pillar-trunked cabbage palmettoes and through a tunnel of live oak, laurel oak, and grape. The dwarfed, knotted trees pressed tightly against each other, clamping a hedge over the road. The forests of Bald Head are about six hundred years old—very old in terms of Atlantic maritime forests—and riding through them gave me the sensation of being deep within a maze. My brief passage into the culture of the wealthy began to fade; I imagined the tram winding me back to a not-so-distant past when Bald Head was unclaimed and undeveloped and giant sea turtles were more common on the beach than human beings.

Fossil records show that as early as 175 million years ago, the middle of the age of reptiles, a few species of giant tortoise developed the ability to survive in the seas. Some paleontologists believe marine turtle fossils from 90 million years ago, the time of the largest dinosaurs, may have been early species of *Caretta,* the genus to which the loggerhead belongs. Other scientists argue that the fossils do not show enough anatomical detail to be certain. But it is clear that sea turtles evolved long before mammals, and perhaps as long as 160 million years before man.

The loggerhead and five other species of turtle—the hawksbill, leatherback, Kemp's ridley, olive ridley, and green turtle— bred prolifically in the Atlantic before humans began harvesting their eggs and relishing their meat. Loggerheads, the most abundant North American species, once nested on sandy beaches from Virginia to the Caribbean. They were especially prolific along the Florida Atlantic coast, which still is believed to be the largest rookery in the world.

The nesting ritual of the loggerhead is utterly common but difficult to observe. Sea turtles normally come ashore well after dark and reenter the water before dawn. When a female turtle emerges from the surf, she crawls to the dunes, inspects the sand, and—if satisfied with the location—thrusts her front into a dune and uses her rear flippers to dig a round nest about two feet deep. A person who happens on her before she begins to deposit her eggs will almost certainly spook her back into the surf. Once she begins to lay, however, she goes into a trance; virtually nothing will disturb her until she has produced about 130 small, round eggs. She corks the nest with a lid of sand, rests for a few minutes, and returns to the surf.

Between sixty and seventy-five days later, the eggs begin to hatch. Bit by bit each turtle scratches out of its shell with a small spine on the tip of its nose. Not until all the eggs have hatched will the turtles begin to dig out of the nest, and then they will come in a burst. In the cool of night the sand erupts with life, and a company of reddish-brown hatchlings two to three inches long scampers across the beach. A substantial percentage are snatched up and devoured by ghost crabs and raccoons. Those that survive crawl to the water and duck under the breakers, where they can still be eaten by fish.

What happens next is a matter of some debate. Most biologists believe loggerhead hatchlings swim frantically for the Sargasso Sea, the warm, salty gyre that lies just east of the Gulf Stream and reaches more than halfway across the Atlantic. The gyre's northern edge is roughly on the same latitude as the mouth of the Chesapeake Bay, and it is bounded on the south by equatorial currents. To reach it the turtles must swim at least fifty miles and cross the Gulf Stream. It is widely thought they achieve this without food or rest, although some biologists argue that the energy provided by the yolk of their eggs cannot sustain the hatchlings for the entire trip.

Once they have crossed the Gulf Stream, the loggerheads spend their early years floating on huge mats of *Sargassum*, the bushy brown seaweed common in the open Atlantic. Often the mats are carried by currents to the east Atlantic, where biologists have found loggerheads that weigh between twenty and thirty pounds near the mouth of the Mediterranean. When the turtles have matured to a weight of about forty pounds, they ride equatorial currents back to the western Atlantic. Or so many scientists believe. The issue is debatable, because biologists have been unable to observe large populations of loggerheads less than three or four years old. Once the hatchlings plunge into the sea, they simply drop from sight.

Neither is it known for certain when loggerheads reach sexual maturity, although it is believed they mate for the first time between the ages of ten and thirty years. Thereafter, females become fertile every two or three years. In a fertile season a loggerhead female will lay four or five nests, and each time she must drag herself onto the beach. Scientists estimate that only one in every hundred hatchlings will live long enough to reproduce.

The reproduction rates were probably much higher before the widespread development of the southeast coast of the United States. Marine turtle meat was considered a delicacy by early American settlers, and turtle eggs, which have whites that do not harden when cooked, were used to make unusually moist pound cakes and breads. Hides were tanned for shoes and handbags, and the beautiful plates on the shell of the hawksbill were fashioned into tortoise-shell jewelry. However, it was not until the Florida coast was thickly settled in the 1940s and 1950s that the population of sea turtles began a precipitous decline. Turtle steaks and soups, always a specialty of the region, became increasingly popular in the 1950s, and bakeries began to market specialty products made with loggerhead eggs. At the same time, a wave of oceanside development severely decreased the areas where loggerheads could safely nest.

Despite an aversion to bright lights and developed beaches, turtles occasionally nest in the most populous areas, usually with disastrous results. When a loggerhead nest hatches, the young turtles instinctively make for the brightest horizon, which on dark, empty beaches is the starlight and moonlight reflecting off the surf. Before the establishment of turtle hatchery programs, beaches and streets in resort cities sometimes began to swarm with loggerhead hatchlings on still September nights. The hatchlings clambered toward the lights of restaurants and motels with resolute determination—even when turned around and placed in the surf. If they survived an onslaught by ghost crabs, the next day they were eaten by fish crows or they dehydrated and died.

Each year the number of nesting loggerheads on the Atlantic coast steadily decreased. Although no one is sure how many loggerheads live in the Atlantic, nesting surveys indicate that the number of turtles coming ashore to nest fell by as much as 75 percent in the thirty years after World War II. By the late 1960s southeastern states began to ban the killing of loggerheads and the harvesting of their eggs. Marine scientists began recommending that fishing trawlers, which accidentally catch and kill thousands of loggerheads each year, use nets with special doors that enable sea turtles to escape. And in 1978 the loggerhead was listed by the federal government as a threatened species.

Since the early 1970s wildlife biologists have started programs to monitor loggerhead nesting on federal and state preserves in North Carolina, South Carolina, Georgia, and Florida. Most of the projects are operated on slim budgets and staffed by students or volunteers who search for loggerhead nests and, when necessary, excavate the eggs and rebury them in areas safe from predators, encroaching roots, and high tides. Frequently the programs move the nests to fenced hatcheries.

The protection programs were heralded as a major step toward correcting the pressures of overfishing. Yet the earliest efforts unwittingly may have caused more harm than good. For several years some programs dug up nests and stored the eggs in styrofoam boxes that protected them from fungi and kept their temperatures from fluctuating. Wildlife experts believed keeping the eggs at a constant temperature of about 82 degrees Fahrenheit would increase the proportion that hatched. However, in the early 1970s a French biologist discovered that the sex of a marine turtle is determined not by the embryo's chromosomes but by the temperature at which the egg incubates. Biologists in the United States began checking the sexes of loggerheads hatched from eggs stored in styrofoam and found a disproportionate number to be male. They increased the incubation temperature of another group to about 90 degrees. All the hatchlings that emerged were female. The eggs kept above ground had been exposed to consistently lower temperatures than they would have been in sand—and the hatchery programs had produced nest after nest of males. If the practice of incubating eggs in styrofoam had continued, the species' reproduction rate might have dipped to an all-time low.

Ever since, the techniques for managing loggerhead stocks have been the subject of vigorous debate. Among North Carolina wildlife experts, Cindy Meekins is known for her adamant opinions on how loggerhead protection projects should be run. As I neared the headquarters of the Bald Head Conservancy program, I had the feeling I was in for a remarkable evening, turtles or no.

The wood-frame houses that headquarter the conservancy's turtle program are perched side by side on a dune far from the bustle of Bald Head's only marina and inn. To their west was a tract that would be developed soon, but for now the forests there were dark and quiet. On the island's eastern end, the largest trees stood leafless and brown, burned the previous fall by the salty rain of Hurricane Diana.

Meekins had been waiting at one of the houses. Round-faced and blue-eyed with short blond hair, she is thin and feminine, but with a solidness that comes from years of strenuous outdoor work. Frequently she slips into the precise, formal manner of speaking common among scientists. On Bald Head she is known as the turtle lady, a nickname that seems too flippant, given the force of her personality.

In 1982, while completing a master's degree in coastal biology at the University of North Carolina at Wilmington, Meekins took a seasonal job with the Nature Conservancy to establish a loggerhead protection program on the Bald Head beach. To accomplish the task she was given a three-wheeled Honda cycle with wide, studded tires, a stack of data sheets, and a drafty, cramped trailer for quarters. From the beginning of nesting season in late May until the end of hatching in late September, she rode the beach alone all night, every night. In the next three years she built the largest and best-funded of the seven loggerhead programs in the state.

Since 1984 Meekins's year-round salary has been paid by the nonprofit Bald Head Conservancy, and each summer she hires three college interns to conduct the nightly patrols she once ran alone. The students live dormitory-style in one of the blue houses. Meekins works seventy-plus hours a week on public relations, administrative chores, and escorting Bald Head residents on nightly hikes to look for nesting turtles. In the winter she compiles nest data, attends conferences, and prepares for the coming season.

I had dropped my pack next to the guest bed in Meekins's room and wandered to the living room to find her reclined in a deep chair. "It's hard to get a full night's sleep this time of the year," she sighed, "but it's also a very exciting time. Strangely enough, we've had a high proportion of false crawls the past couple of days, and no one is sure exactly why." In a false crawl the turtle returns to the surf without depositing her eggs.

"Does it have anything to do with the phase of the moon?" I asked. I had heard that turtles nest in greater numbers when the moon is full. Only a sliver would rise that night.

"That's an old wives' tale. There's absolutely no validity to it," Meekins replied. "There are lots of misconceptions like that about turtles. But at least people are interested in them now, and that's a great improvement from my first year here. The cottage owners were completely in the dark; so were the developers. By and large the people we've dealt with since then have been tremendous. But it's taken some work to get things to a manageable point."

Almost all the nests are moved, she added, because erosion has drastically narrowed the beach. If left alone the nest cavities would almost certainly flood in high tides. The interns patrol twelve miles of coastline. Nests found within the five-mile stretch that lies inside a state park are moved to nearby dunes, but nests laid on private beaches are taken to a hatchery surrounded by a wood-and-chicken-wire frame.

The interns work as speedily as possible to reduce the mortality rate. Just after an egg is laid, the embryo floats to the top and attaches itself to the shell with a thin filament. If the egg is turned over, the embryo will be crushed. "It's thought that the embryos are free-floating only for the first six hours. That's spelled out in the handbook we use," Meekins said.

I asked whether moving most of the eggs to the hatchery might produce a disproportionate number of females or males.

"You have to remember that eggs laid early in the season are going to incubate at different temperatures than the ones laid in late July," Meekins replied. "As far as we can determine, we are getting enough temperature flux to ensure some variation in sex typing. Of course, ninety percent of our turtles may be male. That's the pattern up here at the northern end of their range. In Florida many more of the hatchlings are female."

She stood up suddenly and stretched her hands toward the ceiling in a gesture that emphasized her strength. "I've got to wake up," she said. "Want to see the beach before it gets pitch dark?"

The temperature was dropping. As I looked east across the water, the breeze grew stronger and the night began to smell of rain. Meekins finished her jumping jacks and slapped her arms against her sides. "I hope I don't have any smart alecks on the turtle walk tonight," she said. "One reason we have to be so strict with regulations is that this beach is going to be used with increasing frequency as the island is developed. We've already had some problems this year with people scaring turtles back into the water before they've nested. There are a few people every year who refuse to go by the rules. But we're just not going to tolerate it.

"Records show turtles used to nest in Virginia, which means their range has already decreased by an entire state. We think the decrease was caused mostly by development and a decline in the turtle population. That's why the Bald Head Conservancy is so determined that development here be managed. The bottom line is that we are going to preserve the beach for turtles. If that means we have to pass an ordinance restricting people from coming on the beach at night, we'll do that. And whatever other measures it takes."

I was to ride that evening with Jennifer Bender, a twenty-two-year-old intern from Norlina, North Carolina, who had graduated from Wake Forest in June with a bachelor's degree in biology. Bender was large-boned and strong, with a manner of speaking that was light and full of humor. She had also worked with the program the previous summer. At 9:25 we donned raincoats and long pants, then sprayed our wrists and necks with insect repellent. Two other interns, Kim Vanness and George Kosko, were to take a second three-wheeler.

We pulled out onto a narrow paved road, my back against the wooden box that contained stakes, wire, and a wooden rod used to probe the sand for air pockets surrounding the eggs. The Honda's red headlight barely illuminated the road. Loggerhead eyes do not detect red light, so the interns had covered the lamp with a filter. From my position in back of Bender it seemed that the darkness had softened and shrunk in dimension. The butterflies in my stomach were inexplicable.

In front of us the scarlet beam from the other cycle bounced off the dunes. We passed the boxlike enclosure of wood and wire mesh that formed the hatchery and rode onto the beach.

"You're bound to see something tonight, even if it's only a false crawl," Bender said over her shoulder as she turned the cycle south toward the tip of Cape Fear. "I'll be surprised, though, if those two turtles that came in last night don't come up and nest immediately. You know they're out there, just waiting for the conditions to be right." I glanced toward the surf, which was calm and lit with pale blue-green phosphorescence. Without warning, Bender released the throttle and let the cycle glide to a stop. Before us was a set of deep slashes in the sand that led straight toward the dunes but doubled back in a meandering path. "I'd have stopped earlier if I'd only seen one set of tracks," Bender said, "but there she goes." A dark, oblong lump moved across the sand near the tide. We got off the cycle and silently approached from behind. The cumbersome animal paused, aware of our presence but presumably too tired to lunge into the waves. In the red flashlight beam her shell appeared black and lusterless. I stood close behind her, afraid to move lest I should scare her more.

"Go ahead and touch her," Bender said. I leaned over and placed my hand gingerly on her smooth, cool shell. She slid forward a few feet, then stopped. Bender followed her and wiped her hand across the crest of the shell, creating a swath of phosphorescent sparks. "These aren't particularly bright," she said. "Sometimes you can write your name in them." The turtle shoved herself forward with her flippers and disappeared into the surf.

"Off to a good start, even though it was just a false crawl," Bender said, remounting the bike. "Some people ride almost all night and don't see that much." I realized I had been holding my breath. Having convinced myself I would not see a turtle, the encounter had rendered me speechless. Bender turned the bike up the beach toward the dunes and traced the tracks. "That's so we know we've already checked it out. It gets confusing if we don't run over the tracks as soon as we find them."

"Was that one of the same turtles that came in last night?"

"There's no way to know, but probably. She's got to be ready to nest."

We rounded the island's southeast point and drove west toward the Bald Head Inn and the Cape Fear River. The beach rose and dipped in red ridges before us. Peering into the soft night, I barely had time to brace myself for jars and bumps. Lightning continued to flicker on the south horizon, and the air grew moist. We had ridden for more than an hour when we came upon the other cycle parked next to a single set of tracks. Vanness and Kosko stood near a thicket of brush beside a large loggerhead that had thrust itself into the brambles. "Hey, Jen, look at this big mamma," Kosko called.

We scrambled off the bike and up the beach. "Good Lord, that's the biggest I've seen in a while," Bender said. And indeed the turtle looked much larger than I had expected. Vanness had measured her shell length at forty-five inches. Patches of a thick, mosslike algae coated portions of her back, and flesh protruded in great pink folds from the bottom of her shell. Her flippers and neck were scaly, rough, and darkly blotched. A liquid the consistency of honey dripped from her eyes. "Those are the tears they use to keep sand out of their eyes and to excrete salt," Kosko said. "She's really crying." The turtle emitted a low groan. "Did she nest?" I asked.

"Yep. She's all through. See that depression?" I turned to see a shallow hollow about five feet by five feet. "The eggs are in there somewhere. Luckily we saw her just as she was finishing up, so we have a pretty good idea of where they are." The turtle groaned again and began moving toward the surf. At the back of her shell I could see a wide, fleshy stump of a tail. She moved her flippers alternately but quickly so that it looked like she was wriggling—if an animal with a carapace can wriggle.

Vanness and Kosko had already begun scooping out a hole in the shallow depression. Gnats swarmed in my eyes and nose, and I pulled up the hood of my jacket. Within minutes Kosko had located the eggs. He pulled two of them out and plopped them into my hand. Round and white, they were no greater than three inches in diameter, the size of Ping-Pong balls. One dented under the pressure from my thumb. "Don't worry," Bender said, seeing my sheepish look. "A lot of them give like that. It doesn't hurt the embryo's development."

It was time to continue our patrol. I positioned myself on the cycle and readied myself for a long ride. I had begun to fear that my chances of seeing a turtle at her nest were growing slimmer with each passing hour. I began scanning the waves. The phosphorescence in the foam had intensified. With the blue of the lightning to the west, the glowing waves to the east, and the wide beam of our diffused red light, the night was cast in two muted, jarring hues. We crested a ridge and Bender stopped.

"Aha," she said. "I see tracks going up, but there's none coming back."

Halfway up the dune I could see a dark shape. I got off the bike with the intention of walking toward it, but Bender cautioned me back. "Right now's a real critical time, because if you approach her before she starts laying she's likely to go back into the surf."

We leaned against the cycle, and I slapped a mosquito that had landed on my cheek. "Buggy tonight," Bender said. Overhead the lightning grew brighter, but no thunder sounded. I eyed the lump in the sand. It appeared to be moving to the north, parallel with the dune. Finally it stopped and I stood up, restless.

"Let's do it," Bender said.

She grabbed her flashlight and walked slowly toward the dark shape, but veered south well before she reached it. "Look at this," she groaned over her shoulder, "look at this. We've been watching a bush." To her left a turtle was positioned over the hole that formed her nest. To her right and farther up the dune was the shape we had been watching—a clump of myrtle.

"But it moved," I said.

"We just thought it moved. This red light can do funny things to your eyes."

We crouched in back of the turtle. Pure white barnacles that glistened with phosphorescence were strung down her shell like uneven strands of pearls. Through a gap between the animal's belly and the opening to the nest, we could look inside at the wet, round eggs. The turtle sighed a hard, raspy breath, curled up her back flippers, heaved her shell, and produced three eggs. She flattened her flippers, curled them again, and pushed out two more. The gap was about five inches wide, plenty wide enough for a person to reach inside. I remembered reading that raccoons had been known to steal turtle eggs as they were being laid. I watched closely as more eggs squeezed out. This was a sight from the archives of evolution, a sight too precious to be lightly forgotten. The sides of the nest were round and damp, and I could see scrapings where the turtle had pushed away the sand. Eggs fell from her in pairs and landed with a plop, forming a neat stack in the cavity's middle.

I put my hand on the turtle's shell. Unlike the larger animal we had seen earlier, her shell was clean of algae and sand. "She's an old girl," Bender said softly. "See how her shell is more dome-shaped than the others? That's usually a sign of age."

I walked around to the turtle's side and trained the red light on her eye, which stared straight ahead, unblinking and dull. She had thrust herself half into a dune, which had crumbled around her. Her front flippers and large, flat head rested on a shelf of sand. Her mouth was a jagged, tightly closed line. Loggerheads feed on crabs, jellyfish, and seaweeds, and their powerful jaws can crack a horseshoe-crab shell in a single bite. To me, the mouth looked no more oversized than the rest of the beast. She let out a hard, grating breath. Her eye moved; her left back flipper scooped a lump of sand into the hole. "She's done," Bender said.

I walked back for a last look at the heap of eggs. Bender moved into the dunes to search for a spot to relocate the nest. Carefully, laboriously, the loggerhead shoved sand into the cavity with her back flippers, shifting her body from side to side with each swipe. She dug her front flippers deeper into the sand, presumably to keep from sliding down the dune. The motions were tediously slow; for me, knowing we would dig up her work within minutes of her return to the surf, the process was painful to watch. I flipped off my flashlight and sat down. The turtle heaved with another deep sigh and began breathing loudly, but with a more regular rhythm. The sound was harsh and resonant, like the sound of breath through a snorkel tube. Pulses of lightning outlined her shell. The irregular flashes tinted the seeds of the grasses, the ridges in the sand, the ghostly foam of the surf. We were miles from civilization, miles from anything resembling modern time. Without warning, she moved her front flippers, smearing sand over the area to camouflage the location of her eggs. Finished, she rested and sighed.

I followed three yards behind when she finally turned and began crawling back toward the water. Bender, strolling by with the tools she would use to move the nest, pulled a tape measure from her pocket and strung it across the turtle's carapace from front to back, then from side to side. "Thirty-seven by thirty-two," she said. "What you have here is a Joe-typical turtle." The turtle resumed her laborious crawl, stopping every ten feet. The resonant breathing continued. She moved faster as she neared the water, pausing a final time as the first wave hit her, raising her head and remaining motionless for thirty seconds, maybe longer. I could still see her when the second wave broke over her shell, but by the third wave she was gone.

Bender had begun to dig with her hands when I climbed back up the beach to the nest. "This sand is full of oyster shells, which really makes it hard to feel for the eggs," she said. "Geez, if we hadn't seen this turtle laying, we might have been here looking for the eggs all night." She dug with her hands for several more

minutes, until she uncovered the small, moist balls. Before extract-
ing them she lined the bottom of a plastic ice cooler with sand from
the nest. "Whenever we relocate eggs we always include a little of
the sand from the original nest," she explained. "I don't think
anyone knows for sure if it makes a difference, but it's something
we like to do."

The eggs were closely packed, and Bender could bring out
three and four at a time. I put my hand into the nest cavity and
cautiously pulled out two eggs. They were covered with sand and
a transparent liquid. "You need to handle them carefully," Bender
said, "but remember that she dropped them down two feet into the
nest. They're not as brittle as chicken eggs." Together we extracted
seventy-eight eggs, an unusually small number. After Bender
measured the nest's dimensions, I felt the rounded walls of the
cavity with my hands and was surprised to find the air inside moist
and warm, as if it had been heated by someone's breath.

We carried the cooler up a small dune to a flat area that
seemed well out of reach of the tide. "This is the part that makes
me nervous," Bender said, "because I feel a tremendous responsibility to make sure the eggs are in a safe spot." She began scooping
out sand to form a pear-shaped cavity twenty-three and a half
inches deep and twelve inches in diameter—the exact size of the
original nest. She arranged the eggs inside, packed sand over the
top, and covered the sand with a wire netting with openings large
enough to allow hatchlings to crawl through but small enough to
keep out foxes and raccoons. I marked a stake with the numerals
167, the number of the crawl, and inserted it into the dune.

The lightning had intensified by the time we had loaded the
gear back on the cycle and resumed our patrol. "Time for a
midnight break," Bender said, flagging down Vanness and Kosko.
We drove to the beach in front of the blue houses and went inside
for snacks.

The kitchen's fluorescent light irritated my eyes. Squinting
and sniffling from the breeze, Vanness tore open a package of
Lorna Doones, a delicacy someone had brought back from town.
We had just consumed our first cookies when the wind gusted with

a ferocity that sent us scrambling to close windows and doors. Shutters banged against the side of the house, and within minutes the sky began to throb with blue light that leaped and spread like the flickering of fire. Thunder cracked nearby, and we heard the approaching roar of rain. It hit the house in a burst, pouring over the gutters in thick streams and seeping through the windows on the southern wall. The atmosphere pulsed with light; it seemed that there was more electricity than darkness in the sky. Any thoughts of continuing the patrol had been banished. All we could do was hope instinct and fright would keep the turtles off the beach.

I could not help thinking of the fury of that night two months later as I boarded the ferry for a second trip to Bald Head. The thinly overcast dome seemed a pallid version of the lightning-filled sky that had driven us from the beach. The air was damp and limp.

The hatching season was at its peak, but the interns had gone back to school. Instead of riding the beach all night to watch for loggerheads erupting from the sand, I would join Meekins on her nightly check of the hatchery at 9:30. If none of the nests in the enclosure happened to be ready to hatch I was out of luck. And even if some of the clutches had broken out of their eggs, the turtles would not catapult through the sand covering the nest. As we waited for dusk, Meekins explained that for some reason most of the nests in the hatchery had developed pockets of air at the top of the cavities. When the hatchlings were ready to dig out, they could not reach the sand overhead. To compensate for the problem, she had started opening nests by hand after the eggs had incubated for seventy days.

"Usually if I just stick my hand down four or five inches—not enough to disturb the eggs, if they haven't hatched—I can see a head or two," Meekins said. "Then they all come pouring out. It looks like we may have built the hatchery on an overwash fan. The sand is very coarse, and that may have affected the way the nests held their shape. The nests in the state park are hatching out with no problems."

I had half-hoped to be able to see the hatchlings from the eggs laid by 167, the number assigned to the turtle that had nested as I watched. But barely sixty days had passed since that visit, and a nest laid by turtle 127 had hatched only the night before. "We're almost halfway through," Meekins said. "Every time a turtle makes a crawl, we give her a number. We had more than two hundred crawls and a hundred and thirty-three nests, a few more than last year. We thought we had a hundred and thirty-one, but the interns missed two nests that were laid near the inn."

Since Meekins and the interns hadn't known about the nests, they were surprised when someone called to tell them baby loggerheads were crawling in the roads, the yards, and the marshes near the inn. "They were everywhere, even back in some of the freshwater ponds. People helped us collect them as fast as they could. I have no idea how many there were. That's what it would be like all the time if we didn't run this program. Absolute chaos."

It was time to go. A quarter-mile off the beach a trawler rocked with its outriggers extended in a wide V. "There's the enemy," Meekins said. She was not joking. Most of the fishermen I knew scoffed at the notion that the species needs federal protection, because loggerheads are still common sights in south-eastern waters; the turtles chew up crab pots and rip holes in fishing nets, and many fishermen would welcome a decrease in their numbers. As I mounted the Honda behind Meekins, I was surprised to see the headlight shining white against the trees. "I just ripped the red cover off one day," she said. "We don't need it anymore. We even use a white flashlight to lure the turtles down to the water."

There were no sightseers at the hatchery to witness the night's release of baby turtles. As Meekins opened the pen door, she shined her flashlight around the edges in a search for hatchlings and tracks. The short wooden stakes that marked the nests gave the pen the look of a cemetery. A hundred yards to the east I could see that the phosphorescent waves were even brighter than on my previous trip. "Any activity in here?" Meekins asked, stepping into the pen. "Aha. I see some tracks. There he is. ..." A dull brown turtle three inches in length crawled toward the beam of her light. She scooped up the animal and handed it to me. Cool and smooth, it wriggled in my hand. Its flippers moved alternately as it tried to skitter across my palm, but when I held it aloft by the shell its movement changed to the rhythmic butterfly stroke it would use in the surf. At Meekins's direction I placed it inside a wooden frame that surrounded nest 149.

"None of these are sinking in, so I guess we'll have to check the ones that are farthest along by hand." She bent over and began gently scooping out sand. About eight inches down she uncovered a turtle head. "Okay, these are ready to go." She pulled out the lead turtle and two others, then shined her light into the small cavity for me to inspect.

The sand below was writhing with life. Tiny flippers appeared from all directions and sank beneath tumbling grains of sand, rising and squirming in a wild attempt to break through to the top. Heads gaped and stretched toward me as rivulets of sand poured down. I reached in and brought out four of the animals. Four or five more immediately filled in the gaps. "They've been patient for so long," Meekins said. "Now every ounce of energy is geared toward getting out." Hurrying to free the leaders so those at the bottom would not be injured, I pulled dozens of turtles to the surface. Sand clung to their moist limbs and shells. Until hatching they had maintained a fetal position, and their shells, although stiff, were slightly curled. Each had a small yellowish nodule on its belly, the last of the yolk. I lowered my cupped palm into the warm sand and let it fill with turtles. Gently I pulled the hatchlings out and again curled my hand into the nest. I could feel turtles squeezing in between my fingers, like water seeping through cracks. Scraping at the edges of the hollow, I uncovered six hatchlings that seemed to be having difficulty digging out of packed sand.

At length they stopped breaking the surface, and I could feel no more wriggling limbs. In less than five minutes I had extracted seventy-five turtles. They bumped against each other in the frame, following the flashlight beam like a school of minnows rising to the surface for food. A few that had turned over on their backs pressed their tiny rear flippers together in a gesture of self-defense. They looked like miniature versions of Winnie the Pooh's friend Piglet. I had difficulty imagining them as three-hundred-pound adults.

We put the hatchlings in four buckets and started toward the beach. It is Meekins's custom to release hatchlings at a different point every night in hopes of reducing predation by fish, and we walked north to a wide stretch of beach. "Someone asked me the other night if I didn't feel horrible releasing these poor baby turtles into the surf to fend for themselves," Meekins said. "I said, 'listen, if I can get them this far I feel like I've done them a big service.'"

The sand near the water lit with sparks beneath our steps. Fifty yards north of the hatchery Meekins stopped and set down the buckets. "I'll get in the water with the light to make sure the turtles head in the right direction. Try and release as many of them at once as you can." She kicked off her shoes and strode ankle deep into the surf, leaving me to dump four buckets of turtles simultaneously.

I gathered the buckets around me and watched her dark silhouette. The flashlight beam turned toward me. "Ready?" she called.

I lifted two buckets and tipped out their contents gingerly, spreading turtles across the sand. The ones that landed upright fanned out immediately, and not all toward the surf. I emptied the last two buckets and began righting turtles that lay on their backs and turning others toward the surf. Their frenzied movements never stopped, even when I picked them up, as if the purpose of their lives was to get somewhere, anywhere. I reached for a turtle to my right, lost my balance, and stuck out my foot to save myself from a fall. "Watch where you step," Meekins called sharply. I couldn't blame her; I could have easily killed six or seven hatchlings, maybe more.

The majority of the turtles were toddling toward the surf. Dark shapes dotted the sand as Meekins played the beam of light across the beach in a search for stragglers. I moved carefully up and down a five-yard area, collecting wayward hatchlings as quickly as possible. Within minutes the final turtles had scampered to the water's edge. The surf was rising and strong, and the spent waves swept sharply to the south, carrying the turtles in a wide arc. I took off my shoes and waded out beside Meekins; pricks of light dotted the foam that surrounded my feet. Despite the coolness of the night, the ocean was as warm as it had been in midsummer. A small hatchling ventured down toward the water, only to be caught by a wave and deposited neatly back on the beach. Again it crawled down, and again it was knocked back. Meekins and I chuckled. The turtle's struggle had all the comic appearances of a small child trying to tackle a giant. "If they can get out a little ways and then stay low, the waves will break right over them," Meekins said. The straggler caught a wave on the ebb and rode past us stroking furiously, a baby on a water slide. Another wave broke over it, but it did not reappear.

I watched the phosphorescent breakers silently for several minutes. "That was some sort of show," I said.

"No it wasn't. It's not a show. We have people coming out here all the time who think it's a show, and they're the ones who can do the most harm because they don't take it seriously. A natural wonder, an awesome sight—you can call it anything like that. But please don't describe it as a show."

That was the last of my dealings with turtles this year, or so I believed as I rode the ferry back to the mainland. But ten days later I learned that the Pea Island refuge crew had encircled two loggerhead nests with a wire mesh to corral the hatchlings as they emerged. The turtles were to be taken to the state Marine Resources Center in Manteo and kept for a year to gain strength before being released. They were due to hatch any day. One night just past 12 o'clock I went out to the beach to see if the sand over the nests had started to sag in, a sign that the turtles were preparing to break through.

The evening was still and clear and moonless. The Milky Way stretched across the sky in two wide swaths. I picked my way slowly through myrtle and knots of saltmeadow hay, stumbling occasionally as grasses grabbed at my feet. The nests were on the south edge of the tern and skimmer colony, but no birds scolded me as I sneaked over the dunes. All of them had gone, leaving a peace that struck me as thick and unnatural. Anywhere else on the beach the silence would have seemed soothing. Here it only heralded the end of the year's richest season and the coming of cold.

I found the turtle nests with no difficulty. They lay only a yard apart, with cylinders of wire mesh around them. With a flashlight I could see that the sand over them was still packed firm. A ghost crab burrow had been excavated next to one of the cavities, but the crab had been unable to dig deep enough to invade the mesh. It skittered a few feet from the beam of my light, too timid to come close but too intent on the possibility of a meal to be driven away.

The sand showed no sign of collapsing, and the weather was too cool for me to stay on the beach without a sleeping bag. I turned out the light and walked toward the surf with my head back to gaze at the stars. Familiar constellations hugged the horizon—the sprung W of Cassiopeia and the pinched triangle of the Pleiades. Spread between them were specks of light that receded and floated toward me in deep, layered darkness. A hole in the sand caught me unawares, and I flung my arms wide to keep from falling. I turned on the light to see what I had stepped in. When I did, eight ghost crabs scrambled to the edges of the beam.

I shined the light north, then south. Hundreds upon hundreds of ghost crabs froze momentarily and danced away, as closely packed as a living, moving mat. Their numbers extended as far as I could see in both directions. In the diffused beam their shells appeared very white, like chips of plaster. It was an army of crabs afoot in search of food. I thought of the turtles below the sand, pipping through shells, unfurling their bodies as grains of sand trickled around them. The wire mesh surrounding their nests was the only reason to think they would live longer than two minutes.

Whatever turtles were still beneath the sands of Pea Island would have to evade a mob of crabs to reach the surf. The odds of breaking through those lines seemed remote, maybe worse than a hundred to one. And ghost crabs were only one of a dozen threats to the remaining clutches. The survival of any loggerhead still buried in the North Carolina sands would be jeopardized seriously by the events of the coming week.

David Rains Wallace

David Rains Wallace was born in Virginia in 1945 and educated at Wesleyan University and Mills College. He is the author of eight works of natural history, including *The Dark Range: A Naturalist's Night Notebook* (Sierra Club, 1978), *Idle Weeds: The Life of a Sandstone Ridge* (Sierra Club, 1980), *The Klamath Knot: Explorations of Myth and Evolution* (Sierra Club, 1983) and *The Untamed Garden and Other Personal Essays* (Ohio State University Press, 1986). Wallace has also written two novels, including most recently *The Vermilion Parrot* (Sierra Club, 1991). Twice the winner of the Commonwealth Club of California's Silver Medal for Literature, David Rains Wallace also holds the John Burroughs Medal for Nature Writing, awarded for *The Klamath Knot*. His articles and essays have appeared regularly in *Sierra, Wilderness,* the *New York Times* and other national periodicals. Wallace lives in Berkeley, California, with his wife Betsy, who is an artist.

In the selection from *Bulow Hammock: Mind in a Forest* (Sierra Club, 1989), a book that re-explores a subtropical woodland near Daytona, Florida, which Wallace first discovered as a child, the author describes an encounter with a softshell turtle after a torrential deluge. Seeing the turtle at home in its aquatic habitat, perfectly content in a flood that has closed the asphalt highways, brings Wallace an "unaccountable happiness." *Bulow Hammock* is a collection of essays full of such epiphanies, as Wallace, following the path of such notable naturalists as William Bartram and John James Audubon, searches the Edenic woodlands of

south Florida for the marvels of nature in the subtropics. Most compel-
lingly, Wallace finds a curious parallel between the natural history of the
woodlands and the evolution of human consciousness.

The second selection comes from *Idle Weeds: The Life of an Ohio
Sandstone Ridge* (Sierra Club, 1980), which David Rains Wallace wrote
after a stint as a naturalist at a small state park in central Ohio. Wallace
offers Chestnut Ridge (a fictional name invented to preserve the park's
anonymity) as a symbol of the humanized nature that is now ubiquitous
in North America. Chestnut Ridge is what scientists call a "fragmented
landscape," that is, an amputated piece of what was formerly a large
integrated whole. Gone are the elk, buffalo, black bears, wolves and
passenger pigeons, but in this humble relict of a woodland the author
finds beauty, wonder and hope, as it revivifies and naturalizes the human
culture that surrounds it. He chose as an epigraph for the book a passage
from the English Romantic poet William Blake:

> Timbrels & violins sport round the Wine Presses. The little Seed,
> The sportive root, the Earthworm, the small beetle, the wise Emmet,
> Dance round the Wine Presses of Luvah; the Centipede is there,
> The ground Spider with many eyes, the Mole clothed in Velvet,
> The earwig arm'd, the tender maggot, emblem of Immortality;
> The slow slug, the grasshopper that sings & laughs & drinks;
> The winter comes; he folds his slender bones without a murmur.
> There is the Nettle that stings with soft down; & there
> The indignant thistle whose bitterness is bred in his milk
> And who lives on the contempt of his neighbor; there all the idle weeds,
> That creep about the obscure places, shew their various limbs
> Naked in all their beauty, dancing round the wine presses.
>
> *The Four Zoas*

The Softshell
(circa 1989)

Florida's rainy season started soon after I encountered the tortoise, in late May. It was dramatic: a slate blue overcast darkened the west, and a southerly wind drove gray pennants of cloud over the shore at a speed made all the more impressive by the apparent immobility of cumulus banks on the Atlantic horizon.

I watched the sunset at Bulow Creek that evening. In the cold light, the water was gunmetal blue and chrome, and the cord grasses and rushes swayed autumnally over it. A small alligator glided out of the marsh and swam the creek so smoothly it might have been on an underwater track. I wondered how it managed in the current, which seemed pretty strong, the water moving upstream instead of down, pushed by the tide.

I never stopped being impressed by the strength of tidal influence on a creek that was several dozen miles from the nearest ocean inlet, south of Daytona. Within the hammock, about a quarter mile from the creek, was a brackish mudflat. Shorebirds fed on it when it wasn't submerged. Somehow, the tidal water got through the woods into the flat, although there was no sign of a channel, not above ground anyway.

The power of the advancing tidal current caused a startling illusion. It seemed as though something very big was moving up the creek just under the surface, so big that it almost filled the bed. I felt a moment of the vertigo that arises when one stares a long time at running water, then looks at the ground and sees the dry sand or earth appear to eddy and flow.

The rain began as I went to bed that night, at first just a drizzle. A steady pounding on the tile roof awoke me in the small hours. It sounded peremptory, as though the sky was so eager to unload that it had descended to roof level to do it. It continued for twelve hours.

Six inches had fallen by the next afternoon, when the sky lightened, then boiled up into towering thunderheads. The roads looked like canals. A lighter rain kept up for another day, finally thinning to a yellowish overcast that unexpectedly produced window-rattling thunderclaps and twenty minutes of the hardest downpour yet. It flooded my grandmother's yard two inches deep. Her pebbles weren't as absorbent as the neighbors' crabgrass.

The thunderstorm stopped as abruptly as it had started, and I splashed through the flooded roads to the hammock. I didn't expect it to have changed much in a couple of days, but, once again, I hadn't understood it. It hadn't changed in the ways I would have expected. I'd been afraid the sand road would be flooded, since all the paved ones were, but there wasn't even a puddle in it. The sand was firmer than during the dry season: the rain had cemented it.

There wasn't any flooding in the hammock. Swamp rivulets that had dried up during the rainless weeks were full again, but the ones that hadn't dried up seemed no fuller than before. I'd never seen a more graphic demonstration of the spongelike properties of wetland. It was a little eerie. What had the hammock done with all the rain?

Much of it had never even reached the ground. It wasn't that the vegetation had a lot of water on it, in fact it was surprisingly dry for less than an hour after a thunderstorm. The vegetation did have a surprising amount of water *in* it that hadn't been there before. The epiphytes, the resurrection ferns and tree mosses that had been mere blackish incrustations on branches two days before, were now lush, emerald shrouds. Individual resurrection ferns had tripled in size. It was instant rain forest: just add water and stand back.

The downpour had knocked down a few rotted limbs and tattered leaves, but the hammock seemed remarkably undisturbed. Mosquitoes and flies were less in evidence, but birds and frogs called lustily in the canopy, and life seemed encouraged rather than intimidated. A barred owl flew out of a thicket and landed on a branch in full view, behavior I'd seen in the Okefenokee but not the hammock.

A large brown frog sitting on a snag in a swamp rivulet also demurred to flee at my approach. I wondered if it was the ranid species that I'd heard calling at night. It might have been a bronze frog: the distant chorus had had a clacking sound heard among that species. On the other hand, it might have been a southern leopard frog, since its snout had a characteristic shape, or a pickerel frog, since its legs had yellow patches. The frog just sat there, as though daring me to come and attempt identification. Even herpetologists have trouble sorting out southern frogs.

An armadillo rummaged in the leaf litter, also ignoring me, although the sun hadn't set. It thrust its head under the leaves, pushed its whole body into a tree hole, rose like a bear on hind legs to tear at a stump. The sound of its own scratchings seemed to startle it: it suddenly jumped sideways. Then it stuck its head back into the ground.

When I got to the ditch, a songbird was scolding in a tangle of vines. Another barred owl flew out of it and landed in the open. It was facing away from me, but turned its head around 180 degrees to stare. Yet another started calling to the south.

I came to the place in the sand pine scrub where I thought I'd heard frogs in the night. Since it wasn't getting dark yet, I left the path and pushed through the saw palmetto. In a little while, I saw an opening in the brush and started toward it. I wasn't expecting much, a scattering of brackish puddles and rivulets as in other swampy parts of the hammock. I'd misunderstood it again.

I found myself on the edge of a sizeable sheet of water that was translucent black, like obsidian, quite unlike the brown murky water of the brackish tidal swamps. It stretched out of sight eastward. Around it, and in its shallows, grew some of the biggest trees I'd seen in the hammock, not only palmettoes and red cedars, but great, buttressed American elms, swamp hickories, Carolina ashes, and gums. Buttonbushes grew farther out in the water, tall shrubs bearing masses of spherical white flowers, and a clump of willows stood in the sunny center.

It was a sweetwater swamp, isolated from the tides by slightly higher land, and fed by some intricacy of limestone aquifer, some vagrant but copious outlier of Bartram's "salubrious fountains." It glowed in its scrubby setting, the new hardwood leaves reflected in water already green with duckweed, aquatic *Salvinia* ferns and lotuslike floating hearts. Even underwater, the swamp was full of green plants, feathery-leaved bladderworts and stoneworts. The presence of carnivorous bladderworts indicated that it was also full of the water fleas and other zooplankton I missed in the jade swamp.

I walked along the water's edge, expecting to come to the end of it pretty soon, since the creek was in that direction. Yet it kept stretching ahead of me, and it was so different from anything I'd seen in the hammock before that it began to seem unreal. I felt dislocated, as I had felt when trying to follow the path in the dark, although this time it was exhilarating instead of intimidating.

I skirted a palmetto trunk and almost stumbled over a spray of green stems on its base. It was a whisk fern, a very healthy one. I found another of the ancient plants a few yards further, growing on the base of another palmetto along with a little moss garden of liverworts, maiden cane, and red cedar seedlings. I wondered what whisk ferns had grown on the bases of before palmettoes evolved.

I glimpsed something in flight and heard a furtive splash, then a wood duck drake was swimming among the buttonbushes, making peevish sounds. He climbed on a log and peered at me through the foliage. The red skin around his eye gave him an intense stare even at a distance. As I stood still, not wanting to frighten the duck, I noticed other creatures: a brown frog like the one I'd seen earlier, except that this one still had its tail, and a big black cooter turtle. The turtle had its neck craned anxiously, watching me. When I glanced away a moment, it slipped into the water so quietly I was unsure I'd ever seen it. When I looked back at the wood duck, it had disappeared too.

A live oak had fallen in the water, forming a natural boardwalk. I climbed out over its slippery carpet of epiphytes and sat where the main limbs branched from the trunk. The reddening sky intensified the treetops' reflections in the swamp, but its water was so clear I could still see the bottom easily. Even the mosquito fish in it seemed larger and more colorful than those in the brackish swamps. Many of the large females had swollen bellies: more mosquito fish on the way.

I glimpsed a movement at the surface out of the corner of my eye. When I turned to look, I could see nothing but water plants and floating twigs, but I was getting impatient with all these vanishing acts. The spot was about eight feet away, far enough to focus my binoculars on. I did, and saw with a start that there was an eye down there at the surface. Apparently it was unconnected to anything else, like the Cheshire cat's smile. It wasn't the black, impassive eye of a frog or cooter turtle. This eye had a sharpness about it. It was yellow like a cat's, and it kept blinking nervously. When I leaned forward to see it better, the eye disappeared as though the swamp itself had shut it, as though other eyes might start appearing on tree trunks or sandbars.

I waited, keeping my binoculars on the spot. Then the eye was there again. I noticed a dot in front of it. A nostril? I leaned forward again, and as the eye vanished again, I glimpsed a snaky motion underwater, as of a neck being withdrawn.

When the eye reappeared, I knew what it belonged to. A softshell turtle was buried in the waterweeds and fallen leaves, its long neck extended to the surface with only eyes and nostrils protruding. Surface reflection concealed the rest of its strangely beaked and flattened head. To disappear, it had withdrawn head and neck so smoothly that my eye hadn't caught the movement.

I remembered watching softshells in the Olentangy River in Columbus, Ohio, sticking their birdlike heads out of the water as rush hour traffic roared past on riverfront freeways. In wooded areas upstream from town, they'd climb out to bask on the bank a few feet from me if I remained still, but at the slightest movement they'd drop into the water faster than the eye could follow. Softshells can move fast enough to catch trout. They had seemed fabulously unturtlelike, more like little shield-bearing dragons with their flat, leathery shells and catlike eyes. Bartram was fascinated by Florida softshells and devoted two copper plates in the *Travels* to drawings of them as well as describing them in the text, as though to convince himself that this creature truly existed. One of his drawings is so strange-looking that it takes a while to figure out that it is a turtle's head and not some strange mollusk or crustacean.

This turtle evidently thought it had me fooled. It seemed prepared to trade blinks with me indefinitely, but darkness was falling, and I hadn't brought a flashlight. I got off the log and started back toward the path.

Frogs had started calling somewhere, I couldn't tell where. They might have been in the water right beside me, for all I knew, or in my head. The high-pitched trilling, unlike any call I'd heard in the hammock before, was so loud that it seemed to obliterate any sense of direction. It rose to a crescendo that made my ears ring, then stopped suddenly.

It might have seemed ominous, especially after finding the apparently disembodied eye. But coming upon the softshell somehow had evoked the same unaccountable happiness as stumbling on the copulating stinkpots. The thunder-cleared air seemed vinous again, although lighter than the November air had been, a Chardonnay instead of a Beaujolais. Although the sunlight was gone from the woods, they appeared shadowless.

When I got to the marsh, I smelled a sweet, acrid fragrance that seemed familiar, although I'd never smelled it in the hammock. It reminded me of sleeping on the porch of my mother's parents' house in Virginia when I'd visited them in summer as a child. Looking around for the source, I noticed drifts of tiny, white, four-petaled flowers on the path. Sprays of the flowers covered some small evergreen trees, and the smell was coming from them, which didn't explain anything, since the trees were dahoon trees, a species that doesn't grow in Virginia.

The luminous dusk and strangely familiar fragrance made the hammock seem more confiding than it ever had before. Even the jade swamp finally gave up its secrets—at least, I discovered what lived in the flooded palmetto stump besides fly and mosquito larvae. As I passed it this time, a small toad floated calmly on its surface, wearing a duckweed hat. It didn't dive out of sight as I approached, or even when I touched it. It perhaps was too excited about the opening of its breeding season to pay attention to me. I met more of them along the path, little buffy toads with red warts—oak toads. I'd never seen one before in the hammock.

The darkness didn't evoke any of the unease it had on previous occasions. Frog and insect calls sounded less furtive, and the fireflies' light had a robustness, an orange lustre, which seemed new. The sky glowed even after the last red had faded. Drops of water on fallen leaves reflected the glow in little flashes as I passed them, and the hammock seemed full of silver lights beneath the fireflies' golden ones.

Ground Thaw
(circa 1980)

The life of the ridge had begun to renew itself well before the ice storm. The pair of great horned owls had begun to mate, as had the squirrels, raccoons, foxes, mink, and opossums. An eighteenth century philosophe might have been charmed at this—a beneficent Nature providing the joys of sexuality to her children during the bleakest time of year. Modern science sees more significance in a need to time reproductive activities so that the young are born when food is abundant, but there's little doubt the animals enjoyed themselves. Male raccoons and opossums came out of their tree or burrow shelters whenever the weather was bearable to search for females, the raccoons making odd whistling sounds, the opossums clicking their tongues and teeth. Fox squirrels chased one another about the ridge slopes almost every morning, although not as acrobatically as their red cousins the gullies. Copulations were quick, almost anticlimactic, but frequent.

The ridge's invertebrate life never stopped worrying at winter's fraying shroud. Periods of frost were mere suspensions in many activities, which were quickly resumed as the temperature rose above freezing. The winter green herbs and red cedars carried on photosynthesis on warm, sunny days; and tiny yellowish springtails—

insects so primitive they have no wings—underwent population explosions. Round-headed, big-eyed creatures the size of pin-points, they hopped about propelled by switchbladelike tails and fed on algae growing in the sunlit nutrient bath of melting snow. When the temperature fell again, they had mated and left another generation of eggs.

For every springtail, dozens of brown or black oribatid mites scrambled through the dead leaves, sucking the juices of decay. They resembled eight-legged grains of silt. Tiny species of moths and flies emerged from pupal cases, mated on the snow, and left their eggs in the sheltering microclimates of bark crevices or mats of haircap moss. On particularly warm afternoons overwintering butterflies left shelter and fluttered through the woods—purple and yellow mourning cloaks or orange brown hackberry butterflies.

Below the frost line, where the temperature rarely fell below fifty degrees Fahrenheit, life was even less affected by winter storms. The young of some insects were intermittently active. Leathery-skinned crane fly larvae burrowed in moist ground. Orange wireworms, the larvae of click beetles, bored into roots and underground stems, and the brown nymphs of cicadas sucked the sap of tree roots. Tiny, pale centipedes, millipedes, and spiders carried on their affairs in the interstices of soil particles.

Nematodes—microscopic roundworms—performed many ecological roles in the winter soil. Some infested roots, some were predators, some scavenged. They belonged to species adapted to winter conditions and would be replaced by others as the seasons changed. The smallest organisms—bacteria, fungi, and protozo-ans—thrived everywhere the soil was not frozen solid. Even the tree roots continued to absorb water. If frost were to penetrate down the dozens of feet that many roots extended, the trees would die—not from freezing but from desiccation.

Among the few soil creatures fully inactive in winter are the earthworms, which retreat into deep underground chambers and cluster together until the thaw. Earthworms depend largely on leaf litter for food, however, so their retreat may be more from famine than from cold. The short-tailed shrew missed their activity since they were a food staple when available. This was a deprivation for her but a benefit for the ridge woods since she had to depend largely on insect larvae and pupae for food. She rushed about beneath the ridge's frozen skin like a white corpuscle, furiously ingesting the grubs, maggots, and nymphs that could destroy its protective mantle of trees if allowed to become too numerous.

But the quiet life beneath the snow mantle was almost over for the shrew. The temperature rose above freezing for several days after the ice storm and the deathly glaze faded, but unwillingly, still refrigerating itself in shaded hollows. The smell of melting snow permeated the evening air as warm breezes blew, and snow-flattened leaf litter emerged on sunny slopes. Then rain made the small creeks run jade green above their ice. The air was full of glaucous mist, but somehow colors stood out sharply against the snow—the nose and paws of a young opossum floundering up a slushy gully were bright red, its bedraggled fur pinkish beige.

After three days of drizzle, the snow was almost gone. The thawed soil began to sag, collapsing part of the short-tailed shrew's tunnel system and smearing her with mud. She shrieked in annoyance and hurried to her nest to clean herself meticulously. That her fur retain its loft and dryness was very important. Wet, matted fur would allow the heat to escape from her body very quickly, and she would have difficulty finding enough food to regenerate it. She might die of hypothermia like an inexperienced backpacker.

The soggy, collapsing soil pressed at weak spots all over the ridge. A deep pit suddenly appeared over a culvert on the gravel township road. An unwary stroller could have fallen to the waist in it. One windy night blew down six large black cherry trees on the south slope because the soil wasn't firm enough to hold their shallow root systems. They lay the next morning with bushels of soil and sandstone clutched in their upended roots.

In the marsh a cave-in above a blocked drainage tile grew larger. Clouds of silt and sand boiled in the water that welled up in the hole. A huge blue crayfish emerged at the bottom of this turbulent pool and felt around clumsily with its pincers, frightening a much smaller reddish crayfish, which shot to the surface and took refuge on a floating twig. Both had spent winter in deep tunnels beneath the marsh. Like earthworms, crayfish are surface feeders, living mainly on decaying bits of marsh vegetation.

Everywhere on the ridge there was evidence of the soil's stirring and shifting as it thawed. So widespread and rapid were these movements, it was as though the ridge was twitching and stretching as it emerged from the snow cover, as though one stood on an awakening living being. And the soil *was* alive—it breathed, drank rainwater and snowmelt, ate dead plants and animals, and excreted them as mineralized nutrients. It was passing, on different parts of the ridge, through all the stages of life: from a thin, stony birth on abandoned quarries and ridgetop cellar holes, to a vigorous, moldy youth on the reforested slopes, to a firm, stable middle age on the level pastures and hay meadow, to an unsteady senescence on stream banks and eroded gullies.

The soil was like muscle, nerve, and fat around bedrock bone, like the thin cambium of inner bark that every year forms a new growth ring around the stony heartwood of trees. As with the ancient sandstone that underlay it, the soil was inert only to the unobserving eye, permanent only to the uncomprehending mind. It held no certainty, and failure to heed its restlessness had been the undoing of the early farmers whose cabins it had devoured. As with all living things, it was on the move ceaselessly—growing up in the interaction of dead leaves and soil organisms, falling down in the interaction of sand grains and gravity, spreading out toward reunion with its seaside origins.

The ridge soil also resembled other living things in being bounded by the year's rhythms. If it now sank and crumbled in the thaw's rivulets, it would begin to grow when the spring warmth allowed its organisms to multiply and attack the leaf litter in force. Then it would dwindle when the fall of the leaf canopy exposed it to autumnal rains, and sleep its fitful winter sleep to awaken again, perhaps stronger and fatter than during this year's thaw, perhaps not. Like all living things, the soil was vulnerable. There was always the possibility that deteriorative forces would outstrip creative, that gravity and raindrops would defeat leaf litter and microbes.

The Blackhand sandstone origin of the ridge soil made it particularly vulnerable to human disturbance. Acid sandstone soil is a good growth medium for chestnuts and oaks, but lacking calcium, a poor one for vegetables and grains. Cleared and plowed, it disintegrates unless very carefully limed and fertilized into a thin, sandy residue that will grow little except lichens and broomsedge until ash and elm seedlings begin to reclaim it. It is altogether different from the deep, black prairie soil of the Midwest, and trying to crop it is a bit like trying to raise groundhogs for bacon.

BALMY NIGHTS

In mid-February the temperature fell and the soil surface froze again, though not as deeply as before. But the lengthening days were already triggering hormonal changes that swell the gonads of male songbirds and bring about their spring songs. On frosty mornings song sparrows were the first to start, their songs tinkling and diffident. As dawn light turned the old fields a pale cream color, tufted titmice cried "Peedle-peedle-peedle!"; cardinals whistled "Wheet! Wheet! Wheet!"; a few overwintering field sparrows opened their pink bills and trilled "Pew! Pew! Pew! Pewpewpewpewpew!" In the woods bluejays made a peculiar ringing sound: "Tlapit! Tlapit!"

As the sun hit the beeches of the south slope one morning, several dozen crows trooped in from the northeast. They arranged themselves in the treetops with much swaying and flapping for balance and cawed happily. They had returned, "Kr-a-aa-a-k!" said a male crow; he left his perch and chased a smaller female over the silver maple swamp. She ducked and dodged coyly as he dived at her tail. This display of sexuality was too early for crow propriety: two other male crows sped after the amorous individual and chased him back into the trees.

Although the ground still froze at times, the deep frost was over for the year, and the life of the soil was resurgent. This was why the crows had returned. When the sun had thawed the south-facing hay meadow, the big black birds flew down and strutted across it, spearing earthworms and cutworms (the larvae of noctuid moths) that were newly active after their long winter dormancy. Cleaning soil from the worms with their feet, the crows devoured hundreds of them as well as an odd wireworm, centipede, wolf spider, and meadow mouse.

Then the weather became so balmy that even the nights were warm. The moon was new, and on the windless evenings the rustling of earthworms in the leaf litter of the wooded slopes was pervasive and distinctly eerie, as though hundreds of invisible beings were pattering about the dry leaves. The earthworms were eager to taste the newly decayed riches of last autumn's harvest. They thrust their heads from their burrows, grabbed the nearest bits of maple or ash leaf (oak leaves, full of tannic acid, are not as desirable), and pulled them underground. And they left large quantities of castings—feces—on the surface, this earthworm exchange of leaf litter and subsoil being the most important means of soil building on the ridge.

A wide range of predators took advantage of the earthworm emergence. Owls and foxes pounced on the worms; raccoons and opossums grabbed them with nimble fingers; newly emerged garter, ring-necked, and brown snakes yanked them from their burrows. The worms held on to their tunnel walls with stiff bristles, and it was sometimes easier to pull one in half than to get it all out. Woodcocks arrived from the Gulf States and fed predominantly on the earthworms, using their long, prehensile (hinged at the tip) bills to pull them from the soil.

The short-tailed shrew abandoned her lower tunnels temporarily to throw herself onto the sudden abundance at the surface. She felt safe in venturing out in the dark of the moon. She caught night crawlers three times her own length, slashed them with her tusks, and, unable to eat them all, cached them away. Some of the less damaged worms revived and escaped, but she had forgotten them anyway. One pair even remained in the cache to conjugate, clinging head to tail in the mutual exchange of sperm, which insures genetic variation and natural selection in the bisexual annelids.

There seemed to be no end to the food crawling from the ridge. The shrew found moths and flies just emerging from pupal cases, their wings still soft and useless; she found large black blister beetles, their fat abdomens protruding ungracefully from under-developed wing cases, their movements slow and feeble; she found big, hairy wolf spiders in great numbers in grassy patches; she found land snails and slugs, which left shiny mucous trails across tree roots and stones. She filled her stomach in an hour, slept a few minutes, and filled it again. The increment of fats and proteins allowed her ovaries to begin the development that would shortly bring her into breeding condition.

RITES AND GAMES

In late February a warm, soft rain fell for several nights, somehow signaling to a population of spotted salamanders on the south and east slopes. The large, black amphibians with yellow-spotted backs emerged from a subterranean existence that made them virtually invisible the rest of the year and moved toward the spring pool and an oxbow pool below the marsh. (Oxbows are abandoned stream courses that become filled with rainwater.)

The male salamanders were the first to arrive at the pools. They crawled underwater, swam to the bottom, and began prowling about in an odd, stiff-legged way, lashing their tails and twining their bodies into uncomfortable-looking U shapes. Biologists call this behavior *liebspiel*—love play. As they gyrated, the males exuded into the water a sexual attractant from abdominal glands.

When the females arrived in the pools, they smelled or tasted this substance and approached the males. The excited males continued their play before the females, then pressed their cloacae against leaves and twigs, attaching to them clear, gelatinous objects about the size and shape of plastic pushpins. Inside each of these was a bead of white glandular secretion mixed with spermatozoa. The objects were spermatophores, the sperm packets that represent an intermediate evolutionary stage between the wasteful external fertilization of frogs and fishes and the chancy direct fertilization of mammals and birds. Many amphibians and most insects use them.

The jellylike objects had an attraction for the females. They crawled over the spermatophores, squatted, and picked them up with the lips of their cloacae. Inside the females the clear gel melted and the sperm emerged and was stored in crevices in the cloacal wall. As eggs descended from the ovary ducts, the sperm fertilized them. Mucus from cloacal glands covered the buckshot-size eggs, and the females laid them in packets, which they attached to underwater twigs or leaves. The packets would absorb water and expand to baseball size.

The weather began to clear and cool; somehow the spotted salamanders anticipated this. They left the pool on the last warm night just before the temperature fell. At dawn a thin film of ice covered the oxbow pool. The only evidence of the salamanders' breeding were the eggs—already somewhat camouflaged by silt and green algae—and some scattered whitish stuff resembling crumbled chalk—the leftover spermatophores. The presence of the green algae boded well for the eggs. It was a species of algae especially adapted to life on spotted salamander eggs and— perhaps by increasing the oxygen content around the eggs through its photosynthesis—it actually makes the embryos develop better. Growing in the rich nutrient bath of the egg membranes, the algae also benefit.

The day warmed, and the bright weather was a message for the ridge's chipmunk population, recently awakened, too, from its winter sleep. As the sun reached its zenith, the chipmunks emerged en masse from their inconspicuous burrow entrances under logs or stones. They were ready for *their* mating orgy, and it would be a good deal less sedate than the salamanders'.

In fact, it was downright bacchanalian. There were frenzied pursuits, squeaky shrieks of passion or rage, tail-twitching harangues delivered from atop rotten stumps. Brawling rivals tumbled down slopes, kicking and clawing at each other. This went on throughout the afternoon as dozens of male chipmunks nosed about searching for females in estrus. The females were coy and sneaky, however, some- times giving several males the slip before letting one have his thirty- second way with her in some secluded nook.

A pair of gray foxes that denned in a brushy area of the southeast slope knew about the chipmunks' spring celebration and took good advantage of it, hunting in daylight for a change. The striped rodents were so excited that they could be approached easily. The foxes moved quietly along the slopes, dispatching and snapping up the males that blundered within pouncing distance. It was a fleeting abundance, however. The next day dawned cold and gray, the brief chipmunk estrous period was over, and the foxes went back to nighttime pursuit of the ever skinnier and less numerous cottontails. Of course, this was made easier by the fact that the cottontails were beginning their own breeding season and were often unwary. But there were no bonanzas. The female fox was carrying pups and needed all the food she could get.

The owls were nesting by this time, and the crows knew it. They watched the owls closely, especially in the early morning. Hardly a dawn went by without an explosion of caws when a roosting owl was discovered and driven from its cover in the gullies or pine plantations. The crows' excitement was uncannily similar to that of a crowd at a football game when an unexpected touchdown is made: it had the same near-hysterical quality.

The crows would chase the displaced owl, long lines of them strung out over the treetops with much flying back and forth. Finding the owl's general location for the day seemed to satisfy most of them, and they turned to the performance of aerial displays before slipping away quietly to feed. Sometimes a small group would return to vilify the owls later in the day, and another mass scolding might occur before the evening return to the roost. If the crows found a chance, they would raid the owls' nest and throw their eggs or owlets to the ground, but the owl pair had managed to conceal the nest's location from them so far. The owls knew where the crows roosted, though, and had already captured several of them at night. A crow's intelligence makes it hard to approach in daylight, but at night it is blind, almost helpless, and easy prey for owls, which are thus among the few predators really dangerous to crows. This is why crows hate owls so much and mob them at every opportunity in daytime, when owls are—although far from blind and helpless—at least sluggish and vulnerable.

A red-shouldered hawk wandered past the ridge during one of these owl-mobbing mornings. This resulted in some confusion.

Nearly as large as a red-tailed hawk but with a banded tail and red on the shoulders instead of the tail, the red-shouldered hawk was sitting in a white oak just below the maple grove as the sun rose. A migrating flock of grackles surrounded it, scolding the hawk with a cacophony of squeaking and whistling. Annoyed, the hawk took wing. The noise ceased abruptly as the grackles left their perches in pursuit. The whistling was replaced by a sighing as of wind in treetops—the sound of several hundred grackle wings beating in unison.

The hawk flew across the township road, and the grackle flock veered away and left it in peace. The tranquility was short-lived, however. Two crows on their way to the owl mobbing spotted the hawk as it rose above the trees and dived after it. By happenstance the hawk fled toward the gully where the owl was being persecuted. On arrival there, the two crows were confused, suddenly being confronted with two victims instead of one. They perched in a tulip tree to consider this embarrassment of riches while the hawk alighted in a red oak across the gully and then watched as the crow flock cawed and dived at the big owl.

Evidently this activity appealed to the red-shouldered hawk for it left the oak and made a pass at the owl, shrieking like the rustiest of iron gates in its excitement. The owl, petulantly ensconced in a white pine, paid no attention to its new persecutor, and the crows were too excited about the owl to bother with the hawk. Joining the attack on the owl was actually a good way of diverting the crows' attention from itself, but it's doubtful the hawk did so on purpose: hawks are not very intelligent.

The hawk circled screaming around the owl several more times, then dived into the woods, where it landed in a tree and looked back as though perplexed by the whole affair. When the owl at last broke cover and the crows voiced an ecstatic outburst of caws, however, the hawk circled the gully again, its wings taut and quivering with excitement. But the owl merely flew quietly away through the pine plantation in search of another roost.

Thoroughly aroused, the hawk flew to the ridgetop and stalked a rabbit in a poison ivy thicket, until the rabbit was frightened away by a pair of dogs chasing a groundhog. The dogs

harried the groundhog into a clump of multiflora and nosed
around it patiently, waiting for the rodent to venture out. The
hawk gave up on this confusing round of attacks and continued its
northward migration.

THE FINAL SNOWFALL

The weather warmed again at the beginning of March, and the
increasingly long twilights took on an extraordinary softness. The
leafless woods receded into distances that seemed faraway and slightly
melancholy, while warm breezes full of the sweetness of greening grass
moved across the pastures. Around the marsh the silver maple flowers
burst their buds—thousands of unpetaled clusters, some with bright
red pistils, some with yellow stamens, some with a few of both. The
grasslike leaves and pink flower buds of spring beauty appeared on the
south slope, and a golden haze of slippery elm flowers spread over the
brush tangles of the west slope.

As dusk faded into night, these brushy places generated
peculiar sounds: first a series of nasal squawks, then a protracted
whistling that ended abruptly in a twittering and soft roaring. After
a silent interval, the squawks would start again and the whole
sequence would be repeated. Sometimes the squawking came
from one location while whistling and twittering went on in
another.

Male woodcocks made these sounds as they performed their
mating display, sometimes with females watching, sometimes
without. The squawks were their calls as they strutted about small
glades with tails spread and breast feathers puffed up. Sometimes
they tripped over goldenrod stems in their excitement. The
whistling was the sound of their wings as they took off and circled
high into the gloaming, while the twittering and roaring were
respectively vocal and wing sounds as the birds dived headlong
back to their strutting ground.

As the new moon waxed and grew brighter, the woodcock
raptures went on well into the night. Amorous male groundhogs
left their homes and crept about the quarries searching for the
burrows of females. Unlike the chipmunks, they were phlegmatic

about mating. There were few fights between rivals. Groundhogs often climbed trees to eat the buds at this lean time.

The short-tailed shrew responded to the changes in the air. Her ovaries matured and began to produce egg cells, and the scent-producing glands on her flanks that usually marked her tunnels dried up. At other times the scent served as a repellent to other shrews: in its absence male shrews could respond to the attraction of her estrous state without fear.

Several males lived in the vicinity. Driven by their own swelling testes, they soon found her. With much twittering and nimble, if short-sighted, pursuit, they courted her, and all won her at one time or another. Shrew ovaries are sluggish, and the upheavals of repeated copulation are needed to shake the egg cells loose from the ovary walls. Finally five egg cells descended the Fallopian tubes and met the spermatozoa of the various males. The fertilized ova then attached themselves to the uterine walls and began to multiply and grow at a fast, shrewlike pace.

The prospective mother became hungry and irascible, and the males abandoned her in favor of another female that had just come into estrus. The prospective mother was somewhat worn out by their attentions anyway and welcomed a return to her normal, frenetic pursuit of food, a pursuit made more difficult by the changes in her body.

Winter interrupted the thaw once more. Thunderstorms broke up the soft weather as a front of cold air moved in and forced the warm air upwards into cumulonimbus clouds. At one moment the evening was quite still—the air a little heavy, with a rosy gray light—then a clap of thunder sounded, the sky darkened abruptly, and a heavy rain thumped down. Undeflected by foliage, the rain flooded the earthworms' burrows and drove the short-tailed shrew out of the less well-drained parts of her tunnel system. Earthworms came to the surface in great numbers as the flooding exhausted the oxygen in their burrows, and predators took advantage of this after the rain had stopped. By morning, ground that had been littered with worms was once more clear of them, the survivors having reentered the burrows.

After the thunderstorms, the evening was cold again and the earthworms stayed underground. The sky broke up into chilled fragments of a transparent, almost colorless blue, and opaque clouds piled up above the western horizon. As the sun set, shafts of platinum light slanted northward and the sky turned a faint salmon color below the gray cloud layer.

It snowed the next chilly morning, big flakes that quickly whitened the ground. In the swamp, festoons of snow lay on silver maple flowers that had already set fruit—small, fuzzy samaras like yellow green mouse ears. On the upper slopes the snow temporarily buried some spring beauty blossoms and the newly emerged leaves of fawn lily and cutleaf toothwort.

Rick Bass

Although Rick Bass now lives in the high, elk-filled mountains of northwestern Montana, just a short walk from the wilds of Canada, his personal and literary roots reach across the continent to the sunny, white-tailed deer country of south Texas where he was born and raised. It was in the Texas hill country, as a youngster, that Bass learned the art of storytelling from listening to his grandfather and older relatives recount adventures and spin yarns at the family hunting lodge. Bass's fond recollections of these early yearly expeditions are memorialized in his first book *The Deer Pasture* (Norton, 1985).

As a result of this unique apprenticeship, there is a strong oral quality to Bass's nonfiction and fiction narratives, with a conversational idiom; a digressive, rather than discursive mode; and the frequent use of the second person to engage the reader. In this orality, he comes straight out of the southwestern literary line that runs back through Edward Abbey and Mark Twain to Thomas Thrapp and James Pattie. With respect to the contemporary scene, Rick Bass has more in common stylistically with southwestern writers such as John Nichols, Larry McMurtry and N. Scott Momaday than with writers of the northern Rockies such as William Kittredge and Tom McGuane. Bass is characteristically southwestern in his independence, his restlessness, his humor, his vitality, his sunny outlook, his distrust of unchallenged authority and his disdain for affectation and pretense. All of Rick Bass's subsequent books—*Wild to the Heart* (Stackpole Books, 1987; Norton paperback,

1989), *The Watch* (Norton, 1989), *Oil Notes* (Houghton Mifflin, 1989) and *Winter* (Houghton Mifflin, 1991)—have steadily built upon the promise of *The Deer Pasture* and have borne witness to the persistent influence of his home region.

In this essay from *Wild to the Heart,* Bass relates a backpacking trip he made with the Mississippi Sierra Club into the twelve-thousand-acre Sipsey Wilderness, which is located along the Sipsey Fork of the Black Warrior River in northwestern Alabama. The region constitutes a transitional zone between the pine woods of the Coastal Plain and the hardwood forests of the Appalachian Mountains. Characteristically, Rick Bass focuses as much on the people with whom he is traveling as on the natural history of the southern Appalachians. In this is the unique beauty and power of his writing.

Sipsey in the Rain
(circa 1987)

I'm supposed to meet Jim Trunzler and the Mississippi Sierra Club in the Bankhead National Forest Friday night. They're leaving from Jackson, a five-hour drive. I'm leaving from Tuscaloosa; I was in a business meeting all day, so I'm already halfway there. I don't know who'll get there first. They have farther to drive, but they've been there before; they know the way. This will be my first trip.

I didn't know you could backpack in the South. I thought you had to go out West, to Colorado or even Montana, or at least to north Georgia, to the Appalachian Trail. When I saw on a bulletin board in my office building where Jim and Co. were going to lead a trip to this Bankhead area (north of Birmingham), I called him up; I met him for lunch. He drew me a map on the back of a napkin. He told me to meet them there around midnight Friday. He asked if I was afraid of owls. I told him no.

Also, I did this: I lost the napkin.

Steering with my knees—it is dusk, and I am driving through the North Alabama mountains of Nowhere (last town was Samantha, pop. 27)—I unfold my eastern United States road map and squint. My car's interior dome light is out, so I have to hold a penlight in my teeth to see. I drive slowly; I look up and check the road as I drive, but there is no traffic out. Why I don't pull over and look at the map sitting still I don't know.

Yes I do know—it's because I'm in a hurry. It would be a real feather in my cap to find a good backpacking place this close to home. I grew up out West, and have discovered that if I go more than three weeks without a camping trip, my left eyebrow begins to twitch. A month, and my stomach makes funny noises in public. Five weeks and I drool and sometimes babble incoherently and without warning feeble poetry about mountain larkspurs and aspen.

I've never found out what happens after six weeks.

I wake up once during the night, but the tent is dry. I go back to sleep.

Morning. Still raining. I lie on my back and listen to it *pit!* against the tent before remembering I left my breakfast squares in the car. I pull on my boots and crouch like a sprinter and bolt for the car, but once outside I'm surprised to find it's only misting.

When you're closed in a tent, it always sounds like it's raining harder than it really is.

Delighted at this good fortune, I dance out across the pine straw, turn a whirl, jump up and down, and do a little dance, sort of a stamp-stamp-stamping dance.

I would not have done it if anyone had been watching. It felt good to be in the woods again. I sat on a rock and ate two blueberry energy bars.

Hint: if you are ever driving out of your campsite on a Saturday morning on your way to meet some other people and you do something really dumb like not watch where you are going, so that you drive off the road and get stuck in the mud, then you will do well to remember that the only way to get out is to jack the car up and put rocks and logs under the wheels.

Do not ask me how I know this, I just know.

After I got the car unstuck, I was pretty muddy, so I went back up in the woods and stripped down and stood there in the mist and toweled off with my tee shirt and then real quickly put some clean dry clothes on. It felt good; it was like a shower without a shower curtain.

I would not have done that either if anyone had been watching. I ran back down the hill feeling refreshed and clean, running fast so I would not get wet. It felt good to run so fast.

It was a good morning.

I found Jim and Co. by the smell of Jim's cherry pipe smoke. They were breaking camp; they were wearing rain gear, and cooking under a fly. They looked happy too—no eyebrow tics or growling stomachs this weekend. I noticed that none of them were eating blueberry energy bars however, and I felt guilty. I wondered how they had gotten their fire started with wet firewood.

There are two basic philosophies concerning the preparation and consumption of food on a backpacking trip. The first, and most glamorous, is to spend a week or so beforehand dawdling over cookbooks and mulling through grocery stores, picking up spices and cheese graters and odds and ends and knickknacks, and then planning a very detailed, very elegant menu.

In camp, spend a lot of time preparing it, spend even more time cooking it, eat it slowly, and then sit back and smoke a cherry pipe and rest easy for a while before cleaning up all your utensils. Total time: two hours, forty-eight minutes.

Or, you can do this: cram your pack with blueberry energy bars and raisins and Vienna sausages. Total time: twelve minutes.

Some people eat better when they are camping, some eat worse.

I sat under the fly with them and waited for them to finish cooking and eating and cleaning up. They kept offering me food; I kept telling them I had already eaten.

I began to consider changing philosophies.

Jim introduced me to everyone. I tried to remember their names as they told them to me. Jim's hiking partner was Eck. "Eck?" I said. "Eck," she nodded. "Like the sound a frog makes," she said. She did not explain what it stood for, or what her real name was—that might have been it—and I did not ask. She was four feet, eight inches tall.

Another guy had a moustache, and another a beard. One girl had on a bright new blue rain suit. There were seven of us.

We put in at a place called Bee Branch, up on a ridge. The plan called for us to go down the ridge toward Thompson Creek—more of a river, really, especially today—and follow it for a dozen or so miles before coming out of the woods at the Thompson Creek Bridge, where we had left one of the cars.

On the trail, we talk and surge and shift and chatter; our packs are heavy, and it is still misting, but we are dry, and our stomachs are full. It is cool; there is a frost warning for that night. Fat white dogwood petals float like snow out over the creek on the ends of slender limbs; viewed from a distance, the limbs are invisible, so that the petals look suspended in midair.

Everyone wears ponchos. I ask the girl in the blue rain suit ahead of me what her name is and she tells me it is Sue. The trail drops steeply.

Suddenly, we are in a canyon. I am beside myself with joy. Slick rock walls, sheer faces, wet with leaking springs; tall cliffs, like out West! There are dogwoods everywhere. The blossoms hang motionless over the canyon, and our boots fall silently on the thick carpet of fern and moss. There are huge leafy trees everywhere; it is like a drizzling rain forest. Thompson Creek sounds wild. There are felt-covered green boulders everywhere, the smallest ones as big as refrigerators, and we pick our way around them.

The lure of the creek is irresistible. We will not stop until we get there.

We pass a tree bigger than the rest and pause to marvel at it. Five of us ring it and try to encircle it by holding hands, but cannot; a sixth is needed, and then a seventh. We cheer when we link up, though; we have it trapped. We stand there a moment and listen to it grow. Bill, the guy with the moustache, remarks that this tree is probably older than all of us put together. We look up at the top, or at least as high as we can see, and the understatement of his guess makes us dizzy.

There are some big trees down in the creek bottoms of the Sipsey Wilderness Area. We argue a while before finally deciding that this one will be 1017 years old this June fifth. We all agree that it would make a very loud noise if it ever fell. Doc (the guy with the beard) says that it would probably rattle windows in Birmingham and cause power outages in Atlanta.

May the woods never hear such a noise.

We reach the creek. It is like a rain forest; it is still raining lightly, but we are used to it—it is mystical. The moss-covered canyon walls box us in; a waterfall spouts over the top and showers down into the creek. It is a big waterfall; a rainbow spray mist surrounds the waterfall for many yards.

We sit on boulders and snack on peanut butter on wheat crackers and dried coconut and banana chips and watch the mist stipple the river. I look back up at the big tree and become dizzy again. It is centuries older than we. Castles were built over in Scotland, grew old and rotted and fell to the ground as it was growing. Growing a little bigger each year.

Deer that have been dead three hundred years had passed under its boughs.

Had anyone suspected, when they first saw it as a seedling, that it would ever get that big?

Had there ever been anyone to see it as a seedling in the first place?

There are no paintings, no hieroglyphics on the wall to indicate tribal civilizations. Either that, or the rain washed them off. It rains a lot in the Bankhead National Forest in April. Bring a poncho, or a blue rain suit.

A turkey gobbles, just once, and far off. We all look at one another happily, as if we had been given a gift—a real turkey gobble! At ten-thirty in the rain!

Surely it is going to be a very good day.

A green-and-yellow frog spooks and springs out of some ferns—bounds once, twice, three times—and then he is in the river and we all look at Eck: he called her name before jumping. Eck giggles. We rise, and move on.

I am in the lead; a raccoon trundles across the path in front of me, scolding at the mist. I am beside myself. I am the only one who sees it.

We stop for lunch a few hours later; these Jackson folks are an eating crowd. It's still raining, still misting. We've all got rain gear, though, and our packs are dry: the rain might as well give up and go away. I look all around me as we rest. Everywhere, great sprawling roots of unidentifiable trees clutch the green felt boulders like angry fingers; they are literally growing out of the rocks. It's amazing, it's like a hidden world, where nature does things you've never seen.

More hiking later on. We come to a side creek that can only be described as "swollen." It looks angry; it looks in pain. It makes a loud rushing sound at us as we stand on its banks. It tells us to go away.

A slender tree has been felled across it. The tree is green and limber, and slick with rain; it is barely wider than a man's foot. There's nothing to hold on to, either—no hand rails. The side creek is perhaps twenty feet wide at this point, but it is obviously the only place to cross. Jim takes his boots and socks off and tightropes across. No problem.

Jim was a member of the 1964 U.S. Olympic Gymnastic Team. He stops and lights his pipe and then does a little dance when he gets out over the middle of the creek. He bows; he does another little kick-dance, the kind the Russian vodka dancers do on top of tables. We are not amused. The women talk of turning back. I try to pretend that is a silly thing to consider; I try to pretend that I'm not glad they're suggesting it. I wonder to myself if we all closed our eyes and wished on the count of three, whether or not we could make Jim's sapling break. He's left his pack on shore; he's trying it out without the pack first, for safety's sake.

He's thirty-seven years old; he should be ashamed of himself.

In the end, we form a sort of conveyer belt. All the guys line up across the log, straddle-legged—one foot facing east, one west—and pass everyone's packs down the line. Then we all walk gingerly and shakily to the other side.

It is the ladies' turn now. They go one at a time, with a rope tied around their waists; we hold the rope and watch, nervous ourselves.

Jane goes last. Jane cannot swim. We are extra nervous with Jane. She doesn't fall in, though, and we all cheer when she is across. We shoulder our packs and look back at the big creek and marvel for a moment; it is the first time a lot of us have done anything like that. One minute we were on one side, and then we were on the other. Just like that.

Feeling coltish and giddy with leftover excitement, we start up the steep hill. "That was fun," says Eck. I look at her carefully to see if she is being sarcastic, but I swear I don't think she was. But then you could expect as much from a girl named Eck.

It stops raining shortly before dark, as we are making camp for the night. I say making camp; what camp really consisted of was this: unrolling our sleeping bags under the overhang of the Big Cave.

It's probably got a name locally—Throne Room of the Gods, or Thunder Palace, or something like that—but for us, it was the Big Cave.

It was big enough to sleep a dozen, easily.

We were the only ones in the cave that night; north of that swollen creek, we were the only ones in the entire Wilderness Area. We began casting about for semi-dry twigs and branches. It was a challenge.

We get the fire going. It cheers us even more than we already are. Though it is still daylight, a bottle of white wine is produced. Dusk hangs over the river below in a quiet, satisfied mist; bats and night birds chatter and swoop across its surface with great energy, with great excitement.

Jim is a foreign car specialist; Doc is a neurosurgeon. Jane is an architect, and Eck's a schoolteacher. We sit with our feet dangling over the cliff and pass the bottle like bums. It's fun. We stand up and take turns trying to imitate the little dance Jim did on the log this afternoon. We sit back down and watch the river, and watch the night come in. We go back to the fire and add more wood to it. It blazes; it lights up the cave. We grow more cheerful still.

Jim cooks pizza for all of us; it's his surprise. He has, he tells us, brought seven different kinds of cheese. He busies us all with the preparations: mixing dough, grating cheese, cracking eggs. I am instructed to slice the eggplant.

There is (as there is in all of us) a small streak of the bizarre in Jim Trunzler. It needs letting out every now and then; it needs a release of the tension. I politely chose to view this abnormality of bringing eggplant pizza as a minor illness, and (politely) avoided mentioning it to him. I washed my hands in the little waterfall that spattered down off the cliff above us; I sliced the eggplant.

Baking in the fire, in foil, it smelled good. He cooked it for thirty minutes.

Is it possible for someone to go twenty-four years under the mistaken impression that he doesn't like eggplant?

Yes.

After the eggplant there were jokes, of course. We laughed; we talked. The fire faded, and we yawned. The river's cadence pitched and changed occasionally; changing water loads from the day's numerous earlier rainfalls did this. There were no sounds other than the river; we were too close. There were no stars either; there were too many trees around to see the sky.

No one had a watch. We went to bed. It could have been eight-thirty, or it could have been quarter past one.

What did it matter?

Breakfast, and some of us are back on the ledge, watching the sun come up. We're discussing those two philosophies I talked about earlier, the ones about cooking. Behind us, Jim is cooking blueberry pancakes—we can smell the blueberries. I open another can of Vienna sausages and drain the oil over the edge of the cliff.

But my spartan breakfast leaves me free to do this: while everyone else is cleaning up, while they are still cooking even, I get my pack all ready to go and then leave it in the cave and wander down the talus slope, down to the river. The sun's up pretty good now; it's a warm Sunday morning, not bad at all for the week after Easter. I sit on the rocks in my shorts and a tee shirt and read a paperback about a cattle rancher in Montana. There's a little breeze; the river music is relaxing too, and slowly, I move through the chapters.

Again, no watch. Perhaps I read for fifteen minutes; perhaps two hours.

I'm not sure why I looked up, or how long he'd been sitting there watching me. I think I was in his spot, or where he wanted to be; I was in the brightest, warmest patch of sunlight on the entire talus slope. I recognized him immediately as a patch-nosed garter snake. He noticed me looking at him, and flicked his tongue, and then—I swear I am not making this up, he really did this—looked embarrassed. He turned and slithered in and out of some rocks, down into some brush.

A butterfly comes sailing by ninety-to-nothing, a black-and-yellow barred one, comes sailing across the spot where that snake sat coiled not twenty seconds ago. I am awed at the workings of this event. It is like Fate showing off. I like butterflies, I like them a lot, and yet I find myself wanting to cry out to the snake. "Wait! Come back! If only you had waited a little longer . . ."

The butterfly breezes past, never even slows down.

I refocus; I am startled to see the snake again, just a little farther down the slope. He hasn't left after all; he's watching the swallowtail. I can tell he's watching it because his tongue is not flicking. He's got it folded back in against the roof of his mouth, and he's just sitting there, spellbound, thinking about how good that particular kind of butterfly tastes. The butterfly flits, dips, pauses at a flower, then glides toward the snake.

I can see it coming before it happens. Awed and aghast, I shout a warning, but they ignore me. They rise toward each other like friends, the butterfly drifting and the snake striking.

The snake misses. (I like to think it was my yell that threw him off.) The butterfly leaps higher into the air, terrified, and careers off crazily into the woods. The snake coils back, tests the air again with his tongue, glares at the spot where the butterfly was a second ago, and then races off into the woods himself.

Embarrassed again, no doubt.

Eck comes down to the creek to see what I was shouting at. "A bear," I tell her. She turns and runs back up to the camp.

But really, there might be bears in the Sipsey after all; who knows? It's a wilderness area; it's wild. Last night I dreamed of bears.

Are there bears in the Sipsey? Is it truly that wild, that free?

I don't know, but I do know this: one time I dreamed of a friend I hadn't seen in over ten years, a friend I didn't know still existed, and the next day, I saw him on a city street.

On the way out, I watch the shadows carefully; I sniff the air and scan the path for tracks.

I do not find any, but that does not mean they are not there; it does not make the Sipsey any less wild, or any less free.

They were probably still hibernating.

Conger Beasley

Conger Beasley has published two novels and two books of poetry. His essays and articles have appeared in the *Washington Post,* the *North American Review* and *Orion Nature Quarterly*. In this essay from *Sundancers and River Demons: Essays on Landscape and Ritual* (University of Arkansas Press, 1990), Conger Beasley provides readers with a meditation on one of the great North American rivers, the Missouri. In the author's youth, the Missouri "was a creature to observe from a distance and to cross as quickly as possible; it was not a place to linger in idle contemplation or recreational enjoyment. It was an unbridled monster in dire need of hobbling." Thirty years later Beasley canoes on a river that, like himself, has "changed in character and shape." The river "no longer is as wide as it once was; neither does it flood as torrentially." Despite being tamed by dams and water diversion projects, the Missouri is still wild in places: "You have to search for [these places], but they are there. Great blue herons still poke for frogs along the banks. Kingfishers rattle noisily between the trees. ... Turkey vultures hover over the bottomlands. ... Fish erupt from the scuddy current. ..." Beasley is moved to an eloquent defense of the river and the region: "The Midwest is a sadly misunderstood place, routinely dismissed by Californians and Atlantic seaboarders, scorned by Rocky Mountain enthusiasts, and grudgingly defended by its own inhabitants. In a culture that celebrates spectacular surfaces, such a quiet, unruffled landscape is easy to ridicule." The essay ends with a fine description of a beaver that Beasley sighted along the Missouri a few years ago, an indication of the resilience of the historic river the trappers called "The Big Blue."

The Return of Beaver to the Missouri River
(circa 1987)

In an autobiographical volume entitled *The River and I,* John Neihardt recounts the first time he ever looked upon the Missouri River. It was sometime in the late 1880s, and the place was Kansas City. The river was in full flood, a "yellow swirl that spread out into the wooded bottomlands," demolishing entire towns. "There was a dreadful fascination about it," Neihardt remembers, "the fascination of all huge and irresistible things. I had caught my first wee glimpse into the infinite. ..."

Some seventy years later, in the spring of 1953, I stood on a bluff in St. Joseph, Missouri, and watched the last great flood on that unruly river ravage the bottomlands between my home town and the hills of distant Kansas. Augmented by several weeks of ferocious rains, tributaries in Iowa and Nebraska had disgorged an unprecedented volume of water into the Missouri, which quickly overflowed its banks. Levees crumbled, dikes collapsed, water swept across wheat and alfalfa fields, carrying houses, cattle, barns, and automobiles with it. From bluff to bluff between the two states, a distance of maybe five miles, the river was stippled with foamy whirlpools and entire trees. I remember watching the procession in stunned silence with my father and his friends. All my life (I was then twelve) I had heard of the river and watched it from passing cars and trains and even viewed it once or twice from airplanes, but I had never been on it in a boat or (God forbid) swum in it. That was unthinkable. The river was too capricious to attempt such a feat. There were boiling eddies that could devour the strongest swimmer, deadly snags and sawyers that could rip open the stoutest hull, animals with pointy teeth that could tear off a leg or arm. No, the river was a creature to observe from a distance and to cross as quickly as possible; it was not a place to linger in idle contemplation or recreational enjoyment. It was an unbridled monster in dire need of hobbling.

"That sure is a hell of a lot of water," remarked one of my father's friends.

"The airport's gone. Elwood's under water. A few feet more and it will wash over the Pony Express Bridge," said another.

"Yeah, but this won't keep up for long," declared a third. "Once they close off those dams up in Dakota, this ole river's gonna get trimmed down to size."

I think of that exchange now, thirty years later, whenever I launch my raft or canoe out on the river. Within the scope of a few decades it has changed in character and shape. It no longer is as wide as it once was; neither does it flood as torrentially. Periodically, it spills over its banks and inundates the lowlands, but it no longer rolls from bluff to bluff or sweeps through entire communities, stranding people in trees. Rarely does it bring the media rushing to its cresting banks. The dams up in South Dakota and the Army Corps of Engineers have taken care of that. Over the years the Corps has deepened the channel and made it more accessible to barge traffic. More recently, the Corps has lined the banks with a solid wall of riprap and installed wingdikes which jut out into the water at right angles; silt, building up behind these protrusions, progressively narrows the river's width. Gradually, the Corps has exerted more and more control over the river, reducing it in size to a tawny ribbon whose least impulse can be carefully monitored. In the process commercial fishing has become almost nonexistent, and the meandering oxbows—remnants of the river's earlier path—have dried up, drastically reducing the acreage of precious wetlands, prime nesting places for waterfowl.

"You know what that river has become?" a man said to me recently in a bar in Kansas City. "An irrigation ditch, that's what. A goddamn irrigation ditch!"

He had grown up in St. Joseph in the 1920s and '30s, and had fished on the river as a boy. Once, on his sixteenth birthday, he had swum the width, from Kansas back to the Missouri side. When he told me that, I gazed at him with speechless admiration. When I was growing up, swimming the river was the most daring thing a boy could do, more daring than stealing the old man's car for a joyride or crawling through sewer pipes under a cemetery or putting your hand on a girl's breast or even engaging in BB-gun wars.

Despite considerable changes that have severely modified its character, the river is still regarded with trepidation by most people who live near it. The reasons for this are mystifying. Recently, as I was tying my canoe on top of my car, my neighbor—an amiable man in his sixties, a veteran of the Battle of the Bulge—strolled over to help me adjust the ropes and tie the knots. "Where you headed?" he asked after pronouncing the boat secure.

"I'm going on the river."

"The Missouri!"

"Yep. A day float down from the mouth of the Platte."

He pulled carefully on his cigarette. "Well, you want to think twice before doing that, don't you?"

"Why?"

"It's dangerous. There're whirlpools that can easily upset a canoe the size of yours."

"Have you ever been on the river?" I asked.

"No. But I grew up around here, and I know when to stay away from a place that doesn't want me."

As I drove to the river I thought about what he had said. He had encouraged me to enjoy an outing on Smithville Lake, a reservoir located northeast of Kansas City, filled with power boats and water skiers and beer-drinking people swaddled with layers of fat. Their presence aside, there's something about still water that doesn't engage my imagination the way moving water does. A river flows from point to point and around the next bend; scenes unfold in slow procession with subtle variations. The sense of motion is invigorating.

My neighbor's remarks recalled the look of incredulity on my father's face the first time I told him I was going on the river. I might just as well have put a gun to my head and pulled the trigger, he declared, for all the chance I had of surviving.

"But you don't understand," I protested. "The river has changed since the time you took me up on the bluff to watch the flood. You can still die there, I grant you. But it's not the power it once was."

"You're crazy," he concluded with a shake of the head. "You're crazy to tempt fate that way."

When the reality alters, the rhetoric seems to harden into place. At least that's what I concluded after talking with my father and neighbor—two men of the same generation and similar backgrounds and experiences. The Missouri River—the lower portion of it at least, from Gavin's Point Dam in South Dakota to its juncture with the Mississippi—is but a slip of its former brawly self; nonetheless, the popular perception of it remains the same. The folklore of the river still evokes images of greedy whirlpools and menacing trees and aquatic carnivores. Elements of these images persist, though in sadly reduced form. Added to these fears, of course, is the relatively new one of pollution, though like many rivers in the United States the Missouri is less contaminated now than it was twenty-five years ago, primarily because the stockyards of Omaha, St. Joseph, and Kansas City no longer pump their refuse directly into it. But the rhetoric persists, almost as if people need to believe all the bad things they've heard. The river is still configured in the local imagination—and not just by people my father's age—as an excess in need of correcting.

The fact of the matter is that the Missouri has been "corrected"—overcorrected to a fault, I would say: dammed, diked, dredged, and drained to suit the needs of the dying barge traffic industry—so it will no longer flood valuable property along the banks; so it will no longer serve as a breeding ground for superfluous fish and wildlife. Certainly as a cultural and recreational resource it has been sadly ignored. In Kansas City, for example, there is virtually no access to the river within the city limits; there is no museum or park along the banks where the river can be viewed and appreciated. Memories of the devastating 1951 flood are still vivid here; while that kind of destruction will never occur again, does it really make sense to construct more wingdikes and drain more oxbows and lay down more riprap so that, within the city boundaries at least, the river will purl harmlessly as water through a sluice?

Enough water flows past Kansas City in a single day to satisfy its needs for an entire year. When I tell this to my river-running friends in New Mexico and the arid Southwest, they express envy and delight. But when they actually view the river and see the wingdikes with the sandbars filling in behind them and the miles of concrete chunks lining the banks, they shrug and turn away. The river isn't very interesting, they seem to say. It isn't very wild.

And yet parts of it still are. You have to search for them, but they are there. Great blue herons still poke for frogs along the banks. Kingfishers rattle noisily between the trees. Borne by sultry thermals, turkey vultures hover over the bottomlands, scouting for carrion. Fish erupt from the scuddy current in flashes of sun-dappled scales. And the river still churns along its ancient bed, down from the Dakotas, across the loamy, fertile midsection of the continent, to its fabled confluence with the Mississippi. Always, even in its present denatured form, there is a sense of movement, of process, of rhythm ... of a metabolism older and wiser and more meaningful than anything yet invented by human ingenuity.

Historically, the Missouri River has defined one segment of the progressive western border of the American continent. It provided the pathway into the heart of the northern plains and brought trappers and explorers to the verge of the Rockies. In states like the two Dakotas it marks the boundary between one form of terrain and another. East of the river, the land is sectioned into small undulating farms with a distinct Midwestern feel; west of it, the grass diminishes in height, the range opens up to the

horizon, and the sky arches endlessly like a yawning mouth. When
the Teton Sioux first crossed the river in significant numbers in the
mid-eighteenth century, their culture changed dramatically. For
decades in southwest Minnesota they had been a woodland
community, dwelling in deep pine forests, hunting and fishing on
lakes, content with occasional forays onto the plains. Once they
crossed the river their transformation into a fierce warrior society,
the most respected of all Plains Indians, was assured. Armed with
French rifles and mounted on Spanish horses, they created,
through legendary heroes like Crazy Horse and Sitting Bull, a
reputation for valor that endures to this day. Ahead of them lay the
Badlands and the Black Hills and battlefields like the Rosebud and
the Little Big Horn. Behind them, frothy and unpredictable—a
Rubicon of the sensibility that forever distinguishes the western
imagination from all others on the continent—flowed the massive,
untidy, indefatigable Missouri.

Unquestionably, George Caleb Bingham was the premier artist
of the Missouri River, if not the entire border region, and in the
Metropolitan Museum of Art in New York City hangs one of his finest
works, "Fur Traders Descending the Missouri." It depicts a man,
probably of French extraction, and a boy, most likely a half-breed,
sitting in a pirogue laden with furs. The time is early evening; roseate
tints from the descending sun tinge the river's placid face and the trees
in the background. The man smokes a pipe and dips his paddle in the
water, more to steer than to accelerate the pirogue's speed. The boy
leans against a hide-covered chest and stares dreamily into the artist's
eyes. On the bow, tethered by a short rope, sits one of the most
enigmatic figures in all of American painting ... a dark, bristly, wolfish-
looking animal with pointed ears and a glistening snout that appears
to be looking down at its reflected image in the water—or is it staring
into the artist's eyes?

Blake's tyger holds less portent for me than this creature. I like
to think that, intentionally or not, Bingham captured in this
curious figure the true feeling of wilderness that the Missouri River
once held for explorers and adventurers. That feeling has been
described accurately and at great length by observers from Lewis

and Clark to John Neihardt and James Willard Schultz; but no
where else for me in all the art and writing produced by the region
does it exist so powerfully. Whenever I bemoan the loss of the
river's freedom, I look at that painting and am content that
Bingham at least was able to capture a portion of what it once was
and to pass it on for others to savor. Whenever I paddle my canoe
on the silty current, I imagine the animal sitting in the bow, staring
back at me with all the irony and inscrutability that two hundred
years of bitter history can produce.

The Midwest is a sadly misunderstood place, routinely dismissed by Californians and Atlantic seaboarders, scorned by Rocky
Mountain enthusiasts, and grudgingly defended by its own inhabitants. In a culture that celebrates spectacular surfaces, such a quiet,
unruffled landscape is easy to ridicule. "I don't like to go west of
the Alleghenies," a lawyer in New York once told me when I was
a student there. "Missouri, Kansas ... places like that. It's the same
old thing, over and over and over again."

But it's not. The rivers of southern Missouri differ from the rivers
of eastern Kansas. The foliage along the banks, the soil composition,
the fish and animals vary in subtle, yet significant, ways. A
sensitivity to the nuances of topography sharpens the eye and instructs
the mind in the difficult task of making distinctions between organic
forms. There is a moral here. The way we perceive landscape can
have a direct bearing upon the way we perceive society and the
human beings who comprise it. Dismissing a landscape because it
does not conform to preconceptions is a prejudice as galling as
dismissing people because of the color of their skin or the beliefs
they profess. It violates the biological urge toward multiplicity and
diversity that energizes our planet. By adjusting the rhetoric of
perception to the reality of the fact perceived—by making the two
more consonant and therefore truthful—our sensibilities can be
sharpened and refined, and wherever we go in the world, instead
of adopting the prevailing stereotype, we can encounter the reality,
the genuine forms, that reside underneath.

One evening, after floating all day down from Atchison, Kansas,
a friend and I passed under the Leavenworth bridge just as the sun was

about to set. Our destination was Parkville, Missouri, a small town a
few miles upriver from Kansas City. The time was late summer; a full
moon was due to appear in about an hour, and despite the obvious
dangers of floating at night, we intended to do just that, guided by the
moonlight and the phosphorescent markers on the channel buoys.
Barge traffic had been light that day, but we needed to be wary of the
occasional tree limb that bobbed just under the surface.

The moon, huge and full, came up over the trees on the east
bank. The light spilled onto the leaves and spread in a wavering beam
across the water. We watched with fascination as the sky and river
seemed to swell under the eerie light. On the west bank, willows and
cottonwoods stood out in bold relief; between them, dark and moist
as the entrance of a cave, the shadows were alive with sounds.

Suddenly, closeby, there was a loud crash as if a rock had been
chucked into the river, followed by another and another, echoing back
and forth and far downstream. "What the hell was that?" my friend
exclaimed; and I confess that at that moment images of river demons,
passed on to me by another generation, surfaced in my brain. A
moment later I saw a creature with a sleek head and flat tail slip off the
bank and disappear into the water. "Beaver," I muttered, almost in
disbelief. One of the stories I had heard as a boy was that the beaver
had been trapped out in these parts, along with the otter and mink,
leaving only the muskrat, a durable species.

Additional explosions sounded up and down the channel,
signaling our presence. "Beaver," I whispered, and suddenly I had
a vision of the river as it once was—wide, tumultuous, shoally with
islands, teeming with birds and fish and animals. If this were 1832,
their pelts would fetch hard silver down in Westport or in the
trading posts of Blacksnake Hills. But it wasn't; that era, with its
magnificent vistas and murderous events, was over. The future
stretched before us with the same chimerical uncertainty as the
river's path in the moonlight. Tonight we were just drifting along,
enjoying the sights, the steady current, the moist air that lapped
against our cheeks. As if in acknowledgment, more beaver boomed
their warning signal. We laughed and called out to them. This
time, I thought, we'll share the river together.

John Hildebrand

John Hildebrand received his Master of Fine Arts in Creative Writing from the University of Alaska, Fairbanks, and currently teaches at the University of Wisconsin, Eau Claire. His articles and essays have appeared in *Sports Illustrated* and *Outside*. In 1988 John Hildebrand published his first work of nonfiction, *Reading the River: A Voyage Down the Yukon* (Houghton Mifflin), which describes a solo trip he made down the entire length of the Yukon River in a canoe. The book met with critical acclaim and has been reissued as a paperback. In "Wading in the North Woods," which originally appeared in *Outside* magazine in April 1989, John Hildebrand takes us on a tour of the Upper Peninsula of Michigan. This is Hemingway Country and many of Hemingway's best-known stories originate here, including most of the stories from *In Our Time* (Scribner's, 1925) and the always popular "Big Two-Hearted River." Hildebrand's search for the geographic center of these stories leads him to a better understanding of both Hemingway and the North Woods. These northern Midwestern forests have inspired two other important nature writers: Sigurd Olson, who wrote of northern Minnesota, and Aldo Leopold, who kept his famous "Shack" very close to Eau Claire where John Hildebrand now teaches. There are wolves and moose, black bears and beautiful loons in the North Woods, and Hildebrand's love for this wilderness is more than evident here in "Wading in the North Woods."

Wading in the North Woods
(circa 1989)

As a child I was told that the Upper Peninsula of Michigan was shaped like a running wolf. I see now that this is nonsense. It's only because the state's lower half looks like a discarded mitten that anyone tries to make the upper half into an animal. But a map can be a kind of Rorschach test. If people fool themselves into seeing a wolf caught in mid-leap between three Great Lakes, well, it just says something of our expectations for the place.

The Upper Peninsula is wild enough to accommodate running wolves as well as other things the Midwest supposedly lacks—like mountains and coastline. In the western part of the peninsula, the Porcupine Mountains rise to just under two thousand feet, the highest range in mid-America. To the east is Pictured Rocks National Lakeshore with its sand dunes, wave-cut arches and caves eroded out of the rugged Superior coast. And far out into Lake Superior itself is Isle Royale National Park, a granite atoll of the Canadian Shield that has both moose and timber wolves. Personally, I like driving across the UP's pine plains and stopping at dinky towns with French names like L'Anse or Grand Marais to order the local specialty, a greasy meat pie called a pasty, to go. But most of all I like camping along the rivers.

A river, the thinking goes, is as good as its name. And nowhere do the rivers run more evocative than in the Upper Peninsula. There is the Yellow Dog, the Salmon Trout, the Ontanagon (four branches) and the Manistique. But the most beautiful of all, in name at least, is the Big Two-Hearted River. The words sound mysterious and vaguely Indian. They also form the title of Ernest Hemingway's classic story of trout fishing and angst in the North Woods.

A few summers ago I went looking for Hemingway's river. A map wasn't necessary, the river's course having been fixed in my memory since I was twenty and read the story in a dusty volume of *The Hemingway Reader*. I drove across the Upper Peninsula until I came to Seney, a few cottages and a cafe straddling Highway M-24. The story begins with Nick getting off the train at Seney to discover the town devastated by fire. Nothing remains but scorched earth and the heat-split foundation of the Mansion House Hotel. Walking down the tracks, he finds the river alive and flowing beneath a bridge. *It stretched away, pebbly-bottomed with shallows and big boulders and a deep pool as it curved away around the foot of a bluff.* Nick watches trout holding in the current beside the log pilings until a kingfisher swoops upstream. Then he picks up his heavy pack and rod case and sets off across the hilly, burned-over countryside to hit the river far upstream.

Full of anticipation, I followed the trackbed of the Soo Line west out of Seney until it crossed the iron bridge. Here then was Nick's river! It slipped beneath the bridge, a clear brown river louvered in slats of light from the cracks between the crossties. But not a single trout was holding in the current; the river bottom wasn't pebbly but clean, ribbed sand, and forget about boulders. Ahead the river flowed through country without a hint of a hill.

No kingfisher made its obligatory flight upstream.

Literature, of course, follows its own meandering logic. One just assumes, wants to believe, that the river in the story was the same as the one in the title. It isn't. Only one river flows through Seney, and it is the Fox. The Big Two-Hearted, a real enough trout stream, lies far to the northeast in another county. To hike there from Seney in a day through swamp and thick woods is flatly impossible. Which river, then, did Hemingway have in mind?

In 1919, the summer of his twentieth year, Hemingway still limped from a mortar wound received the year before on the Italian front. Recuperation took the form of trout fishing on streams near his parents' cottage at Walloon Lake. On the final trip of the summer, Ernest and two friends took a ferry across the straits to St. Ignace and then a long, swaying train ride across the pine flats to Seney. For a week they camped on the banks of the Fox River above the town, catching trout and reveling in the absolute freedom that would soon dissolve before the onslaught of employment and marriage.

The Fox then was the story's germinal river, but it was not the one I had imagined in all those years of vicarious wading. Down-hearted, I headed for the car.

Twenty-two miles north of Newberry and a couple of miles above Pine Stump Junction on County Road 407, a state forest sign beside High Bridge reads BIG TWO-HEARTED RIVER IMMORTALIZED BY ERNEST HEMINGWAY. The river's watershed lies in northern Luce County, a sparsely settled region of lakes and pineries. Rising in spring-fed lakes, the river takes on the color of the cedar swamps and tamarack forests in its path, so that, passing beneath High Bridge, the water is a transparent brown with big, smooth boulders making white rents in the fast stretches. Hemingway may never have laid eyes on the Two-Hearted, but he certainly imagined it in perfect detail.

Most of the watershed is within the boundaries of Lake Superior State Forest, and the Two-Hearted itself has been desig-nated by the state as a Wilderness River; what private lands remain are held by a handful of venerable sporting clubs. Four state forest campgrounds lie between High Bridge and the river's terminus at Lake Superior. A good day's canoe trip is the seventeen-mile run between Reed campground and the bridge at the river's mouth. But my plan was to fish the headwaters where the Two-Hearted's main branches angle in from opposing compass points and count-less logjams deter all but the most manic canoeists.

Fly rod in hand, I struck off from High Bridge along a sandy road through the jack pine. It was a hot day. The heat fairly radiated off the white surface of the road. Already I was sweating beneath a Duluth pack overloaded with a camping outfit from an era when the mark of an outdoorsman was the sheer volume of junk he lugged into the woods. The second-growth forests of northern Michigan lend themselves to that kind of low-tech approach. You want canned goods, khaki and wool clothes and a good canvas tent. You don't want to look like the latest thing in backpacking, done up like a Gore-tex® Easter egg. After an hour, though, my back was killing me.

Turning south toward the river, the road climbed up and around forested ridges. I rested my pack on a cut bank and watched a swallowtail butterfly flutter down the hot road. A wind ripped through the treetops and the road moved in and out of shadow. The river could not have been far off.

This was the Michigan woods that Hemingway was trying to write about in Paris in 1924. Living in another country seemed to sharpen the memory of his own. Mornings he would write at a cafe and in the afternoon walk to the Musée du Luxembourg to look at the French Impressionists' paintings. In a letter to Gertrude Stein, he mentioned a long story he had written about trout fishing and how in it he was "trying to do the country like Cézanne."

The story is a somber reflection of the trip Ernest had taken five years earlier to the Fox River. Not only is the landscape altered, but Nick is now alone as he hikes upriver from Seney to make his camp beside a meadow where the river runs into a swamp. The war is never mentioned but it hangs over the story like the pale mist rising from the swamp. Very little happens in "Big Two-Hearted River," but the way Hemingway wrote about the country was something new. The short, simple words blend together like flat brushstrokes of pigment on a landscape of light and shadow. The graceful repetition of words creates a strange sense of depth: *There was the meadow, the river and the swamp. There were birch trees in the green of the swamp on the far side of the river.*

The road crossed the North Branch on a plank bridge then climbed to a sandy bluff where the river cut close in an oxbow curve. I staked out my canvas tent with a view to the river, lost elsewhere in solid alder. Over a campfire, I opened a can of spaghetti and another of beans and wondered how many young men in khaki shirts and impossible packs make this pilgrimage, their lips silently reciting each scene as it's reenacted. Nick Hiking Across the Pine Plain. Nick Making Camp. Nick Opening the Can of Spaghetti and Beans.

The next morning I was up early and flopping down to the river in my waders. In the spring and fall, anadromous rainbow trout, or steelhead, ascend the river from Lake Superior to spawn. But aside from lingering rainbow smolts, this is brook trout water. The river was frigid, even through my waders. False casting line to reach upstream, I addressed the fly to the pool below a sandstone ledge and came up tight on a trout. The fish made a short, heartening run before sagging in my net. It was no salmon-like monster of the sort that bends Nick's fly rod double, but a nice brookie, its sides flecked with vermillion dots and golden coronas.

At the confluence with the North Branch, I sloshed up the lesser stream. No singular swamp intersects the Two-Hearted such as Nick confronts, but stretches of the North Branch possess the same dark, constricting qualities. There are always plenty of trout in streams like this, scarcely fished trout leading unlikely lives in brief pockets of water. The going is tortuous, cedars criss-crossing the river, the banks unwieldy with timber. When an open stretch of water presented itself, I quickly broke my leader on a submerged root. Annoyed, what I really wanted to feel was some deep reaction to this wading, some link with the story so that my heart would tighten with *all the old feeling.*

After Hemingway left Paris and returned to this country as its resident literary lion, he lost interest in Michigan. The years were divided among the Florida Keys, Cuba and finally Idaho. The North Woods, he complained, had changed too much from the wilderness he had known as a boy. Maybe so, but people change in ways the country doesn't, and the Two-Hearted remains the river we want it to be.

With the one good brookie for breakfast, I waded back to the confluence. I would head back to camp now, fry up the trout and reread the story to find out what Nick would do next. Scrambling over the trail, I heard a racheting song overflow the riverbanks as a kingfisher swooped upstream.

Dan O'Brien

Dan O'Brien, who was born in 1947, lives on a ranch in South Dakota where he divides his time between work as an endangered-species biologist and teaching literature and creative writing. O'Brien received graduate degrees from the University of South Dakota and Bowling Green University. His first collection of short stories, *Eminent Domain,* won the Iowa Short Fiction Award and was published by the University of Iowa Press in 1988. O'Brien has subsequently published one work of nature nonfiction, *The Rites of Autumn: A Falconer's Journey Across the American West* (Atlantic Monthly Press, 1988; Doubleday paperback, 1989), and two novels, *Spirit of the Hills* (Crown, 1990) and *In the Center of the Nation* (Atlantic Monthly Press, 1991). Almost all of Dan O'Brien's writing has focused on the region around his home in the Black Hills of South Dakota. In *The Rites of Autumn* he describes his attempts to teach an injured peregrine falcon how to fly and hunt in the wild; the journey leads O'Brien across the American West, from his home near Rapid City to the Charles Russell National Wildlife Refuge in Montana, to the Front Range of Colorado, to the Llano Estacado and Laguna Madras of Texas. In this marvelous passage from the book, the author's love of the land, and for the falcon he is trying to save, is strongly evident, as he relates his successful hunt for a ruffed grouse and then the falcon's first successful hunt for a pheasant: "... I looked closely. Her eyes were slightly deeper, her feathers tighter, and her grip on the pheasant more intense. In some immeasurable way this was a different peregrine from the one who had disappeared into the dusk an hour before."

The Grasslands
(circa 1988)

It would have been faster to drive around the Black Hills, but there was a place in the center of the Hills that I visited every autumn and this would be my last chance. With the pickup loaded again, we started up Boulder Canyon toward Deadwood. This road is in a perpetual state of disrepair and winds as it climbs the several thousand feet to the old gold mining towns. The largest hard-rock gold mine in North America is still located in Lead and is the main employer of the area. But as in most of the mining and energy-related economy of the West, the wealth doesn't seem to stay in the area. As in the oil towns, the uranium towns, and the coal towns, the promises of prosperity have never really come true and the Deadwood-Lead area of South Dakota, for all its charm and history, seems depressed and gray. The only real gold in the Black Hills is the autumn aspen leaves. And even those, on that late October day, were past their prime. I wound away from the mining towns into gravel roads and could see by the drifts of fallen aspen leaves that winter would arrive any day. I was late for my annual ruffed grouse hunt.

There is not a lot of good ruffed grouse habitat in the Black Hills because the aspen is being replaced by pine. What habitat there is does not get heavy hunting pressure and so the grouse remain tame. The place I go to is the site of an old forest fire with logging trails cut through the second growth timber. The area is hilly and the hunting hard. I never find more than a few grouse and usually only get shots at one or two, but the beauty of a hunt in the Hills at this time of year is enough to keep me coming back autumn after autumn. Because the grouse are tame they are easy for dogs to handle, perfect game for puppies. Ruffed grouse would be a good lesson for Spud.

We stopped along a logging road miles from the nearest blacktop, and I let Spud and Jake out while I pieced together the shotgun my father had given me. I ran my fingers over the chip in the stock and remembered the morning, twenty years before, when I had dropped it while trying to take it apart in the dark. The sharp pain in my left ear came back to me and I shook my head. It had been a terrible time; a time that would be nice to forget. But that was impossible because everything I was or did went back that far in my memory. It was really all that was left of my father, and in a way it had given me the freedom to start moving. If I traced the genesis of this trip with Dolly far enough back, I would find the old shotgun. I ran my finger over the stock again and then down along the barrels. It was not a fine shotgun and many times I had thought of getting a better gun. But this gun and I had a lot of history. I glanced down at Spud, who was looking up at me as if he wondered what was going on, and thought that this might be the day he would become part of that history. Then I put a handful of shells in my pocket and snapped a bell to Spud's collar so I could tell where he was in the brush. I touched him on the back of the head and told him to go on. Jake moved up to heel and we walked up the hill through the golden aspen leaves.

Spud took off and in no time his bell was out of hearing. He had never hunted in thick cover before, and he would have to learn. Though Spud liked to run, he liked people even more. Instead of trying to call him in, I sat down in a particularly thick spot and waited. Jake and I were partially hidden when Spud charged past us. I didn't say a word. In a few minutes he was back, looking a little more worried. He stood for a moment in a clearing and I could see that he was concerned that he might be lost. He charged off again, but in a moment he returned. This time he was clearly afraid that he was alone. He made several starts in different directions, then I heard him whine. That was enough. I stood up. When he saw us he bolted headlong into the thicket where we had hidden and leapt into my arms. Leaping into arms was against the rules, but I couldn't help holding him for a few seconds while he licked my face.

We tried it again. Spud moved ahead, through the aspen and the spruce. This time he stayed close and checked in frequently. We walked to the top of the rise, then followed the edge of the tallest timber. When we found an abandoned logging road, we followed it to a clearing where someone, a miner perhaps, had built a shack. It was mid-morning and the sunlight filtered through the trees in such a way that the weathered grain of the siding cast shadows on itself. It was one of thousands of little buildings that had been built in the Black Hills in the last hundred years. Nature had reclaimed the area, and now the building was only a place for a great horned owl to live.

I didn't linger at the shed. Spud was working a particularly nice edge between a group of aspens and a tiny meadow and I moved to stay up with him. But I couldn't help wondering what the builder of the shed had in mind. Had he planned to get rich in these hills? It was likely: If so, the shed was a monument to the folly of that notion. I was thinking about this when I noticed that Spud's bell had gone silent. I moved ahead quickly and looked into the juniper bushes growing along the edge. It was still in my mind that Spud might have wandered out of hearing or that he had just stopped to rest when I saw grouse droppings. Jake, still walking at heel, raised his head and tested the breeze. His tail came up and began to wag double-time. Ruffed grouse had obviously been using that area, and for the first time it seemed possible that Spud had found one and was on point. I began to search hard. I finally spotted a black and white tail pointing skyward from the center of a patch of brush.

I made Jake sit and stay, then moved toward Spud as quickly as I could without making too much noise. Finally I could see that Spud was frozen in a curved position, his head lower than his rear and turned to the side as if he had been moving perpendicular to the scent when he hit it. I shifted around so that the grouse was more likely to flush into the open. When I was within five feet of Spud's nose, I stopped and looked hard into the grass and brush. For a long time I saw nothing, then I caught the flick of the grouse's tail and heard it make a putt-putt sound. The sound made Spud's ears come up even higher, and he swelled with excitement but didn't move. It was proof that his nose had not lied to him. "Easy," I said, sliding shells into the twenty-gauge. I closed the gun and moved to flank the grouse.

Even though I knew that it was ready to fly, the sound of its wings startled me. Spud jumped in as the grouse pounded free of the brush. It turned sharply to miss a pine tree and careened back toward the shed. It was an easy shot and it crumpled not far from where Jake waited. The sound of the shotgun and the falling grouse were too much. Jake broke and scooped up the grouse before it had stopped rolling. Spud, being inexperienced, had not watched the bird down and ran off frantically in the wrong direction. I stepped into the clearing and met Jake who brought the grouse to me posthaste, his tail arched and his head high and proud.

I knelt and took the bird. The big dog wiggled all over, then got a grip on himself and regained his dignity by lying down as I inspected the grouse. Spud returned and nosed the bird as I turned it in my hands. I marveled at the delicate brown feathers of its neck, spread the tail and saw by the continuous black band that it was a male. It was probably a bird of the year, recently dispersed from its family group. Somewhere close, there was a log that this bird would have used to drum in females in the spring. Now the log would be used by another grouse. I made a note to myself to come back in late April and listen to the thmm-thmm-thmm. Then I spread the wings and tried to grasp the phenomenon of evolution that had produced this bird. These cup-shaped wings, pounding against a log, could call a female from a great distance, yet the sound was somehow ventriloquistic and hard for predators to find. The drumming is also produced at forty cycles a second, well within the auditory range of the grouse but too low to be heard by the great horned owl that probably lived near the old shed. Nature is a process of selection; everything fits at least as snugly as the works of a watch. The grouse whose wings beat at fifty cycles a second were all gone, and so were the people who built the shed.

The three of us walked back to the truck and I gave Spud and Jake a drink of water. Dolly stood on her perch. I could see by the bulge at her neck that there was a little duck still in her crop from the day before. She would not be interested in flying that afternoon. That was fine, since I wanted to camp near the North Platte and try her the next day in Nebraska. It was afternoon by then and had begun to cloud up. After I cleaned the grouse, we loaded up and made our way to the blacktop road. By the time we left the Black Hills the clouds were dark, and it looked like snow. When I returned in seven weeks, the Hills would be buried under four-foot drifts. We were leaving just in time.

Because it is so sad I don't visit Fort Robinson, Nebraska, very often. But since it was on my way I decided to drive past. It was a pilgrimage I did not relish, a little like a Christian going alone to Calvary, complete with the outrage of a senseless murder but without the neat justification that it was done for our salvation. Fort Robinson is the place Crazy Horse was murdered. In the latter 1870s it was a military post, established to protect whites moving into the Black Hills. It was also a depot for gathering and shipping the Indians to reservation compounds. The beauty of the land where the fort stands hides the shame of its history.

It was evening when I reached the pine-covered ridge northwest of the fort. I stopped the pickup and looked at the valley below, trying to imagine what it must have been like when thousands of Sioux were loosely held there by the soldiers of the fort. The military had known just how to manipulate the Sioux. They had turned many chiefs against each other and ruled them through rumor and intrigue. All the other Indians had already surrendered before Crazy Horse could be convinced to come into the fort.

Indian emissaries, chiefs who commanded respect, were sent out with pack trains of food and supplies to the starving camp of Crazy Horse. They pleaded with him to give up his freedom and join the others in captivity. He was promised his own agency for his people and told that they would be allowed to hunt in the autumn for their winter meat. It was the offer of a yearly hunt, and the fact that his people were starving to death, that convinced Crazy Horse. He was the last of the free Sioux, and all the agency Indians turned out to watch his tattered but proud people march along the valley beneath my truck.

He was the most respected of all the Indians then. Mari Sandoz, in *Strange Man of the Oglala*, quotes an officer who watched the procession as saying, "By God! This is a triumphal march, not a surrender." What made Crazy Horse triumphal was his wildness, his unconquerable freedom. The soldiers hated and feared him for it. Indians loved him for it, but some envied him because even in captivity he refused to give up. Crazy Horse never received the agency he was promised and was not allowed an autumn hunt. He was murdered a few months after his arrival, as the soldiers tried to put him in chains. Just who killed him is not clear. But it is clear that his death was humiliating, coming at the hands of frightened, jealous people within the walls of the fort. The names of the men who plunged the knives or bayonets into him and the names of those who held him are lost. It seems likely that they were both white and Indian. Looking down on the fort from the ridge, I could imagine the claustrophobia of Crazy Horse's last moments and knew that it was envy that killed him. It seemed to me that killing Crazy Horse was an act very much like that of a farmer who, after witnessing a peregrine falcon stoop from the heavens to catch a duck, creeps up on it while it feeds and kills it with a rusty pitch fork.

I did not go near the fort. I drove around it and headed south. By the time I reached Alliance it was very dark. I gassed up at a 7-Eleven and drove to the Crescent Lake Wildlife Refuge. Spud and Jake checked the area out while I fried the ruffed grouse in an iron skillet over the Coleman stove. I ate until I could hold no more, then unrolled my sleeping bag and pad on the ground and slid the .357 under my pillow. Before I turned in, I weighed Dolly. Because she had eaten a lot of duck the afternoon before, I had not fed her all day. My hope was that after a day without food her weight would be right for flying her at pheasants or grouse. She weighed twenty-nine and a half ounces. That was too much, but it was cold and she would burn more calories than usual. She would be close to the right weight by the next afternoon.

In the morning I put the coffee on the stove and walked until I could see the water of Crescent Lake. A large flock of sandhill cranes stood near the edge, and I scanned them with binoculars, hoping to see a whooping crane among them, but had no luck. On the other side of the water was a flock of Canada geese. It was unlikely but not impossible that they were the same flock that had shared the pond with us in Montana.

It was now the first week in November and although the ponds in Montana were frozen, Nebraska's Crescent Lake was frantic with life. I could see five species of ducks, the cranes, the geese, red-wing blackbirds and several species of shore birds. For some birds, this would be as far south as they would go. But the majority would move on, like us, into Colorado, New Mexico, and Texas. A few—Dolly, perhaps, among them—would go on to Central America.

The morning was cool, but the bright sun promised to warm the day, insuring that any ice formed during the night would not last. It was a clear, blue prairie day with the wind already picking up. I went back to my little camp, blocked Dolly out, turned Spud and Jake loose and poured a cup of coffee. After finishing my first cup, I went to the lake and scooped a bucket of water for Dolly's bath. There were three weeks until the North American Falconers' field meet would be held in Kearney, Nebraska, and I planned to spend that time flying Dolly in the pastures and grain fields flanking the North Platte River. Unless the weather turned bad, I could expect to find plenty of game for her. If the Indian summer lasted,

I would be able to stay long enough to see a few old friends at the field meet.

My plan was to join Kent Carnie and Jim Weaver in New Mexico in any case. So if the weather forced me out of Nebraska I would go to Colorado and spend the extra time with Kris. The longer I was out, the better that sounded.

I sat and watched Dolly take her bath, and the more I sat, the more I liked the place we had found. By the time Dolly jumped from the bath pan to her perch and spread her feathers to dry, I had decided to stay awhile. I began unloading and setting up camp. Spud and Jake returned from a swim in the lake and I tied them up so that when we were ready to go hunting, they would be around to go along. Before Dolly's feathers were completely dry and preened, the camp was livable and the dogs snoozed contentedly in the afternoon sunlight. I sat down in my chair with the tent shielding me from the breeze and was asleep in seconds.

I awoke to the sound of Dolly's bells. It was late, time we were out hunting and Dolly bated with anticipation. When I weighed her, she was a half-ounce heavier than usual, but late in the day this was all right. I fixed the radio transmitters to her legs and loaded Dolly, Spud, and Jake into the back of the pickup. Because the country was new to me we should have been out earlier, looking for ponds or likely places to run Spud in search of pheasants or grouse. I drove too fast, thinking that there was a good chance that we would not find anything until it was too late. The lake was much too large, but I thought certainly there would be a pond close by with ducks. I found none. The more I looked and found nothing, the more irritated I became, the faster I drove and, no doubt, the more game I missed. Finally I began to lose hope. I had forgotten that the days were shorter in Nebraska because of the latitude. The sun had begun to set and in a few minutes it would be too dark to fly.

Suddenly, a rooster pheasant sailed across the dirt road ahead of us and into a five-acre swale surrounded by harvested cornfields. If we had more time I would have driven right past. Pheasants are notorious runners and can be very hard to locate. The chances of us finding the rooster were only fair. But on the other hand, the pheasant was obviously going to roost for the night and there was a good chance that there were more pheasants in the low marshy grass. I decided to take the risk and pulled the pickup off the road.

Because it was late, cool, and nearly dark, Dolly flew hard, pumping her wings without stopping until she was very high overhead. She was in such good position that she commanded most of the swale, and I decided to let both dogs out. There was only one patch of cover that a pheasant could fly to, a line of trees a half mile away with nothing but harvested corn in between. Pheasants are not good long-distance flyers and I was sure that Dolly could overtake one before it reached the trees. We walked slowly from one end to the other, planning to flush the pheasants out toward the trees. The sun sank lower and the dogs crisscrossed in front of me, but no pheasants came up.

By the time we reached the other end of the swale, it was nearly too dark to see Dolly. Apparently we had missed the rooster. Jake, who had stuck closer to me, sniffed hard at the patches along the end of the swale, likely places for the rooster to have run into. I called Spud in, trying to encourage him to do the same, but he ran frantically back into the harvested corn. I lost my temper and screamed at him to come back and look for the pheasant. He returned and sniffed around for a few seconds while I debated calling Dolly down to the lure, but in no time Spud was back out in the corn stubble. I had resolved to call Dolly down and then catch Spud and punish him, when he froze on point in the stubble. It was only a flash point because the rooster sprang into flight, heading for the trees immediately, and I lost sight of both him and Dolly in the last rays of sunlight.

The first thing that I did was to call Spud in and apologize to him. Being a dog, he forgave my lack of faith without question. Then we waited to see if Dolly would come back. I rated the chance of her catching the rooster at fifty-fifty and although it would have been nice for Dolly to make a kill, I would have been happy to see her coming back. The thought of her out in the open, feeding on a pheasant in the dark, frightened me. She would be difficult to find and night is a dangerous time for a peregrine on the ground.

She did not come back and after five minutes it was too dark for her to fly. We returned to the pickup to get the telemetry receiver. I left Spud in the pickup because he was too rambunctious for a night search in strange country. Jake stuck close to me and, though his black coat made him invisible in the night, it was nice to know that he was there. I got a signal immediately and the rhythmic beep-beep was reassuring. As long as there is a signal, the falcon does not seem to be lost. The signal is directional, and it indicated that Dolly was somewhere near the small grove of trees that the pheasant had probably tried to reach. As Jake and I started across the cornfield, I thought how comforting the beeping of the transmitter was. Silence would be the worst sound possible. Then I heard another sound, and a chill ran up my back. I turned the receiver off and identified the bass tones of a great horned owl. Suddenly I wanted silence. But the hoots continued and it was clear that they were coming from the same direction as the transmitter signal.

I quickened my pace, listening first to the owl and then to the receiver. Dolly was not moving, which might mean that she had caught the pheasant. But the owl was not moving either, which might mean it had caught Dolly. Peregrines cannot see well at night, and they are preyed upon ruthlessly by great horned owls. In the daylight peregrines will kill great horned owls, if given a chance, but a peregrine wrestling a pheasant in the dark is defenseless against a great horned owl. I had taken the flashlight from the hawking bag when we left the pickup. Now I turned it on hoping it might frighten the owl. I could just make out the silhouette of the trees against the sky when a second owl began to hoot. This was not unusual; great horned owls are often found in pairs or family groups. The line of trees was a likely nesting territory and because great horned owls do not move much, they probably used it all year long. Over the years the owls of that tree grove might have caught many young falcons and small hawks they saw catch game just at dark. Only birds of prey with experience would recognize the danger hidden in the trees.

The receiver indicated that we were close to Dolly, or what was left of her. Enough time had elapsed that the owls could have made a meal of her, and I was sick as I searched the ground with the flashlight. I cast the beam over the ground where Dolly should have been but saw nothing. Then I rechecked the receiver, and again, it indicated that I was very near the transmitter. For one terrible second it occurred to me that the owls had eaten part of her and carried the rest of her to the trees, leaving only the leg with the transmitter. I ran the flashlight beam over the ground again and saw nothing. The owls continued to mock me from the trees. Then I noticed Jake raise his head and smell the air. I took a couple more steps and he sat down, the way he was trained to react when Dolly was on the lure or a kill. I looked intensely on a line directly into the breeze from his nose, took another step, and heard a hawk bell. Dolly was less than five feet in front of me. She lay perfectly flat, her wings outstretched and her head turned to the side. For an instant I thought she was dead. But one dark eye looked upward at me and glistened at the edge of the flashlight beam. She adjusted as I approached and the bell sounded faintly.

When I sat beside her she stood, revealing the rooster pheasant. It was dead, but not a feather was out of place. Probably Dolly had seen the owls in the trees just after she killed the pheasant. She had lain down so the owls would not see her or the pheasant. Her instincts had saved her, and I did not dwell on how close it had been. I wondered what she had felt like, lying on her face in the corn stubble knowing that death was out there in the blackness and that her only chance was to remain absolutely still until dawn. Now, with Jake and I near, and the pheasant illuminated by the flashlight, she began to eat very much like normal. But I looked closely. Her eyes were slightly deeper, her feathers tighter, and her grip on the pheasant more intense. In some immeasurable way this was a different peregrine from the one who had disappeared into the dusk an hour before.

Gretel Ehrlich

Gretel Ehrlich, who was born in 1946 and raised in California, received her education at Bennington College, the UCLA Film School and the New School for Social Research. She first came to the Big Horn Mountains of Wyoming in 1976 to make a film about sheepherders. While in Wyoming Ehrlich's close companion passed away and she decided to stay in the area, which has been her home ever since. She lives with her husband Press, an outfitter, on a cattle ranch in the Big Horns. Ehrlich's books include an essay collection, *The Solace of Open Spaces* (Viking, 1985), which received an award from the American Academy of Arts and Letters, and two works of fiction, *Heart Mountain* (Viking, 1989) and *Drinking Dry Clouds* (Capra Press, 1991). In this selection, the lead essay from *The Solace of Open Spaces*, Gretel Ehrlich provides readers with a vivid sketch of her world in the Big Horns. The land is a place where "winter lasts six months" and the cold is so severe that her "jeans [freeze] to the saddle" and she feels "like the first person on earth, or the last." Not surprisingly, the people of the Big Horns "feel pride because they live in such a harsh place" and are "strong on scruples but tenderhearted about quirky behavior." Ehrlich's prose is distinguished by its many fine images and metaphors, which produce a concrete sense of place. The Big Horns will forever be "Ehrlich Country," and her book is a fitting tribute to the beauty of the land, which has the power to transform, inspire and heal the human spirit.

The Solace of Open Spaces
(circa 1985)

It's May and I've just awakened from a nap, curled against sagebrush the way my dog taught me to sleep—sheltered from wind. A front is pulling the huge sky over me, and from the dark a hailstone has hit me on the head. I'm trailing a band of two thousand sheep across a stretch of Wyoming badlands, a fifty-mile trip that takes five days because sheep shade up in hot sun and won't budge until it's cool. Bunched together now, and excited into a run by the storm, they drift across dry land, tumbling into draws like water and surge out again onto the rugged, choppy plateaus that are the building blocks of this state.

The name Wyoming comes from an Indian word meaning "at the great plains," but the plains are really valleys, great arid valleys, sixteen hundred square miles, with the horizon bending up on all sides into mountain ranges. This gives the vastness a sheltering look.

Winter lasts six months here. Prevailing winds spill snowdrifts to the east, and new storms from the northwest replenish them. This white bulk is sometimes dizzying, even nauseating, to look at. At twenty, thirty, and forty degrees below zero, not only does your car not work, but neither do your mind and body. The landscape hardens into a dungeon of space. During the winter, while I was

riding to find a new calf, my jeans froze to the saddle, and in the silence
that such cold creates I felt like the first person on earth, or the last.

Today the sun is out—only a few clouds billowing. In the
east, where the sheep have started off without me, the benchland
tilts up in a series of eroded red-earthed mesas, planed flat on top
by a million years of water; behind them, a bold line of muscular
scarps rears up ten thousand feet to become the Big Horn
Mountains. A tidal pattern is engraved into the ground, as if left by
the sea that once covered this state. Canyons curve down like
galaxies to meet the oncoming rush of flat land.

To live and work in this kind of open country, with its
hundred-mile views, is to lose the distinction between background
and foreground. When I asked an older ranch hand to describe
Wyoming's openness, he said, "It's all a bunch of nothing—wind
and rattlesnakes—and so much of it you can't tell where you're
going or where you've been and it don't make much difference."
John, a sheepman I know, is tall and handsome and has an
explosive temperament. He has a perfect intuition about people
and sheep. They call him "Highpockets," because he's so long-
legged; his graceful stride matches the distances he has to cover. He
says, "Open space hasn't affected me at all. It's all the people
moving in on it." The huge ranch he was born on takes up much
of one county and spreads into another state; to put 100,000 miles
on his pickup in three years and never leave home is not unusual.
A friend of mine has an aunt who ranched on Powder River and
didn't go off her place for eleven years. When her husband died,
she quickly moved to town, bought a car, and drove around the
States to see what she'd been missing.

Most people tell me they've simply driven through Wyoming, as if there were nothing to stop for. Or else they've skied in
Jackson Hole, a place Wyomingites acknowledge uncomfortably
because its green beauty and chic affluence are mismatched with
the rest of the state. Most of Wyoming has a "lean-to" look.
Instead of big, roomy barns and Victorian houses, there are
dugouts, low sheds, log cabins, sheep camps, and fence lines that
look like driftwood blown haphazardly into place. People here still

feel pride because they live in such a harsh place, part of the glamorous cowboy past, and they are determined not to be the victims of a mining-dominated future.

Most characteristic of the state's landscape is what a developer euphemistically describes as "indigenous growth right up to your front door"—a reference to waterless stands of salt sage, snakes, jack rabbits, deerflies, red dust, a brief respite of wildflowers, dry washes, and no trees. In the Great Plains the vistas look like music, like Kyries of grass, but Wyoming seems to be the doing of a mad architect—tumbled and twisted, ribboned with faded, deathbed colors, thrust up and pulled down as if the place had been startled out of a deep sleep and thrown into a pure light.

I came here four years ago. I had not planned to stay, but I couldn't make myself leave. John, the sheepman, put me to work immediately. It was spring, and shearing time. For fourteen days of fourteen hours each, we moved thousands of sheep through sorting corrals to be sheared, branded, and deloused. I suspect that my original motive for coming here was to "lose myself" in new and unpopulated territory. Instead of producing the numbness I thought I wanted, life on the sheep ranch woke me up. The vitality of the people I was working with flushed out what had become a hallucinatory rawness inside me. I threw away my clothes and bought new ones; I cut my hair. The arid country was a clean slate. Its absolute indifference steadied me.

Sagebrush covers 58,000 square miles of Wyoming. The biggest city has a population of fifty thousand, and there are only five settlements that could be called cities in the whole state. The rest are towns, scattered across the expanse with as much as sixty miles between them, their populations two thousand, fifty, or ten. They are fugitive-looking, perched on a barren, windblown bench, or tagged onto a river or a railroad, or laid out straight in a farming valley with implement stores and a block-long Mormon church. In the eastern part of the state, which slides down into the Great Plains, the new mining settlements are boomtowns, trailer cities, metal knots on flat land.

Despite the desolate look, there's a coziness to living in this state. There are so few people (only 470,000) that ranchers who buy and sell cattle know one another statewide; the kids who choose to go to college usually go to the state's one university, in Laramie; hired hands work their way around Wyoming in a lifetime of hirings and firings. And despite the physical separation, people stay in touch, often driving two or three hours to another ranch for dinner.

Seventy-five years ago, when travel was by buckboard or horseback, cowboys who were temporarily out of work rode the grub line—drifting from ranch to ranch, mending fences or milking cows, and receiving in exchange a bed and meals. Gossip and messages traveled this slow circuit with them, creating an intimacy between ranchers who were three and four weeks' ride apart. One old-time couple I know, whose turn-of-the-century homestead was used by an outlaw gang as a relay station for stolen horses, recall that if you were traveling, desperado or not, any lighted ranch house was a welcome sign. Even now, for someone who lives in a remote spot, arriving at a ranch or coming to town for supplies is cause for celebration. To emerge from isolation can be disorienting. Everything looks bright, new, vivid. After I had been herding sheep for only three days, the sound of the camp tender's pickup flustered me. Longing for human company, I felt a foolish grin take over my face; yet I had to resist an urgent temptation to run and hide..

Things happen suddenly in Wyoming, the change of seasons and weather; for people, the violent swings in and out of isolation. But good-naturedness is concomitant with severity. Friendliness is a tradition. Strangers passing on the road wave hello. A common sight is two pickups stopped side by side far out on a range, on a dirt track winding through the sage. The drivers will share a cigarette, uncap their thermos bottles, and pass a battered cup, steaming with coffee, between windows. These meetings summon up the details of several generations, because, in Wyoming, private histories are largely public knowledge.

Because ranch work is a physical and, these days, economic strain, being "at home on the range" is a matter of vigor, self-reliance, and common sense. A person's life is not a series of dramatic events for which he or she is applauded or exiled but a slow accumulation of days, seasons, years, fleshed out by the generational weight of one's family and anchored by a land-bound sense of place.

In most parts of Wyoming, the human population is visibly outnumbered by the animal. Not far from my town of fifty, I rode into a narrow valley and startled a herd of two hundred elk. Eagles look like small people as they eat car-killed deer by the road. Antelope, moving in small, graceful bands, travel at sixty miles an hour, their mouths open as if drinking in the space.

The solitude in which westerners live makes them quiet. They telegraph thoughts and feelings by the way they tilt their heads and listen; pulling their Stetsons into a steep dive over their eyes, or pigeon-toeing one boot over the other, they lean against a fence with a fat wedge of Copenhagen beneath their lower lips and take in the whole scene. These detached looks of quiet amusement are sometimes cynical, but they can also come from a dry-eyed humility as lucid as the air is clear.

Conversation goes on in what sounds like a private code; a few phrases imply a complex of meanings. Asking directions, you get a curious list of details. While trailing sheep I was told to "ride up to that kinda upturned rock, follow the pink wash, turn left at the dump, and then you'll see the water hole." One friend told his wife on roundup to "turn at the salt lick and the dead cow," which turned out to be a scattering of bones and no salt lick at all.

Sentence structure is shortened to the skin and bones of a thought. Descriptive words are dropped, even verbs; a cowboy looking over a corral full of horses will say to a wrangler, "Which one needs rode?" People hold back their thoughts in what seems to be a dumbfounded silence, then erupt with an excoriating perceptive remark. Language, so compressed, becomes meta-phorical. A rancher ended a relationship with one remark: "You're a bad check," meaning bouncing in and out was intolerable, and even coming back would be no good.

What's behind this laconic style is shyness. There is no vocabulary for the subject of feelings. It's not a hangdog shyness, or anything coy—always there's a robust spirit in evidence behind the restraint, as if the earth-dredging wind that pulls across Wyoming had carried its people's voices away but everything else in them had shouldered confidently into the breeze.

I've spent hours riding to sheep camp at dawn in a pickup when nothing was said; eaten meals in the cookhouse when the only words spoken were a mumbled "Thank you, ma'am" at the end of dinner. The silence is profound. Instead of talking, we seem to share one eye. Keenly observed, the world is transformed. The landscape is engorged with detail, every movement on it chillingly sharp. The air between people is charged. Days unfold, bathed in their own music. Nights become hallucinatory; dreams, prescient.

Spring weather is capricious and mean. It snows, then blisters with heat. There have been tornadoes. They lay their elephant trunks out in the sage until they find houses, then slurp everything up and leave. I've noticed that melting snowbanks hiss and rot, viperous, then drip into calm pools where ducklings hatch and livestock, being trailed to summer range, drink. With the ice cover gone, rivers churn a milkshake brown, taking culverts and small bridges with them. Water in such an arid place (the average annual rainfall where I live is less than eight inches) is like blood. It festoons drab land with green veins; a line of cottonwoods following a stream; a strip of alfalfa; and, on ditch banks, wild asparagus growing.

I've moved to a small cattle ranch owned by friends. It's at the foot of the Big Horn Mountains. A few weeks ago, I helped them deliver a calf who was stuck halfway out of his mother's body. By the time he was freed, we could see a heartbeat, but he was straining against a swollen tongue for air. Mary and I held him upside down by his back feet, while Stan, on his hands and knees in the blood, gave the calf mouth-to-mouth resuscitation. I have a vague memory of being pneumonia-choked as a child, my mother giving me her air, which may account for my romance with this windswept state.

If anything is endemic to Wyoming, it is wind. This big room of space is swept out daily, leaving a bone yard of fossils, agates, and carcasses in every stage of decay. Though it was water that initially shaped the state, wind is the meticulous gardener, raising dust and pruning the sage.

I try to imagine a world in which I could ride my horse across uncharted land. There is no wilderness left; wildness, yes, but true wilderness has been gone on this continent since the time of Lewis and Clark's overland journey.

Two hundred years ago, the Crow, Shoshone, Arapaho, Cheyenne, and Sioux roamed the intermountain West, orchestrating their movements according to hunger, season, and warfare. Once they acquired horses, they traversed the spines of all the big Wyoming ranges—the Absarokas, the Wind Rivers, the Tetons, the Big Horns—and wintered on the unprotected plains that fan out from them. Space was life. The world was their home.

What was life-giving to Native Americans was often nightmarish to sodbusters who had arrived encumbered with families and ethnic pasts to be transplanted in nearly uninhabitable land. The great distances, the shortage of water and trees, and the loneliness created unexpected hardships for them. In her book *O Pioneers!,* Willa Cather gives a settler's version of the bleak landscape:

> The little town behind them had vanished as if it had never been, had fallen behind the swell of the prairie, and the stern frozen country received them into its bosom. The homesteads were few and far apart; here and there a windmill gaunt against the sky, a sod house crouching in a hollow.

The emptiness of the West was for others a geography of possibility. Men and women who amassed great chunks of land and struggled to preserve unfenced emptiness were, despite their self-serving motives, unwitting geographers. They understood the lay of the land. But by the 1850s the Oregon and Mormon trails sported bumper-to-bumper traffic. Wealthy landowners, many of them aristocratic absentee landlords, known as remittance men because they were paid to come West and get out of their families' hair, overstocked the range with more than a million head of cattle.

By 1885 the feed and water were desperately short, and the winter of 1886 laid out the gaunt bodies of dead animals so closely together that when the thaw came, one rancher from Kaycee claimed to have walked on cowhide all the way to Crazy Woman Creek, twenty miles away.

Territorial Wyoming was a boy's world. The land was generous with everything but water. At first there was room enough, food enough, for everyone. And, as with all beginnings, an expansive mood set in. The young cowboys, drifters, shopkeepers, schoolteachers, were heroic, lawless, generous, rowdy, and tenacious. The individualism and optimism generated during those times have endured.

John Tisdale rode north with the trail herds from Texas. He was a college-educated man with enough money to buy a small outfit near the Powder River. While driving home from the town of Buffalo with a buckboard full of Christmas toys for his family and a winter's supply of food, he was shot in the back by an agent of the cattle barons who resented the encroachment of small-time stockmen like him. The wealthy cattlemen tried to control all the public grazing land by restricting membership in the Wyoming Stock Growers Association, as if it were a country club. They ostracized from roundups and brandings cowboys and ranchers who were not members, then denounced them as rustlers. Tisdale's death, the second such cold-blooded murder, kicked off the Johnson County cattle war, which was no simple good-guy-bad-guy shoot-out but a complicated class struggle between landed gentry and less affluent settlers—a shocking reminder that the West was not an egalitarian sanctuary after all.

Fencing ultimately enforced boundaries, but barbed wire abrogated space. It was stretched across the beautiful valleys, into the mountains, over desert badlands, through buffalo grass. The "anything is possible" fever—the lure of any new place—was constricted. The integrity of the land as a geographical body, and the freedom to ride anywhere on it, were lost.

I punched cows with a young man named Martin, who is the great-grandson of John Tisdale. His inheritance is not the open land that Tisdale knew and prematurely lost but a rage against restraint.

Wyoming tips down as you head northeast; the highest ground—the Laramie Plains—is on the Colorado border. Up where I live, the Big Horn River leaks into difficult, arid terrain. In the basin where it's dammed, sandhill cranes gather and, with delicate legwork, slice through the stilled water. I was driving by with a rancher one morning when he commented that cranes are "old-fashioned." When I asked why, he said, "Because they mate for life." Then he looked at me with a twinkle in his eyes, as if to say he really did believe in such things but also understood why we break our own rules.

In all of this open space, values crystalize quickly. People are strong on scruples but tenderhearted about quirky behavior. A friend and I found one ranch hand, who's "not quite right in the head," sitting in front of the badly decayed carcass of a cow, shaking his finger and saying, "Now, I don't want you to do this ever again!" When I asked what was wrong with him, I was told, "He's goofier than hell, just like the rest of us." Perhaps because the West is historically new, conventional morality is still felt to be less important than rock-bottom truths. Though there's always a lot of teasing and sparring, people are blunt with one another, sometimes even cruel, believing honesty is stronger medicine than sympathy, which may console but often conceals.

The formality that goes hand in hand with the rowdiness is known as the Western Code. It's a list of practical do's and don'ts, faithfully observed. A friend, Cliff, who runs a trap-line in the winter, cut off half his foot while chipping a hole in the ice. Alone, he dragged himself to his pickup and headed for town, stopping to open the ranch gate as he left, and getting out to close it again, thus losing, in his observance of rules, precious time and blood. Later, he commented, "How would it look, them having to come to the hospital to tell me their cows had gotten out?"

Accustomed to emergencies, my friends doctor each other from the vet's bag with relish. When one old-timer suffered a heart attack in hunting camp, his partner quickly stirred up a brew of red horse liniment and hot water and made the half-conscious victim drink it, then tied him onto a horse and led him twenty miles to town. He regained consciousness and lived.

The roominess of the state has affected political attitudes as well. Ranchers keep up with world politics and the convulsions of the economy but are basically isolationists. Being used to running their own small empires of land and livestock, they're suspicious of big government. It's a "don't fence me in" holdover from a century ago. They still want the elbow room their grandfathers had, so they're strongly conservative, but with a populist twist.

Summer is the season when we get our "cowboy tans"—on the lower parts of our faces and on three fourths of our arms. Excessive heat, in the nineties and higher, sends us outside with the mosquitoes. In winter we're tucked inside our houses, and the white wasteland outside appears to be expanding, but in summer all the greenery abridges space. Summer is a go-ahead season. Every living thing is off the block and in the race: battalions of bugs in flight and biting; bats swinging around my log cabin as if the bases were loaded and someone had hit a home run. Some of summer's high-speed growth is ominous: larkspur, death camas, and green greasewood can kill sheep—an ironic idea, dying in this desert from eating what is too verdant. With sixteen hours of daylight, farmers and ranchers irrigate feverishly. There are first, second, and third cuttings of hay, some crews averaging only four hours of sleep a night for weeks. And, like the cowboys who in summer ride the night rodeo circuit, nighthawks make daredevil dives at dusk with an eerie whirring sound like a plane going down on the shimmering horizon.

In the town where I live, they've had to board up the dance-hall windows because there have been so many fights. There's so little to do except work that people wind up in a state of idle agitation that becomes fatalistic, as if there were nothing to be done about all this untapped energy. So the dark side of the grandeur of these spaces is the small-mindedness that seals people in. Men become hermits; women go mad. Cabin fever explodes into suicides, or into grudges and lifelong family feuds. Two sisters in my area inherited a ranch but found they couldn't get along. They fenced the place in half. When one's cows got out and mixed with the other's, the women went at each other with shovels. They ended up in the same hospital room but never spoke a word to each other for the rest of their lives.

After the brief lushness of summer, the sun moves south. The range grass is brown. Livestock is trailed back down from the mountains. Water holes begin to frost over at night. Last fall Martin asked me to accompany him on a pack trip. With five horses, we followed a river into the mountains behind the tiny Wyoming town of Meeteetse. Groves of aspen, red and orange, gave off a light that made us look toasted. Our hunting camp was so high that clouds skidded across our foreheads, then slowed to sail out across the warm valleys. Except for a bull moose who wandered into our camp and mistook our black gelding for a rival, we shot at nothing.

One of our evening entertainments was to watch the night sky. My dog, a dingo bred to herd sheep, also came on the trip. He is so used to the silence and empty skies that when an airplane flies over he always looks up and eyes the distant intruder quizzically. The sky, lately, seems to be much more crowded than it used to be. Satellites make their silent passes in the dark with great regularity. We counted eighteen in one hour's viewing. How odd to think that while they circumnavigated the planet, Martin and I had moved only six miles into our local wilderness and had seen no other human for the two weeks we stayed there.

At night, by moonlight, the land is whittled to slivers—a ridge, a river, a strip of grassland stretching to the mountains, then the huge sky. One morning a full moon was setting in the west just as the sun was rising. I felt precariously balanced between the two as I loped across a meadow. For a moment, I could believe that the stars, which were still visible, work like cooper's bands, holding together everything above Wyoming.

———————

Space has a spiritual equivalent and can heal what is divided and burdensome in us. My grandchildren will probably use space shuttles for a honeymoon trip or to recover from heart attacks, but closer to home we might also learn how to carry space inside ourselves in the effortless way we carry our skins. Space represents sanity, not a life purified, dull, or "spaced out" but one that might accommodate intelligently any idea or situation.

From the clayey soil of northern Wyoming is mined bentonite, which is used as a filler in candy, gum, and lipstick. We Americans are great on fillers, as if what we have, what we are, is not enough. We have a cultural tendency toward denial, but, being affluent, we strangle ourselves with what we can buy. We have only to look at the houses we build to see how we build *against* space, the way we drink against pain and loneliness. We fill up space as if it were a pie shell, with things whose opacity further obstructs our ability to see what is already there.

II

West of the
Continental Divide

When I go out of the house for a walk, uncertain as yet whither I will bend my steps, and submit myself to my instinct to decide for me, I find, strange and whimsical as it may seem, that I finally and inevitably settle southwest. ... Eastward I go only by force; but westward I go free. ... Every sunset which I witness inspires me with the desire to go to a West as distant and as fair as that into which the sun goes down. He is the Great Western Pioneer whom the nations follow. We dream all night of those mountain-ridges in the horizon, though they may be of vapor only, which were last gilded by his rays. ... The West of which I speak is but another name for the Wild; and what I have been preparing to say is, that in Wildness is the preservation of the World.

—Henry David Thoreau
"Walking" (1862)

Ed Engle

Ed Engle, a seasonal timber ranger for fourteen seasons with the U.S. Forest Service, lives in Palmer Lake, Colorado. He writes in his first book *Seasonal* (Pruett, 1990) about the many beautiful locales in Colorado in which he has worked: the Upper Arkansas River Valley, the Dolores River Valley, the Glade, Disappointment and Big Gypsum valleys and the wild Coñejos country. In the essay "Timber Beast" Engle eloquently describes the trees he has come to love: "Over the years and through thousands of plots I have come to see trees as individuals ... Once I saw a huge Doug fir towering alone in a stand of aspen. All around it were hundreds of fir seedlings. They were that individual tree's progeny, they could have come from nowhere else—I saw them as that tree's children." Engle concludes that he has "run into spooky ground seeing trees as individuals" and admits that it "isn't something you talk openly about down at the local bar" because they will "cut your drinks off," particularly if you "begin referring to some trees as not only individuals but personal friends." *Seasonal* is a wonderful book, full of such intimations and insights. The essay "Nightjars," which is included here, relates the author's long love affair with the nightjar family, a group of birds "known more for their nocturnal calls than anything else." We are reminded that one of the greatest lyric poems in the English language is John Keats's "Ode to a Nightingale."

Nightjars
(circa 1990)

Disappointment Valley lies just to the north of the flattopped pine country called the Glade. It's a long slide down draws like Wolf Den, White Sands, Ryman, and Box into that brushy place. The pine gives way to Gambel oak, antelope brush, sage, and a host of "invader species" that point to overgrazing. A good bit of it is Bureau of Land Management land and supports the old story that in the beginning the Forest Service took the "good" productive land, meaning timber, and what was left eventually ended up with the BLM. The ranchers would disagree and so would the elk that come out of the San Juan Mountains to winter in the valley by the thousands. The elk were so thick that one winter the Division of Wildlife held a special December hunt to slick some of them off so there would be forage for the cattle come spring. It's called bringing the herd under management.

The valley is imbued with the kind of faraway, edgy beauty of a place that is seldom scrutinized. The view from the Benchmark Fire Lookout up on Glade Mountain is magnificent. To the west and northwest the valley stretches broadly out toward Slickrock and the Big Gypsum Valley and farther still the Abajos and Canyonlands. To the east the valley wanders toward its origin through a roughed-up landscape of gravelly buttes and mesas. It tightens and sways through thicker and thicker oak brush until there isn't much left near the Buckhorn Lodge, which is one of few signs of human life and the location of that country's single radio telephone to the outside world.

The distant view looking that way is dominated by Lone Cone, a twelve-and-a-half-thousand-foot, perfectly conical peak that stands off alone on the divide between the San Juan and Uncompahgre forests. Beyond that are the rugged peaks of the San Miguels—Dunn Peak, Middle Peak, Dolores Peak, and three of Colorado's fourteen-thousand-footers—Mount Wilson, Wilson Peak, and El Diente. The big, flat tabletop known as Black Mesa finishes the scene by hammering at the southern edges of the range.

That is the overview, but the mysteries confine themselves to the smaller draws, benches, and bends that find their way into Disappointment Valley. It's a place that has been peopled in a stingy way, mostly by ranchers, but has seen its share of desperados and the likes of those who don't fit smoothly into the machinery of town life. The chances they've taken are little more than a whisper in a big place and show up in the form of barbed wire, abandoned mining claims, broken liquor bottles, and the memory of water passing under the Daddy Williams bridge. Those who made it may have passed down a homestead or a range allotment or maybe a section or two of scrub along Disappointment Creek. The survivors have gotten bigger, needing more land for more cattle, and the others are just gone.

I took to going down to the edges of Disappointment Valley the summer I worked out of the Glade Guard Station. It was a rocky drive down the Black Snag road with no set boundaries. I figured the valley began where the pines left off, but there was no line of demarcation— simply a change in mood when the forest thinned to a certain point. There was a place where individual trees stood far apart from each other. They were the few that ran up against whatever barrier it was that held their kind out of Disappointment Valley.

I am a ridge person by nature. The idea of running a high line and gathering in the big picture suits me, but I have learned to play a smaller, more repetitive game. I make a point of seeing the same thing as many times as I can stomach it because I know that connections are being made. Look at the same species of lichen a hundred times and you will know some things that are unexpected.

There was a change in perspective in the valley that was as simple as the difference between two birds. Up on Glade Mountain we watched nighthawks carve up the evening sky in huge buzzing arcs. Disappointment Valley was poorwill country. Both birds are from a family known as nightjars or goatsuckers and as a group are known more for their nocturnal calls than anything else. Their lives are a mystery of the night and that suits the land around Disappointment Valley.

The first nightjars I became familiar with were the whip-poor-wills that are a sort of eastern equivalent of the poorwill. The nightjar family is one of a few where many of the species are named for the call they make. I associated the birds with the humid evenings in the woodlands of Virginia. There were spots where I could depend on hearing the loud WHIP-poor-WILL or sharp whip-whip-whip stab through the darkness. The calls put meaning into the name nightjar, which breaks down to night + jar, meaning roughly to jar the night or simply make a harsh noise in the night. The family's other nickname, goatsucker, is come by with more difficulty but relates to a belief, possibly from Europe, that members of this family suck on the teats of goats after nightfall. This hasn't been proven true, but the sight of a whip-poor-will's huge gaping mouth, used to capture insects on the wing, gives credence to the idea. At least it is *big* enough.

An entire lifetime of humid nights can pass in Virginia with the voice of the whip-poor-will as the only tangible evidence of its existence. I chose to try and see one early on and accomplished it on a Boy Scout campout in the Appalachian Mountains. It was twilight fading rapidly to darkness when I heard the voice close-by and took off after it. I was crawling through a mess of honeysuckle and came up for air in an opening and face to face with the bird. It hadn't left its roost yet and was sitting lengthwise on a limb, which I came to find out later is characteristic of the nightjar family.

Even close up the bird was hard to see, being perfectly camouflaged. The whip-poor-will called out a few more times as I stood motionless, then took silently to the air. Their wings, like owls, are muffled by soft feathers to avoid scaring off prey.

I got to where I could occasionally locate whip-poor-wills during the day when they slept, eyes clamped shut, either on the ground or more commonly on a low horizontal branch. The bird is so tough to see with its cryptic markings that I often came close to stepping on them. In the east the bird is still sometimes associated with the larger and less secretive nighthawk, which was actually thought to be the bird making the calls until the early 1800s.

The other great nightjar of the east is the chuck-wills-widow. This bird has the same feel as the whip-poor-will—the soft, hard-to-see plumage, huge mouth, and a name that sounds like the call. The difference is that the chuck-wills-widow is a much bigger bird. The chuck-wills-widow tends to be more of a southerner than the whip-poor-will and my home in northern Virginia was near the end of its range. The long CHUCK-wills-WID-ow even seemed more southern, almost with a drawl, and the sound of it was every mystery I had ever reckoned to come with the night.

There's an interesting hitch to the chuck-wills-widow's diet. While it commonly tends toward the standard nightjar fare of moths, beetles, and other flying insects, it sometimes gobbles down small birds, with warblers seeming a particular favorite. Chuck-wills-widows were not common where I lived and I have never seen one. I know them by the call and an odd association in my mind with the Confederacy. They conjure up the name of John Singleton Mosby, the Confederate raider who stalked the woods around where I grew up and was called the Grey Ghost.

I am caught by the nightjars and it did not leave me when I came west. The nighthawks at the Glade were hard to miss. Sometimes they flew during the day and their pointy wings with the wide white wing patch were easy to spot. More commonly they came out at dusk, often over a point or ridge, and hunted. There are a lot of them out there and the cowboys call them bullbats after the booming roar that is made by the wing feathers during particularly steep dives, most often during the breeding season. It was the poorwills that I was unprepared for.

Of the common North American nightjars the poorwills are the most mysterious and least heard about. It could be due to the fact that they are a western bird common to the arid, brushy uplands. Places like Disappointment Valley. Places where there aren't many people to hear the pooooor-WILL that comes with the twilight but ends by full darkness. Places where people don't talk so much, especially about noises on the edge of darkness. I picked up a standard general duty dictionary once and looked up my favorite nightjars. The whip-poor-wills were there, chuck-wills-widow had an entry, nighthawks were represented, and even the more general terms nightjar and goatsucker appeared. There was nothing for poorwill. The dictionary simply went from "poor white" to "pop" with nothing in between.

My first trip to Disappointment Valley was full of poorwills. I'd left the guard station after supper and made the valley in about thirty minutes. The point of the trip had been to just take a look around, but that wasn't easy. The edge of the valley was grown thick in oak brush and I couldn't find a knoll or a hill to scramble up on for a bigger view. There's a precision of pattern in the way oak grows that can almost always be traced back to the amount of water available to the plants. There in Disappointment Valley the clumps of oak were evenly spaced fifteen to twenty feet apart. It was the kind of exquisite cover that the big mule deer, particularly the bucks, seek out. The ins and outs of that kind of maze leave plenty of escape routes and ample forage. I've seen bucks in those places that I mistook for elk, but hunting them requires a patience that verges on trance and that is why they are there.

I never found a good spot to be and finally lowered the tailgate on the truck and waited for the twilight. It came gradually that clear evening almost like a tide would come over the beach taking a little more sand with each wave. A point came where things were indistinct and I heard the first poorwill of my life. I'd never made an exacting hobby of nightjars and at the time didn't know anything about poorwills, but the almost sad call of the bird reminded me of other twilights spent listening the night in. I strained to locate the bird but couldn't. Within minutes I heard dozens more poorwills echoing one another and finally the air was saturated with their sound. The birds must have still been on the roosts, under cover, because I walked back and forth on the dirt road trying to see just one of them, but they remained invisible. It went on until it was dark enough to see the stars, then the chorus stopped almost completely on cue.

I had figured that the call must be some sort of nightjar if only because it resembled the whip-poor-wills I had heard so many times in the east. I even thought it might be some western relative that had clipped short its speech to go with the sparseness of the land in the same way that the old hardscrabble ranchers spoke in fewer and fewer syllables each season. Whatever the reason, the twilight had been full of the bird's calls—hundreds of them it seemed like.

I turned the truck around and headed out. In the headlights I spotted the poorwills. At first I noticed just their eyeshine, which reflected a deep, almost pagan pink. I'd seen the deep green reflections off a deer's eyes before and even the amber of a cat, but these were new colors and they were everywhere. I picked up the fluttering birds next. They jumped up from the road in two- and three-foot arcs like huge renditions of the moths that they were chasing. I left the lights on and got out of the truck. The poorwills let me get close enough to see that they looked very much like the whip-poor-wills I'd known, only smaller and with maybe a little grayer plumage. They flew silently bending the air with their short tails.

I spent as many twilights as I could in Disappointment Valley and the poorwills came out faithfully with each one. I even managed to sneak down once during the day in an attempt to kick up a few of them but couldn't find any. It could be that they were there, just under my feet, but that their plumage camouflaged them so well that all they needed to do was sit tight and they would become just another rock resting on the ground. For all I knew maybe they *turned into* rocks during the day.

Over the winter the poorwills stayed with me, more like a fragrance that floated through my mind than any kind of exact image. I decided that I would go back to graduate school in ornithology and write my thesis on them. It looked like the kind of scientific deadwater I enjoyed. I searched the literature and found that only one fact had briefly rattled the poorwill's cage of obscurity. It appeared that a couple of the birds had been found during the winter in a rock crevice out in the California desert and that they had been sleeping—deep sleeping. The fact was that they were in hibernation. Hibernation, up to that point, had been unknown in the bird world. There were cases of torpor, a reduced state of metabolism known to occur in some species, most notably hummingbirds, but this lasted at most for a night's time or a few days of unseasonable cold. The poorwills were sleeping the better part of the winter.

Poorwill migration had been sketchily documented, but the two birds in California presented a problem. It might be that all the birds were *not* wintering in Mexico. Biologists went into the field and measured the sleeping birds' body temperatures and found them to be very close to the surrounding environment—like hibernating lizards or snakes or frogs. This was good stuff. The kind of thing that gets a young biologist out of the assistant professor ranks and up to associate professor and tenure country. They started grabbing poorwills and bringing them into the lab and stuffing them into refrigerators to see if they would hibernate. They wrote papers. The birds, indeed, did seem to sleep *very* heavily in the winter. Of course, they could have just asked the Hopi Indians, whose name for the poorwill is Hölchko, which roughly translates to "the sleeping one." Some bird books now state the migratory status of the poorwill as unknown.

I had a meeting in Flagstaff with an ornithologist at Northern Arizona University who was interested in sponsoring my graduate work. He hadn't heard my ideas yet on poorwills and when I told him he said there was no way. "We don't know enough about them for you to study them. It would be too difficult," he said.

It was an interesting problem. Apparently the development of a statistical model would be dicey and that was the new buzz word in biology. I asked why couldn't I just go out and *watch* the birds, maybe laying a foundation for future study. That wouldn't do because the world needed numbers, not old-timey naturalists. We needed to quantify, quantify, quantify. I gave up on graduate school but kept my eyes open.

There is a wonderful series of ornithological papers on the life histories of North American birds that was collected by Arthur Cleveland Bent. The bulletins span decades in the early and mid-twentieth century. The thirteenth in the series is *Life Histories of North American Cuckoos, Goatsuckers, Hummingbirds and Their Allies.* There are some statistics included in the monographs, like numbers and sizes of eggs in an average nest, but more importantly the papers are full of observation. The great ornithologist Elliot Coues contributed this on poorwills in 1874, "This cry is very lugubrious, and in places where the birds are numerous the wailing chorus is enough to excite vague apprehensions on the part of the lonely traveller, as he lies down to rest by his campfire, or to break his sleep with fitful dreams, in which lost spirits appear to bemoan their fate and implore his intercession." A Mrs. Bailey in 1928 described the poorwill's call, "… like the delicious aromatic smell of sagebrush clings long to the memory of the lover of the west."

There is a likeness to poorwills in the drift of certain men into the forest. They are the kind that have somehow managed to end up on the edge of things and are carried into the remote places for vague reasons. They are a mishmash of ramblers, hermits, ne'er-do-wells, sociopaths, half-crazed and crazy souls. They are not truth seekers in any conventional sense and you won't run across any autobiographies of their visions. These are journeys of relief and for damage control. A search for balance. And their legends are like the echo of a poorwill's voice up against the night. They are wildmen.

The idea of wildmen and the forest is nothing new. It's been said that during the Middle Ages in Europe lunatics and the occasional crazies were simply led a safe distance out of town, into the woods, and let go to fend for themselves. There is an entire literature of wildmen as old as the Greek myths or woven smoothly into Buddhist texts. They are here, real or imaginary, hermits like

Hanshan and Shih-te, Don Quixote, Rousseau's Noble Savage, Robinson Crusoe, Tarzan, Sasquatch, the Abominable Snowman, Jesse James, Jeremiah Johnson ... some with hair-covered faces, some kind, some wise, some violent, some raised by wolves ... all riding the tides of our collective thoughts about freedom, passion, and sanity.

For every international wildman there are hundreds more local or regional everyday wildmen. Legends that almost always grow out of facts. Men that run wild in some isolated valley, then disappear or are caught but grow in stature to the point that every man, woman, or child in that country has seen him or talked or shook hands with him. Their children and grandchildren remember. Word gets around. Here in the Rockies and Basin country we take our wildmen seriously; it's open country.

They say Navajo Sam got his name when he was living down south. That was before he took up living in a little make-shift outfit on the Dolores district of the San Juan National Forest. No matter where the name came from it fit perfectly that first day when he came out of the brush on the Navajo Lake Trail. The trail was the main thoroughfare for backpackers heading to a high country lake of the same name that was nestled in a basin surrounded by El Diente, Mt. Wilson, Gladstone Peak, and Wilson Peak up in the San Miguels. It was the summer of 1982 and the year that Navajo Sam decided to start holding up hikers for their lunches. He had a gun, which also fit perfectly; here in the West we also prefer our wildmen to be armed. It emphasizes the point of who is really in control.

Navajo Sam's first victims were a couple of doctors from Grand Junction, Colorado. They said that he never really pointed the gun at them but instead laid it across a rock. They chose to give him their tunafish sandwiches without a struggle and listened to him rant and rave about big government, big business, and the rich guys getting richer. The Forest Service got on the case as soon as the word swept down the Dolores River Valley and throughout southwest Colorado. The newspapers picked it up, too, and it went out on the wires. It was absolutely irresistible.

"Navajo Sam stakes out his claim to the Navajo Basin." If not in the open, then secretly we all kind of applauded him. I don't believe it was the violence that turned us; people stick guns in other people's faces every day and you can get all of that you want by simply watching the Albuquerque news. It had to do with the idea of one man making a stand against overwhelming odds from a wild and remote hideout. Navajo Sam was fighting economics, the government, society, and pretty serious depression. And he was in a position to elude capture—that's the other thing we want in our wildmen. They should be woodswise and crafty, to a superhuman level if possible.

It went on for several months until the hunting seasons came around. Forest Service special agents figured that while Navajo Sam was somewhat of a danger, the greater threat might be that some half-crazed hunters would ride into Navajo Basin, grease him, then pack the body out as a public service, hoping to collect some kind of reward or at least become part of the legend. The agents disguised themselves as elk hunters and picked him up near Wood's Lake.

They threw him in jail in Cortez and charged him with aggravated robbery and felony menacing. A grass roots movement developed to free Navajo Sam and bumper stickers began to appear that said "Free Navajo Sam." A bank account was started to help in his defense. Three weeks later a Dolores County judge freed Navajo Sam for lack of evidence. He was a folk hero. A wildman.

In their introduction to *The Wild Man Within,* a collection of essays on the image of the wildman from the Renaissance to romanticism, Edward Dudley and Maximillian Novak described the wildman as "belonging to the region of the mind that treasured freedom over control, nature over art, and passion over abstract reason." Navajo Sam had walked boldly into that wild country.

It didn't end with the cheering in that Dolores County courtroom. Another warrant was issued when charges were refiled a few weeks later. Navajo Sam high-tailed it out of the area. Even today you'll hear the stories that he's still up there, though, off living in some remote, wild valley, where we'd want him to be. Actually he moved to Wisconsin.

I was working on the Dolores district during the Navajo Sam summer and when the case was closed that autumn I went over to the Hollywood Bar with one of the Forest Service special agents. He was glad Navajo Sam had taken off.

"The hell with justice, we didn't want to be the bad guys that brought a legend in. It's rotten PR and that could hurt us more than Navajo Sam ever could," he said.

The ridgerunner had been gone for the better part of fifteen years when I moved to northern Idaho in 1980, but we hadn't even unpacked our goods in the house we rented in Troy before I heard the legend. My new neighbor, an ex-logger, dropped by to see if he could help out. In the course of conversation he glanced over the rolling hills and mentioned matter of factly that he'd had a cousin who'd seen the ridgerunner over in the Clearwater country. I asked him who the hell the ridgerunner was and he looked at me like I'd just landed from Venus.

The ridgerunner is as much a part of that thickly timbered country as the small logging towns that cling to its edges—places like Bovil, Clarkia, Pierce, Weippe, Headquarters, and Avery. If the ridgerunner isn't part of the conversation on any given day be assured that he is stalking the edge of people's consciousness like the fog and the rain and the forest.

William Clyde Moreland came into the Sawtooth Range of southern Idaho in 1932. Up until then he'd lived a hardscrabble life going from reform school to reform school and sometimes spending a little time in jail for burglaries and the like. He'd managed a fifth grade education somewhere along the way. Odds are he came into the country as a last resort and that first year wintered over in the Chamberlain Basin. There is hard evidence that he tried to steal an airplane down there, but when he jumped into it and started turning keys and cranking switches he couldn't get it to run. He didn't know how to fly anyway. He spent the winter living off deer that he snared using telephone wire he'd ripped off from the Forest Service. He stayed in the backcountry from then on, slowly moving north into wilder and wilder places.

He was seen on the upper reaches of the Selway River in 1936. At some point he made an impression of a Forest Service key in a bar of soap and filed a key out of tobacco tins. He used the key to enter the Forest Service cabins that were located along the trails throughout what was then pretty much roadless backcountry. They say he usually left the cabins a bit messy and had a real taste for jam. He seldom slept in them but rather grabbed some stores and took off back into the forest. Depending on who you talk to, the ridgerunner is regarded as a gentleman who "borrowed" what he needed to get through hard seasons outback or he was simply a wacko thief.

Among the woodsmen, the ridgerunner developed a reputation for cunning, stealth, and endurance under unimaginable hardship. There are stories of his snowshoe tracks disappearing into thin air, his boot prints turning mysteriously into a gaggle of elk tracks, and long winter treks sometimes covering hundreds of miles. There is some truth to all of it. He *was* really out there.

From 1937 to 1942 Moreland travelled the backcountry of the Clearwater and St. Joe national forests, spending a good deal of time around the old Roundtop Ranger Station. By this time the Forest Service knew that somebody was entering their cabins, but it wasn't until the rangers got together that they came to the conclusion that it was in fact the same man. A theft in 1942 of some food, clothes, and bedding at a trail camp led the Forest Service to believe that the ridgerunner was Charles "Baldy" Webber, who was wanted for attempted murder and considered dangerous. The Forest Service set out after the ridgerunner. In 1944 two Forest Service workers ran into Moreland at the Flat Creek cabin. He was cooking dinner and invited them to chow down with him. Afterwards he left and the Forest Service guys called the boss and asked him what to do.

The Forest Service got hold of Morton Roark and Mickey Durant, both skilled Service woodsmen, and asked them to pose as trappers and roam the country in an attempt to bring Moreland in, who they still thought was Webber. They tracked and trailed him into the spring. There were a few narrow escapes. Finally, they tried again in the winter of 1945 and captured him near the Skull Creek cabin. Instead of the highly dangerous desperado they expected to find, they found the ridgerunner, living under a piece of canvas in the middle of winter with a wet sleeping bag. He'd lost most of his teeth and had a touch of scurvy. He'd been running the ridges for thirteen years.

He ended up in jail after a short visit to the state mental hospital, where he was declared a bit on the antisocial side but not really very dangerous. The folks loved him. Anyone who could make it for thirteen years in northern Idaho, summer and winter, was okay with them. He explained the disappearing snowshoe tracks very simply—he had a harness on both ends of his snowshoes and simply turned around and walked back in his tracks. He took to the streams now and then to avoid detection and always travelled on the ridges up above and parallel to the trails. The boot prints disappearing into elk tracks? Be it legend or not it is said that he had a short little pair of stilts with elk feet on the bottom.

After he got out of jail he managed a job with the Potlatch lumbering outfit on the Camp T Flume but blew up a tractor with dynamite when the boss got on his nerves. A local jury wouldn't convict him. In 1952 he took a few shots at a Potlatch foreman and ended up in jail for six months. When he got out he took to living in the bush again and stealing from logging camps and the Forest Service. He also started writing weird letters to the governor and regional forester. In 1956 he was caught in the Canyon Ranger Station that was unoccupied at the time. He ended up in jail for six months again and headed right back into the mountains when he got out.

He eventually stole a .45 pistol and some goods from the Skull Creek cabin in 1957. The FBI was called in and the ridgerunner ended up in the loony bin in Orofino. He escaped in 1959 and was returned. He was released in 1961. A ranger came across him wandering the backcountry after that and asked him what he was doing. He said he wasn't going to stay but had just come back to see if he'd been dreaming all those years. They say he died in 1964, but nobody knows for certain.

I've taken a good bit of the ridgerunner story from an account written by Ralph Space in *The Clearwater Story*. He was the supervisor of the forest from 1954 to 1963 and in on much of what happened to the ridgerunner in his final years. There are other renditions, like the one written by Bert Russell in *Calked Boots*. The facts don't differ radically between the two accounts, but they are worlds apart. Russell, who's logged, cruised timber, and worked the mills, sees the ridgerunner as basically a good ole boy who managed to slide by the government for years by outsmarting them and one upping everyone with a superior kind of woodsmanship. Space sees the ridgerunner as insane and because of that enduring untold hardship. I wrote him in 1982 and asked if he knew any more about the ridgerunner. In his reply he said he had nothing to add to the story but warned me that most people had made Moreland a hero, "describing him as a poor but clever woodsman who eluded all efforts of the mighty Forest Service to catch him. Such was not the case. ... I hope you do not try to make him a hero," Space said.

That would be the obsession. The voice of reason in one ear, the wildman in the other. There are no real people in any of this. It is the kind of thing that floats around on the wind. The grand legend that has been known to outlive governments.

More recently it has gotten ugly. Claude Dallas killed two Idaho Fish and Game Enforcement officers on January 5, 1981, and busted off into the wild country. Some said that he was so strong an outdoorsman that he could live indefinitely out there. The stories started. The legends formed. The wildman crawled out of his box. In the summer of 1984 Don Nichols and his son Dan kidnapped Kari Swenson, an athlete from Bozeman, Montana, and headed into the mountains. They killed a man in the process and wounded Swenson. In a news interview Don Nichols's sister Betty said, "Don's loved the mountains all his life and he knows how to live in them better than anybody I ever knew. They won't starve him out. He doesn't smoke and he doesn't drink, so he doesn't have to come down for supplies. He says he's always warm up there, even in the winter." The wildman scratching at the door.

All of this is unexplainable. These *people* must be crazy. It's the stories and legends that live a life of their own. The idea that there is something like absolute freedom and that it resides in a wild place. A thread so strong that utter deprivation seems acceptable and even murder can get by. The wildman is the story that lives on that edge between twilight and darkness. The shadow of a poorwill jumping through the headlights. Something we don't know enough about to study. A mystery recognized by its voice in the night. A nightjar.

David Petersen

David Petersen was born in 1946 and lives with his wife Carolyn in the San Juan Mountains northeast of Durango, Colorado. A former Marine Corps helicopter pilot, he is a senior editor for *Mother Earth News*. David Petersen also teaches at Fort Lewis College in Durango. His books include *Among the Elk* (Northland, 1988) and *Big Sky, Fair Land: The Environmental Essays of A.B. Guthrie* (Northland, 1988). He has written seven nonfiction children's books as well. In *Among the Aspen* (Northland, 1991), Petersen pays tribute to America's most widespread upland hardwood tree in the tradition of Thoreau's famous essay on the wild apple tree and some of John Muir's passages on the trees of the Sierra Nevadas and the Pacific Northwest. Like John Muir, David Petersen understands that "the clearest way into the universe is through a forest wilderness." In this essay from *Among the Aspen,* the author describes an exciting encounter with a mother black bear and her three cubs, which leads him to an epiphany: "If heaven is to be found right here on earth, as I am inclined to believe it is, surely its throne room is the Rocky Mountain aspen grove."

Heaven on Earth
(circa 1991)

The clearest way into the universe
is through a forest wilderness.
—John Muir

I remember it like a dream.

I'm standing alone in a parklike grove of quaking aspens. I have come here, as on so many evenings before, to see what I can see. Wishing not to disturb the sylvan tranquillity of this special place (only just one of many I have discovered and laid emotional claim to hereabouts, but special nonetheless), I am dressed in camouflage and attempt to keep my movements as imperceptible as the progress of time, as quiet as—what? Well, as quiet as a bumbling, balding, middle-aged human animal can manage.

Just ahead, a predictably ill-tempered gray jay, a large, white-crowned, black-tipped gray bird (*Perisoreus canadensis*), also called Canada jay, Whiskey Jack, and—the most accurate of all its many nicknames, camp robber—screams its harsh familiar curse, then drops from its lofty perch, strokes twice with noisy wings, and sails away, tilting low amongst the stark, upright beams of the quaking aspen forest.

This minor commotion in turn startles to flight a pair of tiny sweet chickadees. (Chickadee: A most beautifully onomatopoetic name it is, given the little gray-and-white bird's distinct, repetitive, all's-well call of *chicka-dee-dee-dee.*) Up the valley a ways—I can't judge just how far—an autumn-enamored bull elk issues a drawn-out bugle ... like a bent high note on a saxophone.

I move slowly on, following a dim but familiar game trail that twists and dodges through the aspens, hoping to catch a glimpse of the bull. Stepping carefully, I stop often to look, listen, test the downslope evening breeze for familiar wild scents: the tangy, pungent smell of autumn aspens; the heavy barnyard funk of elk in rut; the fresh, willowy aroma of the small spring pool that waters this tight little valley with its jungle of aspen-evergreen and lush understory of pine drops the color of dried blood, lady ferns both common and alpine, giant larkspur and cow parsnips, angelica, chokecherry, bearberry, wild raspberry, and other lush living things whose names I have yet to learn and perhaps never will. The going here is quiet, easy, though the undergrowth is so profuse that I can see no more than a few yards in any direction around me.

Suddenly, from out of a tangle of Gambel oak just ahead, an animal appears: roundish, the color of a Hershey bar, furry and fat, the size (more or less) of a badger.

What it is, I realize with a start, is a bear cub, small for this late in the season, but a bear cub nonetheless. I am surprised, elated— but also a little confused.

Before I have time to sort out my thoughts, a second cub comes shambling out of the same island of scrub oak. And a third. And all three are headed straight for me.

Notwithstanding the considerable time I spend alone and quiet in the woods, and even given the generous black bear population hereabouts, my close-up bruin sightings over the past decade have been, as they say, few and far between. The appearance of this wee chocolate trio is great good luck. Still, I am distracted by a couple of curiosities: *Where might be the mother?* And, perhaps a more pressing concern, *how big is she?*

She doesn't keep me hanging for long, making a silent

entrance through a curtain of aspen saplings thirty yards or so up the valley. Fortunately, being upslope, she is also up the breeze from me.

Hump-shouldered and autumn fat, this little sow is by far the most beautifully marked specimen of *Ursus americanus* I've ever seen, more closely resembling a runted grizzly than your average black bear. Most significantly, like her cubs, she isn't black. (In point of fact, I have yet to encounter a black black bear here in the Colorado Rockies, though I know they are about.) Her legs, head, and ample rump are patched over with the same chocolate brown that completely clothes her cubs, but her back is a broad swatch of straw blond, and all of her is mottled with a shifting pattern of light and shadow as she moves beneath the scattered shafts of low-angle evening sunlight fingering down through the aspens.

The sow browses slowly toward me—relaxed, undisturbed, the way such an encounter should be—scarfing up wildflowers, nipping the leaves of giant cow parsnips, using long claws to dig in the dark moist soil for ... who knows what? Bemused. Insouciant. Beautiful.

Standing here like a pine snag amidst her swarming brood of cubs, I feel silly, like some grinning Buddha, and it suddenly occurs to me that my present situation is, well, a mixed blessing.

I know, intellectually at least, that there's little to worry about, that black bears almost never act aggressively toward humans. Almost never, that is, so long as they are treated with the respect due unto large, fast, muscular, well-armed, unpredictable, predatory wild beasts. In fact, truly wild black bears (those that live outside of the protective bounds of parks and preserves) are among the most reclusive of all large North American mammals, wanting only to be left alone, almost always turning stubby tail and fleeing at the first hint of human intrusion. That is why black bears are so rarely seen, even where both they and humans abound, and why they have survived where the more aggressive and visible grizzly has been displaced or exterminated.

And yet, I also know that in this century alone, several dozen people have been mauled by black bears, and at least twenty-three have been killed. And some of those attacks were determined (by the most grisly evidence imaginable) to have been predacious—the bears had stalked and killed these human prey for food. (One singularly unfortunate and incredibly courageous young woman, after being attacked by a black bear, lay playing dead while the bruin slowly ate both her arms; yet, miraculously, she lived to tell about it.)

But banish such horrific thoughts.

The mind works in strange ways when under acute pressure. At least mine does. Just now, a chill September evening breeze and the consequent treetop rattle of sere autumn aspen leaves remind me that another summer has come and all but gone. Winter is just over that proverbial next hill.

Perhaps that is why this family of bears is out and about in broad daylight, instead of napping through this fine fall evening, awaiting the anonymity of darkness to venture abroad; they are maximizing the brief remaining time before the snows come, embarking on a last-ditch fattening spree in anticipation of the rapidly approaching denning season.

Thinking about the extreme cold and deep snow that freeze-frame this high country for a good four or more months of winter each year, I am led to wonder where these bears will hole up. Perhaps right here in this enchanted aspen valley? Within the hollowed hole of some long-dead ponderosa giant? Beneath the shelter of an overhanging rock ledge? Or merely in a natural depression in the earth—such as are created when a heavily rooted tree topples—the snow alone covering, hiding, and insulating them? Black bears, unlike grizzlies, do not actively excavate dens.

The cub nearest me now shinnies a few feet up a small aspen, turns and looks to see if his siblings will follow (which they don't), then backpedals down.

Among the first lessons any right-minded bear mother teaches a new brood of cubs after leading them from the nursery den in April or May is the high art of arboreal acrobatics: tree climbing. Very young black bears are defenseless when away from their mother, and—as evidenced by the trio frolicking this moment around my boots—are filled with the reckless temerity of youth.

Were it not for their acquired agility at virtually flying up trees, black bear cubs almost certainly would fall prey to coyotes, cougars, even boar black bears far more often than they in fact do.

I shift my gaze from the cubs to their mother. The sow continues to narrow the distance between us; she's now maybe twenty yards up the hill—not nearly far enough. I reflect that perhaps it's high time to consider, as the business cliché goes, my options.

Moving only my eyes, I survey the trees around me, sizing them up for climbability ... and am distressed to note the obvious: Discounting one huge ponderosa pine, high-crowned and much too fat to shinny, all the trees within my quick grasp are smooth-barked aspens, and none has limbs (those enticing projections that desperate folk are wont to go out on) low enough to grasp and haul myself up by. Adding the promise of injury to insult, fully a quarter of the aspens surrounding me wear on their pale skins the rough, dark scars of old wounds inflicted by the short, heavy claws of climbing bruins. Not just young black bears, but the adults as well are superb climbers. So much for the flee-up-a-tree option.

The cubs continue to romp nearby. The sow feeds ever closer.

An aggressive self-defense is out of the question. For one thing, I like bears, whether they care for my company or not. On a more pragmatic level, the big hunting knife I superstitiously lug on my frequent solo treks into the backcountry—a carbon steel talisman against all manner of imagined emergencies—is beyond my immediate reach, thrust deep into the bowels of the daypack appended to my tensed shoulders. Just as well, I reckon, since I don't feel like becoming a twentieth-century Hugh Glass—that overly optimistic 1820s mountain man who used a knife in hand-to-claw combat with an out-of-sorts mother grizzly, then spent the next several months gimping around the boonies with a body like Swiss cheese.

But all is not lost, because close or no, the sow is still upwind of me and preoccupied with satisfying her hunger; she hasn't yet "made" me. But it won't be long before she does. It *can't* be much longer now, as near as she is. Bears are dim-sighted creatures that have a hard time distinguishing a stationary object from its background. But their hearing is better than ours, and their sense of smell is unsurpassed in all of nature.

Considering this iffy hand I have been dealt by fate, it's obvious that my best, perhaps my only, bet to avoid being transmogrified into fresh bear plop, is to stand pat until the danger has passed—or until the sow detects me, decides that I'm a threat to her cubs, and calls in the cards. Then I'll probably attempt, pointless though it may prove to be, to wing it posthaste up the nearest aspen, there to tremble in company with the timid yellow leaves.

As the trio of cubs continues to romp roundabouts, circling me as if I were some bearded maypole, and their two-hundred-pound mother grunts and grazes steadily nearer, I strain to remain motionless and to slow the Gatling-gun beating of my adrenaline-charged heart.

And now we approach the denouement. In the retelling, if not in the actual experiencing of this adventure, I long for an appropriately exciting climax ... the discovery; the growling, teeth-clacking charge; my miraculous escape. But lacking any such thing, mere fact will have to suffice.

The sow simply cruised right on past without giving me even so much as a sidelong glance.

Down the valley a few yards, though, she suddenly spun around and bawled; at the signal, the three cubs hurried to her flanks. My guess is that she had finally cut my scent trail. Typically, wisely, choosing flight over a possible fight, she called in her cubs and fled. I watched and listened with mixed relief and sorrow as the sow led her little family at a brisk pace down the valley and out of my life—forever? Probably. A few moments more and my bears were gone, totally gone, their shadowy forms swallowed by the darkening forest.

This, all of it—bears, birds, bugling elk, secret mountain springs and their pellucid pools, the teeming understory of ferns and wildflowers and berry brush and rich green grasses, and most certainly the straight white trees themselves—is the ancient, mystical world of the quaking aspen forest.

If heaven is to be found right here on earth, as I am inclined to believe it is, surely its throne room is the Rocky Mountain aspen grove.

Bruce Berger

Bruce Berger lives in Colorado and has written widely on the American West. His articles and essays have appeared in the *New York Times, Not Man Apart, Outside, Rocky Mountain Magazine, Sonora Review* and *Southwest Review*. Berger's first book of essays, *The Telling Distance: Conversations with the American Desert* (Breitenbush, 1990), was awarded the 1990 Western States Book Award for Creative Nonfiction in a competition judged by N. Scott Momaday, William Kittredge, Jorie Graham and Elizabeth Hardwick. In this essay, "The Mysterious Brotherhood," Berger takes a look at death in the desert, especially as it pertains to the cactus: the cholla, prickly pear and saguaro. "A taste for the desert," Berger writes, "is a taste for ultimates, and death is the backdrop against which all we know comes to brilliance. Cactus tell us nothing of what's ahead, any more than the death of a close friend: all they reveal is process, but process which retains, even in human terms, immeasurable beauty." Berger naturally inherits the tradition of Mary Austin, Joseph Wood Krutch and Edward Abbey, and pays fine tribute to the desert in *The Telling Distance*, a book that gives promise of even greater things to come.

The Mysterious Brotherhood
(circa 1990)

It was a custom in medieval times for saints and scholars to keep a human skull around to remind them of their mortality. That practice seems morbid as we plunge, youth-obsessed, toward the twenty-first century, and the great bonescapes of Georgia O'Keeffe, their elegant folds of calcium and sky, remind us less of death than the deep cleanliness beneath the flesh. To see finality as a kind of radiance, one can turn to the desert not just for the melodramatic bones—which, despite cartoons, are few and far between—but for the quieter revelations of the vegetable world. Those unlikely green lives, each stranded in its claim to water, shed their skins to reveal still deeper miracles.

Cactus are among our most treasured species, yet only cholla has attained posthumous notoriety. The cuddly looking shrubs—actually great fountains of barbed grenades which, in certain varieties, nearly leap out for affection—strew in death the sections of their hollow stems, lattices of holes strung together by a woody fiber like asbestos. The delicacy of the recurrent patterns, the modulations of their holes, their rich patina make them sought after, and they grace the kinds of coffee tables where manhattans are served, find their way into flower arrangements, are positioned as a foil for foliage. They have been strung into lamps, hung up as hat racks, woven into macrame, tricked out as toy covered wagons. They have been stood on end and hollowed with ovals for the insertion of Heidi vignettes in isinglass, seashells and mother of pearl. They have in fact been conscripted for so many forms of kitsch, schlock and inventive bad taste that they seem some Sonoran revenge on deer antlers, abalone shells and Japanese fishing balls.

But it would be too bad to let their abuse obscure one of the desert's most moving cycles. Even as the cholla grows it drops its extremities, and if the pieces are not dispersed by wind, water, the flanks of animals or your pierced skin, they mass themselves under the plant like a field of charcoal. As the plant ages, the trunk turns black, the needles become brittle and the skin begins to peel. The cholla may simply crumble, strewing bits of its stem among the decayed pieces, or tip intact into a small jungle gym. But if it remains on its feet, stripped to its fretted skeleton, it leaves a shape refined as sculpture, lord of its clearing, elegant by day and a spidery presence beneath the moon.

The prickly pear, less noble than the cholla, simply runs out of strength and lays its pads on the ground. If it is noticed at all, it seems a vaguely repellent grey heap. Trodden upon it answers crisply to the shoe, a sensuous crunch like a bite of water chestnut or the slow dismemberment of a champagne cork. The serenity of its depths can call up visions of snakes napping in the cool, scorpions at rest, tarantulas digesting their friends. Menacingly pale, it is most comfortably crossed after making a fair noise, in a state of high alertness. "Here we go round the prickly pear," said T. S. Eliot, and one can see why.

But reach down and examine a pad. The skin, turned sulphurous brown, peels off like cracked cardboard, to reveal a mesh of fibrous sheets, each stamped with a similar pattern like a netting of veins and arteries, laminated sheet onto sheet. Each layer is a faint variation on the last as the holes rework their shapes throughout the pad. Fat green health hides the complexity of the prickly pear, and its disclosure is one of death's small rewards.

The smaller the cactus, the denser its spines, until one reaches the pincushion, one to three inches high, a white thimble usually nestled beneath some larger plant. The pincushion reverses the process by dying inside out, the flesh collapsing to leave a standing cup of barbed lace. Seldom recognized, the spent pincushion is a strange jewel, a crucible of woven stars each sprouting a hook like a talon, delicate as a doll's negligee.

Death on the desert: its forms are extravagant as the species themselves—the barrel's great mashed thumb, the organ pipe's burnt candelabra, the staghorn still more like antlers when stripped of its flesh. But for sheer pageantry the saguaro remains supreme. Largest of the cactus except for its Mexican cousin, the *cardón*, the saguaro reveals itself by painful degrees, breathtakingly. "What will become of ... the huge and delicate saguaro?" asks Richard Shelton in his moving poem, "Requiem for Sonora," but delicacy would not seem a prime characteristic of this stout colossus, one of whose arms, even as I watch in a suburban backyard, has been severed for months, is dangling by a thread, and is blooming furiously. The saguaro can be killed, *is* being killed by destruction of habitat, but the individual, capable of storing up to ten tons of water, taking fifteen years to grow the first foot, surviving a half century before it blooms and attaining a height of sixty feet, seems resilient to an inspiring degree.

We know when an animal like ourselves dies: it is the moment when the heart stops beating. But when does a plant die? When it turns brown? When it falls? When the shape is finally obliterated? The saguaro begins to die even as it grows. King of its habitat, it is home to entire species of woodpeckers and flickers, which riddle it with holes for many other varieties of birds. The injured pulp secretes a thick shell, a petrified leather that offers a comfortable cave for the nesting bird while protecting the cactus, a hole that actually survives the plant in a collectible object called a desert boot. Branches routinely meet with calamity, suffer injury or fall off, to shrivel like crocodiles in the sun, yet the plant grows on, oblivious. The more grotesque its deformities, the more humanly it seems to express itself. By maturity the plant is pocked, gouged, may be missing or trailing branches, or gored to its bare ribs as if it were being eaten by darkness. Remorselessly it thrives. By the time it is actually ready to die, at the age of one hundred fifty or two hundred years, the saguaro may seem the butt of assaults past imagining.

At last letting go, the energy-collecting green skin turns sallow: the plant's least attractive phase. After preliminary jaundice the outer skin deepens, hardens, begins to crinkle, and finally attains a kind of rich parchment. It extrudes a shiny black substance sticky to the eye, glassy as obsidian to the touch, as if it were being caramelized. Peeling skin reveals the inner pulp turning black, a burnt coral brittle to probing fingers. When tapped the skin now gives a report like a primitive drum, and could almost be played like a xylophone. Itself in sepia, the entire saguaro appears to be burning from inside.

At last the flesh is fallen, the skin strewn like old vellum, and the saguaro stands revealed: a white idea. If the specimen has many branches, or the ribs extend too far, the extremities will sheer off, leaving stumps in a variety of crosses and elemental shapes. Occasionally a cactus boot, former home of some flicker or owl, will catch in the ribs, a hole become substance, revealed as if in a structural model. Tough skin at the bottom may hold the freed ribs like poles in an umbrella stand, an immense rattle when shook. But at last the saguaro will fall. It is now only a confusion of hard skin, spines and crumpled flesh, with perhaps a stray boot, though even now the flung ribs may parody its shape in split bamboo.

Object of beauty, toy, curiosity, decoration, cheap firewood, musical instrument, home for scorpions, motive for metaphor— even a dead cactus has its uses. But a taste for the desert is a taste for ultimates, and death is the backdrop against which all we know comes to brilliance. Cactus tell us nothing of what's ahead, any more than the death of a close friend: all they reveal is process, but process which retains, even in human terms, immeasurable beauty. Their odd green lives, if nothing else, bring to consciousness our complicity in a mystery that becomes, even as we reject it, our own:

> Saguaros brave putrefaction like tough meat.
> Chollas strew black fruit while a skinful of char
> Peels into moonlight bleaching on its feet.
> The ocotillo collapses into a star.
> A mesh of fiber loosened by your nail
> Separates into bones of the prickly pear.
> Or lay your hands on a lung. Resemblances fail.
> Death is a common bond we never share.

John Daniel

John Daniel lives with his wife in Portland, Oregon. He was educated at Stanford University and was a recipient of a Wallace Stegner Fellowship in Writing. Daniel has taught at Stanford University and was recently a Visiting Professor at Austin Peahy State University in Tennessee. He is the author of several books of poetry and is the poetry editor for *Wilderness*, the quarterly publication of the Wilderness Society. Daniel is currently working on a collection of essays. In this essay, which originally appeared in the Fall 1990 issue of *Wilderness*, John Daniel takes a skeptical look at what Edward Abbey called "Industrial Tourism" in *Desert Solitaire* (McGraw Hill, 1968; University of Arizona Press, 1989). The author contrasts the communion with nature he experienced climbing Sentinel Rock in Yosemite Valley with the sense of isolation and dislocation he felt while later riding a tour bus on the valley floor with his wife and mother. For Daniel, technical rock climbing offered an "opportunity for an active involvement with nature instead of a passive looking at it." Road-bound sightseers, "on the other hand, are not part of the place they look at. They are observers, subjects seeking object, passing through." This issue will be of increasing concern to the National Park Service in the nineties and beyond: how do we provide for the recreational needs of the burgeoning population while at the same time preserving the natural values people seek in the parks? Some see the answer in tour buses and, more recently, monorails. Others shudder at the thought of such an artificial experience of wild nature. The answer may reside somewhere in between.

The Impoverishment of Sightseeing
(circa 1990)

When I was a boy my family had a weekend cabin on the Blue Ridge of northern Virginia, and it was on one of my hikes in the woods nearby that I experienced a new standard of fear. I was walking alone on a sunny day when I came to a slope of small gray boulders, bare of vegetation. I had skirted this boulder patch on previous rambles, and wondered about it, and now I decided to cross it. As I hopped from rock to rock, a quick buzz from below froze me. *Cicada*, I thought hopefully, but I knew what it was. I jumped to another rock and another buzz sounded, then another. The whole bright strew of boulders seemed to be buzzing around me, beneath me, and one more step, I was sure, would bring lightning fangs. I tried to quiet my tremoring legs, to stand as still and light and thin as it was possible to stand. I'm sure I prayed— prayer was my habit in those days when things weren't going well. I stood for probably half an hour, long after the buzzes had stopped. Finally I boosted my courage, stepped to the very crown of the next rock and accompanied by sporadic buzzes danced out of the boulder field with the nimbleness of dread.

I thought of that childhood ordeal when I visited Yosemite Valley recently for the first time in over a decade. In my mid-twenties

I knew the valley as a rockclimber of high enthusiasm and modest ability. Now, at thirty-seven, I was returning with my wife and mother, neither of whom had seen Yosemite before. I wanted to show them the exhilarating playground I had known. Because my mother wasn't a strong walker, we decided to take our first long look from one of those buses that loop around the valley floor. With its solid bank of windows curving up over our heads, we thought the bus would give us many good views, and it did. But how disappointing those views were, how unaccountably dull. The familiar rock faces were there, as sheer and massive as ever, but *merely* there. As the bus trundled along they paraded through the frame of my window, one after another, as I tried hard to feel excited.

What I saw was dull, I realized after a while, because I was walking the boulder field without the snakes. The places that had once been alive to me, imbued with my zeal and fears, now were reduced to plain visual images, seen for the sake of seeing, *scenes* in the bus window. My wife and mother, viewing Glacier Point and Half Dome for the first time, were more satisfied with what they saw. But I sensed no real enthusiasm from them as the sunny granite shifted in our window view, nor from the other passengers, most of whom were clearly new to the valley. "Look at that," the man in front of us kept murmuring, but listlessly, like a recorded message. "Isn't that a sight. Isn't that a sight."

When I climbed those rocks—only a few hundred feet up most of them—they were not sights but presences. As I focused on cracks and tiny nubbins in front of my face, bright granite expanse was always flaring in the periphery of my vision—all the more vivid, all the more present, for being only obliquely seen. And just as vivid and present was what I couldn't yet see, the challenges that lay hidden where the route disappeared above an overhang or around a corner. It was that perpetual unknown that buzzed me with scary excitement, like the rattlesnakes hidden beneath the boulders— that was what I climbed after, more beautiful than anything I saw with my eyes.

As I looked out from a belay ledge after a hard pitch, the far valley wall wavered and swam with squiggling spots, nothing solid about it, then settled in my vision not merely to stone but to an embodiment of spirit. Having made the pitch I wasn't sure I could make, I was suffused with a sense of body and mind doing exactly what they were meant to do, blended perfectly in their most rightful act. And what was that arched and pinnacled rising of granite I gazed at, shining through a gulf of air, but the world's own most perfect and rightful act?

One July weekend my partner and I tried the Chouinard-Herbert route on Sentinel Rock, a seventeen-hundred-foot face normally done in two days. Mid-morning on the second day, after a bivouac on a ledge, we killed our last bottle of water—we had badly miscalculated our need—and climbed ahead into the ninety-degree afternoon. We became so weak we couldn't finish the climb by dark, though we had reached the easy ledges near the top. We spent another night, sleeping like stones as the brightest colors I have ever seen flamed through my dreams. In the morning we made our way to the top, there to find an enormous, orange-barked Ponderosa pine, standing alone. It seemed to glow from within, a tree but more than a tree, an emblem of being itself. And the stream we finally came to, after what seemed hours of stumbling descent down the dry gully behind Sentinel, was no ordinary stream with a fringe of plants—how *green* those plants were—but the very Garden itself. We knelt there, feeling the icy glow of water inside us with our booming and skittering hearts.

Rockclimbing and mountaineering are unnecessary, artificial activities, invented by a privileged leisure class. Yet the act of climbing can yield an engagement with the natural world that is anything but artificial. That, I believe, is the reason it arose among the European well-to-do of the eighteenth century—it answered a need for reconnection to the wild nature from which they had so successfully separated themselves. Other kinds of outdoor activities answer the same need for many of those who pursue them— backpacking, birding, hunting, fishing, whitewater rafting. What they offer in common is the opportunity for an active involvement with nature instead of a passive looking at it. Climbers and fishermen are not at one with nature but they are immersed in it, interacting with it, and in that sense they are part of their surroundings. They experience a sense of place in nature, or at least that experience is potentially available to them. Those who come to sightsee, on the other hand, are not part of the place they look at. They are observers, subjects seeking an object, passing through.

I don't mean that the population can be divided into two groups, the doers and the lookers. I am both, at different times. All of us at various moments are the man on the bus gazing out and murmuring, "Isn't that a sight." Nor do I believe that that man was completely disconnected from what he saw; he was impressed, perhaps even moved, by the spectacle of Yosemite's walls. But he wasn't moved in any way that energized him much, that evoked any sign of elation or fear or awe. Like me at the time, he wasn't in the *presence* of those soaring faces. And as I watched him and others clicking photographs later, I couldn't help thinking that by recording what they saw they were trying to verify that it was real, and that they were actually there.

I've experienced that odd feeling myself. The first time I saw the Tetons, I was a teenager sightseeing with my family. We sat at an outdoor chuckwagon breakfast place, eating pancakes and staring at the most dramatic mountains I had ever seen, so dramatic my eyes didn't quite believe them. They seemed to have no depth, hardly any substance—I kept thinking they looked like cut-outs someone had propped up on the other side of the lake. Part of my trouble was due, I'm sure, to the fact that an eastern kid was seeing his first western mountains. But I think there was more. I was expecting to experience those mountains, to perceive their full reality, simply by looking at them from a distance. They seemed to lack substance because I was reducing them to an image on the screen of my vision.

I suspect that television—I used to watch a lot of it—had much to do with my perception of the Tetons, as I suspect it has much to do with the way many of us experience the natural world. Television viewers give up the active movements of awareness—glancing around, comparing, looking long or only briefly—to the autocratic screen, reducing themselves to absorbers of presented images. All of us who spend much time in such a mode of consciousness will necessarily transfer it to other areas of experience. When we go into nature we will expect the things we see to reveal themselves, to tender their full value, merely by our laying our eyes on them. And to the extent to which nature seems static and dramatically blank compared to TV entertainment, it is likely to seem disappointing, lifeless and unreal.

Even nature documentaries, despite their educational value, may tend ultimately to diminish the viewer's engagement with nature more than they enhance it. Those who are used to such programs are likely to find real nature—subliminally, at least—disorderly and dull, because its images aren't preselected for visual impact and framed within a screen. Shows about nature may come to seem more real than nature itself. In fact, it may be that for millions of Americans the viewing of such programs, and of television in general, is substantially replacing direct experience of the wild natural world. When an old-growth forest is delivered to the livingroom, some viewers will want to go there. But far more, I think, will feel they have already been.

What that majority will miss, of course, is the unframed sensory texture of the thing itself—the scale of the trees, the pervasive stillness and the filtered ambient light, the dark smells of the forest floor, the feel of moss under their feet. They will miss the varying rhythms of their walking and the unconstrained movements of awareness in such a place. They will miss the primordial alertness that comes in the presence of trees, shadows and small forest sounds, of wildlife seen and unseen. Consuming images rather than the thing, they will have walked the boulder field not only without the snakes but without the boulders and without themselves.

But more is at stake than the quality of our perceptual experience. Diminishing nature to a collection of visual objects, seen on television or firsthand, is not only impoverishing to us but dangerous to the land as well. Nature-as-sight has only an aesthetic appeal to the seer, a pleasing pattern of form and color—what we generically call "natural beauty." There is nothing wrong with aesthetic appreciation, and it can lead to other ways of valuing nature, but it seems to me a very fragile basis for preserving what relatively wild, undisturbed lands we have left. When push comes to shove, the settlement of North America has made clear, aesthetic values have a way of toppling in the practical path of progress. Tall-grass prairie was beautiful to the Ohio Valley settlers, but they plowed it under. The passenger pigeon was beautiful to the hunters who shot it down. Even timber executives see beauty in old-growth Douglas fir, but its beauty doesn't stop them from reducing it to clearcuts.

Appreciation of nature in our society takes two forms above all others. The prevailing form, the cult of utility, shapes and perpetuates our sense of land as something from which to extract uses and materials. The other, the cult of beauty, values land for its own sake, but chiefly for its visual appearance. The cult of beauty has had important, positive consequences—most of our national and state parks were set aside because of their scenic splendor—but it also works hand-in-hand with the cult of utility. Our working assumption as a people has been that except for a scattering of parks and designated wilderness areas, many of them in alpine regions difficult of commercial access anyway, all other land is subject to utility first and other considerations second. On public lands, the much-voiced concept of multiple-use says that scenery and recreation are equal in importance to the land's utilitarian value; but in practice, multiple-use in our national forests means logging first and other uses where logging permits. And in the desert West, which in the eyes of even many nature-lovers still lies outside the category of beautiful, land developments such as mining, oil and gas drilling and the wholesale stripping of forest to create range for cows all proceed with practically no restraint.

When those who oppose such "improvements" invoke only (or mainly) the land's beauty in its defense, they are dismissed as sentimental and unrealistic. And there is a certain justice in the dismissal, because at bottom the cult of beauty shares with the cult of utility the same flaw: it views nature as an object separate from the human subject. The timber or mineral executive reduces nature to a commodity, something to be taken out. The tourist seeking scenic beauty reduces nature to pleasing images, enjoyed and taken home on film. Neither view recognizes nature as a living system of which our human lives are part, on which our lives and all lives depend and which places strict limits upon us even as it sustains us.

That is an ecological view, and though most of us have some familiarity with the ideas of ecology, those ideas remain *only* ideas, abstract and forceless in our lives, if we perceive nature merely as a collection of objects, however lovely. It takes not just looking at nature but getting into it, and into some of its unloveliness as well as its splendor, for ideas to begin to bear the fruit of understanding. The rattlesnakes beneath the boulders instructed me, in a way no book could have, that the natural world did not exist entirely for my comfort and pleasure; indeed, that it did not particularly care whether my small human life continued to exist at all. Being terribly thirsty on Sentinel Rock helped me understand in my body what my mind already knew, or thought it knew—how moisture both makes life possible and sets unequivocal limits on where it can exist. And once I had spent some time in old-growth forests, the profusion of dead trees that had daunted me at first began to elicit an appreciation of how death and life dance to a single music, how a healthy natural community carefully conserves and recycles its living wealth, and so sustains itself through time.

Such perceptions, in their rudimentary way, point toward an ecological understanding of the natural world. Clearly, to fully realize that understanding, we as a people need to follow the lead of the ecological sciences and learn to live by the principles they discover. We need to heal the disruptions we have caused in the biosphere. But it is just as important, even as we scientifically study the inner workings of nature and the ways we have injured it, that we learn how to experience it again, how to apprehend it in its fullness. As Edward Abbey told us many times, you can't do that in a car, and neither can you do it with just your eyes. It can happen only by taking the time to enter the natural world, to engage it, not only to run our eyes along its surfaces but to place ourselves among its things and weathers—to let it exert, at least for intervals in our lives, the ancient influences that once surrounded and formed us.

Enough time under those influences can teach us to use our eyes actively again, as something more than receptacles. They seek a route through trees, across a creek, over a ridge, working in concert with body and mind. They follow the darts and veers of a hummingbird, a lizard skimming across stones, the quick glint of a trout. Things much smaller than El Capitan or the Tetons, things easy to miss, begin to reveal themselves—tiny white flowers of saxifrage, the quarter-sized, web-lined shaft of a tarantula's den, a six-inch screech owl flicking limb to limb in the dusk.

And when later in the evening the owl sounds its soft, tremulous call, and small snaps and rustlings reveal the presence of other lives, the eyes have reached their proper limit. The sense we rely on above all others can never completely know the natural world, for nature's being is only partly what it shows. Its greater part, and greater beauty, is always past what eyes can understand. When I started hiking desert canyons a few years ago, I kept hearing the song of a bird I couldn't see, a long descending series of sharply whistled notes. It was a canyon wren, I learned from the books, but what I learned from the bird was more important. It sang as I woke up, as brilliant sun spread down the great red walls, and it sang as I started farther up the twisting canyon, sloshing through pools and scrambling up dry water chutes, higher and deeper into the carving of time. And what I remember most vividly from those early hikes is no particular thing I saw, no one fern grotto or sandstone spire, no cottonwood or cactus garden. I remember a bird I couldn't see that called from around the next bend, from over the brink of a dry waterfall where the upper walls held the blaze of sky, where even as it steadily opened itself to sight, the canyon receded further and further into the depth of its mystery.

James D. Houston

James D. Houston was born in San Francisco and has resided for most of his life in California and Hawaii. Houston has authored five novels, including *A Native Son of the Golden West* (Dial, 1971), *Continental Drift* (Knopf, 1978) and *Love Life* (Knopf, 1985); and six works of nonfiction, including *Three Songs for My Father* (Capra, 1974), *One Can Think About Life After the Fish Is in the Canoe* (Capra, 1985) and *The Men in My Life* (Creative Arts, 1987). He and his wife Jeanne Wakatsuki Houston, with whom he coauthored *Farewell to Manzanar* (Houghton Mifflin, 1973), have traveled widely in Europe, Mexico, Asia and Indonesia. For the television script based on *Farewell to Manzanar*, which relates the experiences of his wife's family during the World War II internment of Japanese-Americans, they received an Emmy Award nomination and the prestigious Humanitas Prize. His shorter works have appeared in the *New Yorker*, the *New York Times*, *Rolling Stone* and *Manoa*, to name just a few. James D. Houston received the Master of Arts in American Literature from Stanford University and teaches at the University of California, Santa Cruz, where he is Visiting Professor in Literature.

In "Fire in the Night," Houston describes a trek through Hawaii Volcanoes National Park, which protects the historic lava flows between the immense Kilauea Crater and the Pacific Ocean ten miles to the south. This is a region of steaming fumaroles, molten flowing lava and intensive geothermal activity. Traditionally, Hawaiians have viewed the volcanoes as a natural source of spiritual energy and have worshipped the volcano goddess Pele as an incarnation of the life forces of the earth. These native islanders oppose planned geothermal development around the park that would, they believe, threaten the geological stability of the area and violate the sacred domain of the volcanoes. Houston pays fitting tribute to the Hawaiian volcanoes in this fine essay, and comes to see that rocks— inanimate in Western culture—may very well have their own unique form of life too.

Fire in the Night
(circa 1992)

Among geologists and volcano buffs there is a little rite of passage, whereby you stick your hand axe into moving lava and bring away a gob of the molten stuff. In order to do this you have to be where the lava is flowing and hot, then you have to get your body in close enough to the heat to reach down toward the edge of the flow, and it usually means you have to walk or stand for at least a few seconds on some pretty thin crust.

My chance came one night last year, on the Big Island of Hawaii, when I hiked out along the southern shoreline toward the spilling end of a lava tube. I was traveling in the company of Jack Lockwood, a specialist in volcanic hazards with the U.S. Geological Survey. He is a trim and wiry fellow, with wild hair and a devilish grin, a man from New England who has found that island, its craters and its lava fields, to be his natural habitat. He loves it there, he loves the look of the ropey *pahoehoe*, the many shapes it takes. He will stop the car to study the way today's flow has poured over yesterday's, making a drapery of knobs and drips. He will remark upon the metallic sheen in the late sun, and then point out that newer lava can be crumbled with your shoe, while the stuff that came through yesterday has already hardened under a rainfall and thus is firmer.

We parked where the yellow line of the coast road disappeared under a ten-foot wall of new rock. We got out the packs, the gloves, the canteens, the flashlights, the hard-hats. Jack's hat was custom-made, with his name in raised letters on the metal. His hard-toe boots were scuffed ragged with threads of rock-torn leather. I was going to wear running shoes for this expedition, until he told me no. "Where we're going," he said, "the soles could peel right off."

Hunkered on the asphalt, lacing up the high-top boots I'd borrowed, I could already feel it shimmering toward us. Minutes later we were hiking through furnace heat, over lava that had rolled across there just a few hours earlier. Through cracks and fissures you could see the molten underlayer showing, three or four inches below the dark surface.

"You can actually walk on it fifteen or twenty minutes after it starts to harden," Jack said, "as long as you have an inch of surface underfoot."

Soon the red slits were everywhere, and we were crossing what appeared to be several acres of recent flow. Jack plunged ahead with great purpose, with long firm strides, planting each foot and leaning forward as he walked, as if there were a path to be followed and we were on it—though of course there was no path, no prior footprints, no markers of any kind to guide us across terrain that had not been there that morning.

"Jack," I said, "have you ever stepped into a soft spot? I mean, got burned, fallen through?"

He shook his head vigorously. "Nope."

"How do you know where to step?"

He stopped and looked at me with his mischievous eyes, his beard and his squint reminding me of a young John Huston. "You just pick your way and pay attention as you go. It's partly experience and partly faith."

"Faith?"

"You have to put your trust in Pele. Tell her that you come out here with respect, and she will take care of you."

As he plunged on, I wanted to trust in Pele, the goddess of fire, who is said to make her home in a crater about fifteen miles from where we were walking. We had already talked about her, while driving down Chain of Craters Road, and I knew he meant what he'd just said. But I have to confess that at the moment I was putting my full trust in Lockwood, placing my feet where he placed his, stepping in his steps as we strode and leaped from rock to rock.

Eventually the heat subsided, and we were hiking over cooler terrain, though none of it was very old. "Everything you see has flowed through in the last six months," he said. Two and a half miles of the coast road had recently been covered, as well as the old settlement of Kamoamoa, near where we'd parked. Inland we could see some of what remained of Royal Gardens, a subdivision laid out in the early 1970s, laid out right across a slope of the East Rift Zone. In the Royal Gardens grid, cross-streets had been named for tropical flowers— Gardenia, Pikake—while the broader main streets sounded noble— Kamehameha, Prince. Now the access road was blocked in both directions. From our vantage point it looked as if great vats of black paint had been dumped over the highest ridge, to pour down the slope and through the trees, to cover boulevards and lawns.

Our destination—the spilling tube—was marked by a steam plume rising high against the evening sky. When we left the car it was white and feathery at the top, two miles down the coast. After the sun set and the light began to dim, the plume turned pink and red. Spatter thrown up from the collision of lava and surf had formed a littoral cone now outlined against the steam. As we approached, tiny figures could be seen standing at the edge of this cone, like cut-outs against the fiery backdrop.

On one side of the cone, flat spreads of lava were oozing toward the cliff. On the other side, an orange gusher was arcing some thirty feet above the water, while a mound slowly rose beneath it. Beyond that tube, another spill obscured by steam sent lava straight into the water at about sea level. Red-and-black floating gobs spewed out from the steam, or sometimes flew into the air, breaking into fiery debris that was gradually building the littoral cone.

These fires lit the billowing plume from below. As it churned away toward the west, it sent a pinkish glow back down onto the marbled surf, which made me think of the Royal Hawaiian Hotel, where they spend a lot of money on light bulbs and filters trying to tint the offshore waters a Waikiki pink that can never come close to Pele's cosmetic kit.

A video cameraman was there, perched at the cliff edge, filming the build-up on the mound below the arching orange tube. His tripod legs were spindly black against the glow. Nearby a couple of dozen people stood gazing at the spectacle, staffers from Volcano Observatory and the University of Hawaii. They were out there in numbers, Jack told me later, because this was a rare night. Spills like this were usually closer to the surf, and the lava would pour until the mound built up from below to seal off its opening. But this littoral cone was unstable, and part of it had fallen away and beheaded the end of the tube, so the lava was spilling free from high up the cliff, making a liquid column of endlessly sizzling orange.

If you could take your eyes off its mesmerizing arc and turn inland, you could see another glow in the night. It hung above the nearest ridge, light from the lake called Kupaianaha, the source of the lava moving around us. It was a new lake, inside a new shield cone. From there the lava snaked seaward via a channel that looped wide to the east, then back toward where we stood. You could see evidence of its twisting, subterranean path about halfway down the mountain, where tiny fires seemed to be burning, four or five eyes of flame against the black.

We lingered for an hour, maybe more, chatting, bearing witness, sharing our wonder with the others lucky enough to be out there on such a night, at the cutting edge of destruction and creation. We were about to start back when Lockwood said this was probably as good a time as any for me to add my name to the "one thousandth of one percent of the human population who have stuck their axe in hot lava." And with that he began to prowl around a couple of oozing streams, to see how close we could get.

I watched him step out onto some hot stuff that had barely stopped moving, and saw the surface give under his boot. With a grin he jumped back. "That's probably a little too soft."

We moved around to the far side, forty feet away, and approached the fiery mush from another angle. With axe in hand he hopped across the one-inch crust and dug into the front edge of a narrow strip, but it was already cooling and a little too thick to lift. He could only pull it up an inch or so, the front lip already in that halfway zone between liquid and solid stone.

He was pulling so hard he lost his footing and half fell toward the crust. His gloved hand reached out to take the fall, and for a moment his crouching body was silhouetted against the molten stream, while behind him the red-and-orange steam plume surged like a backdrop curtain for his dance. He came rolling and hopping toward me with a wild grin and a rascal eye.

"That's a little too viscous. It's surprising. It's cooler than it looks."

So we moved on, heading back the way we'd come, under a black sky with its infinity of stars, our flashlight beams bobbing across the rocks, while the plume grew smaller behind us.

We dropped down to a new beach of dark volcanic sand, then climbed out of the sand onto that day's fresh lava, where the red slits once again glowed all around us. As we picked our way, in the furnace heat, we came upon a flow that had not been there when we crossed the first time.

"Pele is being good to you," said Jack, grinning, his beard red-tinted underneath. He handed me his axe. "This is perfect. Just keep your back to the heat, and move in quickly."

Which is what I did. The stream was maybe twenty feet wide, seething, creeping toward the sea. I back pedaled up next to it, reaching with the flat chisel end of the metal blade, dipped and scooped into the burning lip. It was smoother than wet cement, thicker than honey, thicker than three-finger poi. Maybe the consistency of glazing compound, or the wet clay potters use. For the first mini-second it felt that way. As I dug in and pulled, it was already harder. It clung to the flow, but I tugged and finally came away with a chunk the size of a tennis ball, which held to the blade as I leaped back away from the heat.

Jack was excited. "Throw it down here, quickly!"

I plopped it between us, on a black slab.

"Now press your heel in hard!"

I pressed my boot heel into the glob, flattening it with a boot print. When the rubber began to smoke, I pulled my foot away.

"Now," he said, with a happy grin, "we'll put this on my shovel blade and carry it to the car while it cools, and this will be your souvenir."

By the time we reached the asphalt road the heat had given way to balmy coastal air off the water. The slits and fissures and plumes and flows were all behind us, and that was the end of our expedition.

But it was not the end of my relationship with that flattened piece of rock. I lived with it for another week, trying to decide what to do. After such a magical night, the idea of a souvenir appealed to me. It was mine, I suppose, because I had marked it with my boot. Now it was smooth, as shiny as black glass, and if I lived on that island I'd probably have it sitting on my desk. But I did not feel right about bringing this trophy back home. I kept thinking about the tug of the lava as I pulled the axe away. Through the handle I had felt its texture, its consistency, and something else that haunted me. A reluctance. A protest. As if live flesh were being torn from a body.

Maybe this was what the Hawaiians meant when they said all the rocks there belonged to Pele and should not leave the island. Maybe the unwritten law that said be respectful of the rocks was another way of honoring that old yearning in the stone. Maybe Pele was another word for the living stuff of earth, and maybe I had finally understood something, through my hands, something I had heard about and read about and talked about and even tried to write about.

Before I left the island I drove down to the south shore again. Sighting from the new black sand beach, I think I got pretty close to where we'd been. I dropped the chunk of lava down into a jagged crevice and asked it to forgive me for any liberties I might have taken, and I thanked Pele for letting me carry this rock around for a while. Then I drove to the airport and checked in my rental car and caught my plane.

I don't tell people about this, by the way. Not here on the mainland. You come back to California and tell someone you have been talking to rocks, they give you a certain kind of look. I'll mention it to Jack Lockwood, of course, the next time I see him. It's easier to talk about when you're in the islands. You meet a lot of people over there who claim to be on speaking terms with rocks. When you're in or near volcano country, it's easier to remember that they too have life, that each rock was once a moving thing, as red as blood and making eyes of fire in the night.

Frank Stewart

Frank Stewart, who has authored several books of poetry, is a professor of creative writing at the University of Hawaii. Stewart also serves as editor for *Manoa, A Pacific Journal of International Writing,* which is published by the University of Hawaii Press. The remarkable essay included here was first delivered at the Midnight Sun Writer's Conference at the University of Alaska, Fairbanks, in June 1990. "The World Between the Waves" is a parallel narrative, shifting between personal reminiscence featuring some of Stewart's favorite wild places in Hawaii and an historical look at literary natural history in the Pacific. Stewart examines the voyages of Cook and Darwin in the Pacific and concludes that "even the most level-headed and scientific-minded of the early naturalist-explorers registered unrestrained wonder at what they saw." This developing "idea" or metaphor of the Pacific was later evident, as Stewart points out, in the journals and books of Henry David Thoreau, who saw the vast, often exotic unknowns of the region as a symbol for the unexplored longitudes and latitudes of the self. At its best, Stewart writes, "Literary natural history ... attempts to awaken us: to 'put nature in our eyes,' so that, for the first time, we see it whole and all at once." The nature writing of the Pacific, as Frank Stewart so brilliantly establishes here, provides readers with a glimpse of a tropical splendor that can be nurtured both inside, and outside, the self.

The World Between the Waves
(circa 1990)

I've spent the past week alternately freezing and burning, hiking the island of Hawai'i from the volcanic coastline to the high rain forests shrouded in cold fog during this season. Now, I'm in the uncertain embrace of Aloha Island Air, feeling the little plane shudder as it climbs through six thousand feet toward the Pacific Ocean. The rising currents from the warm land mass below bounce the half-empty DeHaviland from side to side. Behind us, the small town of Waimea has vanished beneath the clouds, and southwest of it Kona, Keauhou and Kealakekua. The plane banks sharply, giving us a last look at a long volcanic plume that's billowing darkly into the upper atmosphere; it rises from just west of the village of Kalapana, buried during the past month under a steaming plateau of black lava. As the plane banks again, the island's volcanic peaks dominate the view for the last time and are left behind us. They are very old, but not as old as the sea. On this winter morning they are snowcapped in the early light. Flying time to Honolulu will be brief, says the pilot; sit back and relax.

The beach at Kealakekua, where I spent part of the previous day, is smaller than you might expect given its historic importance. The good shelter of the bay comes from its shape, like a fishhook. The longer part is rocky, lying below a steep cliff called Pali-Kapu-o-Keoua, where the early Hawaiians buried the remains of great chiefs. The little calcareous sand beach, called Nopo'opo'o, is nestled in the narrow, inner part of the hook's barb. Here, visitors spread out their blankets; most days there are a lot of visitors and not much beach to lie on.

I've often stood and looked at the cliffs and deep ocean from this spot, the vegetation, marine life, birds and the remains of human history. So much is here that I know I cannot see, or don't yet know how to see, despite several decades in the islands. When I try hard to take everything in together, hold it all in the eye as if it were one thing, a vertigo sweeps the details into a blur. For a while, then, I go back to the parts: the hillside of ekoa, kiawe and 'opiuma; a school of spinner dolphins, glimpsed far out at the point; a wandering tattler skimming low over the water. At the northwest end of the bay, clear in the sunlight, is a white monument to Captain James Cook. And here at the beach's edge a cairn before a barren *heiau*, or Hawaiian temple. Embedded in the cairn is a weathered marker to a crewman on Cook's final voyage, William Watman.

Conscious of the innumerable parts of this vision, yet wanting to know it as a whole, as indivisible as it truly is, I'm reminded of an historical argument in biology, from the 1880s, between the "lumpers and the splitters." In botany in particular, the splitters in their worst excess tried to find as many new and separate entities in nature as possible, even though sometimes this meant seeing every small variant of a plant as a new genera. Often a plant's unusualness was just the result of a local aberration or short-lived hybridization, but they were industriously described, named and endlessly divided into a host of new species, varieties, forms, etc. The lumpers, on the other hand, tended to aggregate living entities into neat, simplified categories; at their worst, they dismissed any of the variations that deviated from these large categories, refusing to make discriminations based on what they considered insignificant differences.

That controversy always seemed to me a reflection of the human condition. Not being a scientist, I don't know all the subtleties of the debate, but I know it's not entirely dead yet, and that taxonomy is still devilishly complicated. And there are splitters and lumpers among writers, doctors, critics, politicians, social scientists and just about everyone else. The problems inherent in perceiving and naming, separating and combining, are perhaps fundamental.

In any case, standing here at the edge of Kealakekua Bay I'm reminded of how difficult it is to perceive in two contrary ways at the same time: to comprehend, all at once, that the whole and the multiplicity are identical and indivisible.

When I first came to Kealakekua, I was intrigued by the cairn for William Watman. Of all the significant occurrences and presences in this bay, many of which profoundly shaped the fate of the Hawaiian Islands, why was Watman's life and death so predominantly marked and not the others? Why wasn't there something here about this great Hawaiian temple, and why wasn't it preserved like the one just south at Honaunau, which had become a national park? No one seemed to know much of the human history concerning either this *heiau* or Watman.

You have to go to Cook's journals to find William Watman. You can read there that he was an old man when he sailed with Cook to Hawai'i in July 1776. He had also sailed on Cook's previous voyage, around the world through the high southern latitudes of the Antarctic. When the voyagers returned to England, Watman had fallen ill, and he was sick again on this voyage, the one that had halted for a moment in the Hawaiian Islands. Still, no one thought Watman's illness was serious. So Cook and the others were surprised and saddened when Watman was seized with a sudden paralytic stroke and died, about ten days after the expedition's ships had anchored here, just offshore.

The priests of the *heiau* seemed to share Cook's sadness, because they agreed at once that Watman should be buried at the *heiau*, in sacred ground. At that time, the temple was a stone platform fourteen feet high, forty yards long and twenty wide. At the end closest to the mountain was a scaffold of poles twenty feet high. There was also a fence made of wooden stakes, many of which were topped with skulls. It was a *heiau* for human sacrifices.

During the burial ceremony, Cook solemnly pronounced the ritual of the Church of England over Watman's remains. Following this, the Hawaiian priests slaughtered animals and performed their own ritual service, placing the burned carcasses into Watman's grave with great solemnity. Years later, the missionaries who came to Hawai'i couldn't forgive Cook for mixing the two services; it set a bad example, they said, for the kind of work they were trying to do, separating error from true faith. And Cook had committed the same mistake almost as soon as he had arrived in the bay, failing to make distinctions between entities—a Christian participating in a pagan religious service in which he himself was referred to as a deity.

Unhappily, less than a month after Watman died, Cook would participate in mixed services again—a few parts of him buried at sea in a Church of England ritual, other parts of him used in a Hawaiian service somewhere on the high bluffs of Pali-Kapu-o-Keoua.

Many other early Western travelers to the Pacific are controversial now, like Cook, or else their lives and deaths are a mystery, like Watman's, either because they left so little trace of themselves, or because people have interpreted and reinterpreted their behaviors and motives. Of these early travelers, the ones that fascinate me most are not the privateers and buccaneers, William Dampier or Abel Tasman, who planted the colonialist flag and searched for "islands of gold and silver," but rather those who were awed by the miraculous plenitude of the natural world, who were spurred by a desire to see and record as many of the earth's plants and creatures as possible.

The great majority of these early naturalists in the Pacific, especially in Cook's era, were observers and collectors and not what we would call scientists. Nevertheless, some laid the groundwork for natural science in the Pacific, and among them were skilled writers whose descriptions of what they saw are often of equal value to the specimens they collected.

Neither their descriptions nor their collections were obtained easily. Early voyagers into the South Seas entered an uncharted region larger than all of Europe, Africa, Asia and the Atlantic Ocean combined. To go there in crowded, overloaded wooden ships required enormous bravery and ambition. Before the 1760s, no Westerners were able to make trans-Pacific voyages without becoming almost hopelessly lost, the ships becoming wrecked on far-off reefs, or the crews dying of starvation or disease. Many of the best-equipped expeditions in this period failed miserably or were simply never heard from again.

With the aid of new navigational technology and with the first, primitive means to combat scurvy and other diseases, however, more and more explorers, like "Foul Weather Jack" Byron in the *Dolphin* and *Tamar*, ventured out in earnest to discover "countries hitherto unknown." Others in this decade included Samuel Wallis and Philip Carteret in the *Dolphin* and *Swallow*, Louis-Antoine de Bougainville with the ships *Boudeuse* and *Étoile*, and of course James Cook in *Endeavour* on his first Pacific voyage. The 1770s saw even more explorations to the Pacific, including Cook's final voyages, on the last of which he was killed by the Hawaiians at Kealakekua Bay.

Increasingly, part of the mission of these explorers was to bring back as much of the undiscovered natural world as possible. They transported this world in the form of "curious objects" and specimens preserved in jars or dried between pages. They also took back their discoveries by means of precise and often beautiful illustrations from life, and by firsthand written descriptions of the plants, insects, fish and mammals they encountered.

Some of these Pacific explorers were skilled enough writers and narrators to render the unexplored world in accurate and often compelling language. Captain Cook was one of these. A scrupulous observer, on his three voyages into the Pacific he tried to measure and describe every phenomenon he encountered. He was self-disciplined, with a constitutional desire for precision. He also knew that his journals would be read by his superiors, and would be published for readers as eager to hear about natural history as about adventure. The account of his second voyage, into the Antarctic, sold out on the day after its publication in 1777; the account of his third and last voyage sold out in three days. At their best, they are careful narratives by an explorer of the first rank, recording the human as well as the nonhuman world. Of his initial glimpse of the Hawaiians on Kaua'i he wrote, in admiration:

> They are vigorous, active, and most expert swimmers; leaving their canoes upon the most trifling occasion; diving under them, and swimming to others though at a great distance. It was very common to see women, with infants at the breast, when the surf was so high that they could not land in the canoes, leap overboard, and without endangering their little ones, swim to the shore, through a sea that looked dreadful.

But you wouldn't know anything about Cook's sensibilities by reading the official account of his first, and in some ways most magnificent, voyage, because Cook didn't write it. The honor was given to John Hawkesworth, an armchair *littérateur* who rose to prominence on his sociability and his wife's fortune. Cribbing from Cook's journal, what Hawkesworth produced in three volumes was not only tedious and verbose, but shamefully distorted. And his lawsuits to prevent those who had been on the voyage from publishing their own accounts were worse than shameful. Still, to a chorus of bad reviews, the work was a publishing success.

The British public's focus at this time was not nearly as much on Cook's accomplishments as an explorer as on the collections brought back by the expedition's "gentlemen naturalists," Joseph Banks and Daniel Solander. It was they, not Cook, who were given heroes' welcomes, audiences with the king, grand parties and honorary doctorates from Oxford. For a long time, the voyage was known popularly as "Mr. Banks's Voyage" or "The Banks and Solander Expedition."

The specimens Banks and Solander collected were extensive—three thousand plants alone, about one thousand three hundred of which had been previously unseen by Europeans; plus, according to Banks, "500 fish, as many Birds and insects Sea and Land innumerable." They were so extensive that Banks was never able—despite all his personal wealth and resources, and his long tenure as president of the Royal Society—to complete a full account of his findings, nor to have his journal published in his lifetime.

When Cook returned from his second voyage, authorization to write the official account of the expedition was again bitterly disputed. Permission was granted first to Johann Reinhold Forster, the voyage's naturalist, but then was withdrawn by the Admiralty and given to Cook, in order for the captain to realize some profit from the long expedition. Forster protested and certain compromises were reached. But eventually, six weeks before Cook's version was published, an unauthorized *A Voyage Around the World* was put into print by Forster's young son, George, who had accompanied his father on the expedition as his assistant and illustrator. He had been just seventeen when the *Endeavour* sailed.

George Forster's account omits all of the technical, seafaring information included in previous expedition narratives and is a well-written contribution to the travel and natural history literature of the period. One modern editor even calls it "one of the greatest travelogues ever written." While this is probably an overstatement, George Forster's rationale and plan for the book were ambitious, as evidenced in his preface:

> The British legislature did not send out and liberally support my father as a naturalist, who was merely to bring home a collection of butterflies and plants. ... From him they expected a philosophical history of the voyage, free from prejudice and vulgar error, where human nature should be represented without any adherence to fallacious systems, and upon the principles of general philanthropy; in short, an account written upon a plan which the learned world had not hitherto seen executed.

George Forster goes on to chastise explorers and naturalists who pursued facts and specimens but didn't attempt to organize and understand them. Such people, he wrote, were "like those minute inquirers, whose life is wholly spent in the anatomical dissection of flies, from whence they never draw a single conclusion for the use of mankind, or even of brutes."

A writer of travel and natural history, he went on to advise, should also be sure to reveal the personal perspective of the author—as he himself was now doing—"for every reader to know the color of the glass through which I looked."

And finally, he insisted—recalling Hawkesworth's literary crimes against Cook's first expedition—a work of travel and natural history should be a "well-told tale" rather than "a lame and tedious narration." In his own case, he said, "without attempting to be curiously elegant, I have aimed at perspicuity."

This quarrelsome preface aside, George Forster could be effusive in his descriptions of natural wonders. Similarly, Banks and Solander, in letters and reports, were nothing if not ecstatic at times. Even the most level-headed and scientific-minded of the early naturalist-explorers registered unrestrained wonder at what they saw. (The modern practice of treating nature with cold detachment would not come into use for another sixty or seventy years.) As Christians, these rational "gentlemen scientists" were encouraged by their faith, as well as by their time and culture, to see a theological design in nature and to respond to it with awe. The pioneer naturalist and taxonomist John Ray had admonished his readers in 1691, in *The Wisdom of God Manifested in the Works of Creation:*

> Some reproach methinks it is to learned men that there should be so many animals still in the world whose outward shape is not yet taken notice of or described, much less their way of generation, food, manners, uses, observed. If man ought to reflect upon his Creator the glory of all His works, then ought he to take notice of them all and not to think anything unworthy of his cognizance.

About seven thousand feet up the side of Mauna Loa, on the island of Hawai'i, I am in a small grove of mamane trees, hiking one of my favorite places and watching for i'iwi and other endemic birds. I never tire of seeing i'iwi. They have flame-like, crimson feathers, and long, salmon-colored beaks that curve downward in a crescent that fits exactly the corolla of certain native lobelias.

There is a local scarlet flower called *nuku-i'iwi*, bill of the i'iwi, so much does it resemble the bird's beak.

Finding the i'iwi in books before I ever saw them in the wild, I was fascinated by their forms and beautiful plumage. I knew through these books that the early Hawaiians made brilliant red capes for their chiefs from the breast feathers of the little honeycreepers. They gave such a cape to Captain Cook when he landed at Kealakekua.

The Hawaiians also ate them, and used their feathers to pay taxes and for barter. Cook refers to this, saying that on Kaua'i he was brought "great numbers of skins of small red birds which were often tied up in bunches of 20 or more, or had a small wooden skewer run through their nostrils."

For a while I got used to seeing the i'iwi in the rigid, silent poses of the illustrations, with their heads tilted back, clinging to the branch of an 'ohi'a or other native tree. Their scientific name would be in crisp italics below them—*Vestiaria coccinea* (the scarlet vestment). When at last I found them in the wild, however, I was amazed at how noisy they were. In life they were raucous, with powerful calls that have been described as sounding like everything from a police whistle to the creaking of a wheelbarrow, from gurgles and squawks to the sound of "a child playing with a rusty harmonica." More than one person has called it "sweet and plaintive." In any case, they are exuberant, not shy in the least, singing while they feed and darting from flower to flower, utterly unlike what I had imagined.

Another small bird found in this mamane grove is the Hawaiian 'elepaio. They are small and brown, curious and approachable. Each of several Hawaiian islands has its own subspecies. While I knew the i'iwi first by its picture, I knew the 'elepaio by its call before I ever saw one. I used to hear them whistling deep in the forest, often in the treetops. Later, after I'd seen the subspecies of neighboring islands—in certain places after searching a good deal, so much have human populations encroached on their range—I still hadn't seen them in this grove or seen this island's subspecies, though I could hear them. I searched without luck.

Then, one day my friend brought an inexpensive bird caller along on our hike and began to screech with it as we reached the grove. The 'elepaio came from all over; they swooped into the trees above us, darted among the low branches to get a better look, and finally landed nearly close enough to touch. There are some mysteries you have to search for a long time, my friend said; others come to find you.

Clearly, many of the early Pacific naturalists were "gentlemen travellers," but that name describes neither the degree of their hardships and daring nor their powers as scientific observers. In truth, the description fits Charles Darwin on his first voyage into the Pacific. Twenty-three years old when he joined the crew of the *Beagle* in 1831, he intended to become a parson when he returned. While the great works he wrote much later are models of scientific argument, the account he wrote in *Voyage of the Beagle* is still a model for certain of the best forms of literary natural history: a combination of close observation of nature, personal narrative, travelogue and speculation.

Darwin's lifetime coincided roughly with the decades of the first systematic exploration of the Pacific, and with the period that's been called the golden age of literary natural history, from 1770 to 1880. Just prior to this time, one scholar suggests, anyone who might want to write seriously about nature was daunted by the awareness that so much of the natural world was still unknown. Just after this time, the tremendous amount of detailed information that had been collected during these decades made the subject even more overwhelming. And, perhaps more important, by 1880 the study of the natural world had increasingly become a subject reserved for specialists, to be conducted in laboratories only.[1]

By 1880, the "old-fashioned naturalists," the nonspecialists, were demoralized not only by changes in methods, new paradigms and a surfeit of data, they were suffered the disdain of "professional" scientists. "The glory of the field naturalist has departed," lamented W. B. Grove in the *Midland Naturalist*. "The biologist or physiologist is the hero of the hour, and looks down with infinite contempt upon the luckless being who is still content to search for species."

The golden age of literary naturalists, in those decades before 1880, was made possible by a large, rural audience of readers who had a practical desire for firsthand accounts of landscapes, plants and creatures. Many of those readers were average people who were themselves amateur naturalists. They expected accuracy and hard information, but also something from the longstanding and humane tradition which saw elements of spirit, or at least wonder, in the natural world. Even writers who were academically trained scientists in this period were free to write about nature using the methods of the literary essay. When individuals appeared whose skills for writing matched their skills for observation—and *vice versa*—it was more than fortunate. The books they produced altered and educated an avid public's understanding of the natural world. At the same time they kept alive a kind of science that was conducted in the field, where phenomena continued to be seen in what we would now call their "ecological context," seeing the parts and whole congruently.

While this period may have been a golden age for literary natural history, memorable nature writing has always been rare. The early Pacific explorers often had a tremendous capacity to find, collect and organize what they came upon, but they were not always writers. And, because of the dangers they faced, even the works of those who were skillful writers—or might have been—frequently were lost along with whatever scientific data they collected. The more we know about them, the more we feel their tragedies were a loss to human history as well as to natural science.

A good example involves the first professional botanist ever to journey into the Pacific, Philibert Commerson. The expedition on which he sailed, commanded by Louis-Antoine de Bougainville, was intended for geographical discovery and a show of the French colors in the Pacific, but it was also designed to be a serious scientific enterprise. On board were various new devices for astronomy and navigation plus the men to work them. Bougainville's two ships were also fitted out to study natural history.

Commerson was thirty-nine years old and a doctor of medicine when the expedition sailed in 1766. It was common for doctors of the period to have a strong interest in herbs and other plants, but Commerson was also the court's highly respected "Royal Botanist and Naturalist." He was, in addition, a moralist and an idealist. In his will, he established a *Prix de Vertu*, an annual award "to whomsoever should have performed, without motives of ambition or vanity and without hypocrisy, the most praiseworthy act of a moral or social kind—such, for example, as a generous sacrifice of his own personal interests."

Commerson had located to Paris after the death of his young wife four years earlier. When the Minister of Marine selected him for the expedition, he quickly accepted, wrote his will and boarded the ship *Étoile* at Nantes. He took with him his faithful servant, Jean Baret, who had been in his employ for two years and was about twenty-six years old at the time.

Commerson suffered violent seasickness from the very beginning of the voyage. With Baret's constant attentions, however, he managed a stormy crossing of the Atlantic. The overloaded *Étoile* and her sister ship, *Boudeuse*, were nearly sunk more than once just reaching the coast of South America. The expedition rounded the Cape, anchored when it could and eventually arrived in Tahiti, eighteen months after leaving France.

At each opportunity, Commerson and Baret combed the countryside for specimens of plants, fish and mammals. From the coast of South America the naturalist sent back to Paris an enormous collection. Unfortunately, few of the plants he collected arrived, and the fish specimens were stored in an attic unopened until well after Commerson's death. But among the flowers that survived was a genus he named after his captain, the *Bougainvillea*.

Everywhere the ship anchored, Commerson continued to gather specimens with the untiring help of Baret, who was seen, according to Bougainville, "accompanying his master in all his expeditions amidst the snows, on the frozen peaks of the Straits of Magellan, carrying, even on those laborious excursions, provisions, arms, and bulky portfolios of specimens with a perseverance and a strength which gained for him from the naturalist the nick-name of his 'beast of burden.'"

At Tahiti, the naturalist was overcome with wonder, and his explorations into what he perceived to be an Edenic island were redoubled. Tahiti had been discovered by Europeans less than a year before and almost everything was new to Commerson. Unfortunately for him, however, his personal life was about to get more attention from the captain and crew than his botanical discoveries. The crew had found Commerson to be high-strung and aloof, standoffish even with the officers. And they had developed suspicions about the naturalist's relationship to Baret—ever attentive, always with him, even sleeping in Commerson's cabin. Shortly after dropping anchor in Tahiti, these suspicions were finally confirmed. The first time the Tahitian men boarded the ship, they were immediately fascinated by Commerson's young assistant; they walked around Baret several times, and began to shout in Tahitian. Their words were, "It's a girl, it's a girl!"

The Tahitian men were delighted at their discovery of Baret's true gender. To her consternation, however, it was soon clear they expected from Baret the same favors the Tahitian women were granting to the French sailors. The captain, for his part, could only be philosophical about the deception. For a time, Baret—Jeanne, not Jean—tried to convince Bougainville that she was an orphan who had come aboard to escape her poverty, and that Commerson had had no idea of her gender and thus should not be blamed. There is no record that the captain or anyone else believed her.

After nine days in Tahiti, the expedition sailed on, a new relationship having been established on board between the crew and the naturalist couple. The captain's clerk noted dryly in his log, "I believe that this girl will be the first of her sex to have circumnavigated the globe." When the ship reached Mauritius, its Pacific journey all but over, Commerson and Baret decided to disembark rather than sail back to France. There, Commerson died five years later. Baret married a soldier on the island and later returned to Europe.

The natural history collections which Commerson and Baret sent back to France were said to have comprised fifty-six cases of specimens—plants, animals and fish from throughout the Pacific—and were said to have been only a portion of over thirty thousand items they collected. The bulk that arrived in France remained unpacked in the attic of naturalist Georges de Buffon. Commerson had described approximately one thousand plants and discovered many species never before seen by Europeans. In 1776, Johann and George Forster named the genus *Commersonia*—a small tree of the cocoa family—after him in tribute.

But Commerson himself wrote almost nothing about his findings or his adventures, except for an enthusiastic letter to Paris praising the beauty and goodness of Tahitian society. One scholar has commented that, though he wrote copiously, Commerson was "far more interested in science than in literary fame—in spite of a lively style that might have produced an interesting travel story." Finally it was Bougainville who wrote the full account of the voyage. Perhaps because he was not a naval officer by training, it contains few details of the navigation. It was a great literary success, much discussed by the leading writers and philosophers of the day, as well as by the general public.

Another example from this era of lost stories and lost natural history involves the expedition of Jean-Francois de Galaud, comte de La Pérouse. Like Bougainville's voyage, his expedition was designed for major scientific work, and comprised two ships, *Boussole* and *Astrolabe*. When it sailed in 1785, the expedition carried a greater number of scientists, naturalists and illustrators than any previous Pacific voyage. And it would be many more years before any expedition would equal it in size and ambition.

The amount of equipment for science and for trading was extensive. The ships carried, for example, one hundred bushels of seeds to be planted, fifty-nine trees and shrubs and ten reams of paper for pressing leaf specimens. Among the books in the expedition's library were twenty-eight volumes about previous voyages, twenty-three volumes on astronomy and navigation, eight books on physics, sixty-five books on natural history, an encyclopedia, a dictionary of chemistry and a complete set of the *Journal de Physique* in twenty-eight volumes.

Among the large stock of items for trading with the Pacific natives were one hundred medals bearing the king's profile, fifty-two plumed dragoons' helmets, four large German organs and twelve smaller ones, two thousand hatchets, one thousand pairs of scissors, twenty-four sets of musical bells, two thousand combs, nine thousand fish hooks, a million pins, seven thousand knives, and fifty thousand needles.

Blessed with miraculously good weather through the Straits of Magellan, La Pérouse entered the Pacific Ocean in February 1786 and reached the Hawaiian Islands in May. He anchored in a quiet bay on Mau'i, which still bears his name, in the channel between that island and the island of Kaho'olawe. There he took on supplies of pigs, bananas, taro and fresh water. The Hawaiians made such a friendly impression on him, he concluded that they would never have killed Captain Cook without having been sorely provoked.

La Pérouse next sailed north, exploring the northwest coast of North America before turning south again. He recrossed the Hawaiian Island chain in November 1786, much to his surprise, and named the small islands he found French Frigate Shoals, which includes La Pérouse Pinnacle and Necker Island.

The expedition reached the coast of China then turned northward, exploring the coast all the way to Kamchatka, where the ships anchored in August 1787. From here, Pérouse decided to send his journals, along with letters from the crew, back to France by land. He entrusted them to twenty-one-year-old Barthélemy de Lesseps, who made the long and hazardous journey across Russia in winter, arriving in Versailles a year later. This decision was one of the last good fortunes the expedition was to have.

From Kamchatka, the expedition turned south again. When they reached Samoa, a dispute arose between a landing party of about sixty crewmen and a group of islanders which may have finally numbered one thousand. In the fray, Paul-Antoine de Langle, commander of the *Astrolabe*, was killed, along with eleven more crewmen; twenty others were badly wounded. Of those who died or would die later from their wounds were three of the naturalists. La Pérouse christened the place Massacre Island.

When the ships reached Botany Bay six weeks later, the state of the crew and of the remaining naturalists was such that little botanizing went on. It was just as well. After *Boussole* and *Astrolabe* left the bay, in March 1788, the two ships vanished and were never seen again. The only record that survived were the journals that La Pérouse had wisely dispatched back to Europe in the safekeeping of others.

Over the next three decades, the Hawaiian Islands were explored by a number of gifted naturalists from Europe and the West. Among the most prominent in this period was Archibald Menzies, who sailed with George Vancouver in 1789, reaching Kealakekua Bay in 1792. Menzies was a tireless collector and was able to climb both Hualalai and Mauna Loa on this trip. The expedition returned to England with the first geographical survey of the Hawaiian Islands.

Several years earlier, Nathaniel Portlock and George Dixon, both of whom had sailed with Cook, had been the first Europeans to enter Kealakekua Bay following Cook's death there. They were keen recorders of natural history and published extensively on what they saw. Others from this period included Adelbert von Chamisso, who sailed with Otto von Kotzebue and arrived at Kealakekua in 1816. Chamisso, along with the expedition's artist, Louis Choris, published rich accounts of the natural history of the Hawaiian Islands.

They were followed by Louis Claude de Saulces de Freycinet who, like Commerson, smuggled a woman aboard the voyage: his twenty-two-year-old wife, Rose. Before this harrowing voyage, she referred to herself as "the gay, the thoughtless madcap Rose." After she returned, her friends noted she had become somewhat more subdued. Not a naturalist, Rose de Freycinet nevertheless became perhaps the second woman to circumnavigate the globe. Because it would scandalize her husband, her journal from the voyage was not printed for more than one hundred years after she returned to France. Freycinet's botanist on the voyage was Charles Gaudichaud-Beaupré, who gathered an important collection of Hawaiian plants on this and a later expedition to Hawai'i commanded by Auguste-Nicolas Vaillant in the *Bonite.*

In 1825, naturalists Andrew Bloxam and James Macrae, along with the artist Robert Dampier, arrived in Hawai'i aboard HMS *Blonde,* commanded by George Anson Lord Byron, grandson of "Foul Weather Jack" and cousin of the English poet. While ascending Mauna Loa, Macrae became the first European botanist to collect and describe the rare silver sword plant, which he called, "truly superb, and almost worth the journey of coming here to see it on purpose." At Honaunau, just south of Kealakekua, Byron was given permission by the chiefs to take away every artifact he wished to have from the *heiau* at the City of Refuge, which he and his crew promptly did. Bloxam then drew and wrote a description of the last known *heiau* in the islands still in perfect condition, just before it was stripped.

Among the early Native Hawaiians who contributed significantly to Western natural history was David Malo, whose work was not translated into English until 1898. John Papa 'I'i also wrote in Hawaiian on many subjects, including the natural history of Hawai'i. The scholar and legislator Samuel Kamakau not only wrote but also collected firsthand accounts by Hawaiians concerning a range of historical and cultural subjects.[2]

❦

By the 1830s, Hawai'i did not seem as distant to many Westerners as it had. Honolulu had become essentially an international harbor, according to one amazed traveler, populated by foreigners from Asia, Europe and America. But it was still not entirely safe for the avid naturalists, and its natural history was far from being thoroughly explored.

Among those who attempted the exploration in this period was David Douglas, who for me embodies a century of intrepid naturalists, and was perhaps the most adventurous of all. His life also illustrates the missing stories of many naturalists in this era, having left only a fragmentary written record of his life. His early and untiring love of natural history would lead Douglas from his birthplace in Scotland to a grisly death, mutilated by a wild bull at the bottom of a pit on the slopes of Hawai'i's Mauna Kea.

Douglas's father was a stone mason, by all accounts honest and skilled, the one who cut the tombstones and fashioned hearths for his Scottish village near Perth. Douglas himself, as a small boy at school, was remembered later with the euphemisms bestowed on delinquents who turn out successfully. When he was young, however, he was described as self-willed, a constant truant, and his obstinate determination to avoid the classroom was said to evince "a contempt for the schoolmaster's thong."

Though he didn't like school, he seems to have loved the countryside and its creatures, owls and hawks especially, which he kept as pets. At age eleven he was mercifully removed from school and apprenticed to a gardener at the palace of the Earl of Mansfield. There, Douglas found his vocation and his element. So suited was he for this new life that, by the time he was eighteen, he had risen to the post of first gardener. At twenty-four he found himself appointed botanical collector to the Horticultural Society of London, now the Royal Horticultural Society. It was a remarkable ascent for a rural Scottish boy born of low means and with no connections. Even more remarkable, he would soon have more plants named in his honor, including the Douglas fir of North America, than perhaps anyone in the history of botany—though many of these were later renamed. In Hawai'i, for example, the botanical names for pukiawe (*Cyathodes douglassi* and *Styphelia douglassi*, now *S. tameiameiae*), hala (*Pandanus douglassi*, now *P. tectorius*), silver sword (*Argyrophyton douglassi*, now *Argyroxiphium sandwicense*), and the pala fern (*Marattia douglassi*) all have included his name in tribute. Douglas was the first botanist systematically to explore the Pacific Northwest and California as well as many parts of the Hawaiian Islands. As a solitary explorer, he was perhaps the most adventurous and well traveled of a century of tough field naturalists known for unbelievable perseverance and bravery. He may have been the first nonnative to have climbed any of the Cascade Mountains, the Blue Mountains of Oregon, both

Mauna Loa and Mauna Kea in Hawai'i, and the first to attempt
Mount Hood. He was sometimes seen traveling with a wild eagle
in a cage on his pack and his pockets filled with reptiles, to whom
he whistled tunes to keep them quiet. The dangers he faced alone,
or with one or two Indian companions, are extraordinary almost
beyond belief—Indian wars, grizzly bears, descents over waterfalls,
starvation, frostbite, drowning, infections and disease are just the
beginning of the list. He often subsisted on berries, ground rats
and wild game; he had been sucked into whirlpools and blinded by
snow and sandstorms, yet he wrote of his worst adventures, "On
such occasions I am very liable to become fretful."

Those who examined Douglas's corpse described its mutilated condition as "mangled in a shocking manner." The missionaries Joseph Goodrich and John Diell reported to the British
Consul in Honolulu, Richard Charlton, "There were ten to twelve
gashes on the head, a large one over the left eye, another, rather
deep, just above the left temple, and a deep one behind the right
ear; the left cheek bone appeared to be broken, and also the ribs on
the left side." In addition to being gored, Douglas had been
trampled badly by the wild bull that stood over him at the bottom
of the pit on Mauna Kea where his body was found. After an
investigation—and continuing suspicions that Douglas had been
murdered and thrown into the pit by a former convict from the
Botany Bay penal colony—the body was buried in the churchyard
of Kawaiaha'o in Honolulu on August 4, 1834. The grave was
unmarked except for a layer of bricks placed over it by Charlton,
and soon its location was forgotten. Perhaps it lies somewhere now
beneath the pavement of Punchbowl Street in downtown Honolulu. When he died, Douglas was thirty-five years old.

Douglas wrote very little for publication; only fourteen
papers are listed in the Royal Horticultural Society's catalog, only
eight of which were published. But he did leave a rough journal,
which was printed by the society in 1914, and reprinted in 1959.
The North American portions were edited and republished in
1980. They are not literary, but between the clumsy lines and

hastily written fragments is an exciting and harrowing story of adventure in the cause of natural science. In a letter describing his ascent of Mauna Loa he wrote:

> A sight of the volcano fills the mind with awe—a vast basin in a state of igneous fusion, throwing out lava in a thousand forms, from tortuous masses like large cables to the finest filamentous thread. Some places in large sheets, some in terrible rolled masses, like the breaking up of a large river with ice—of all colors and forms, showing the mighty agency ever existing in its immense laboratory. The strongest man is unstrung; the most courageous heart is daunted, in approaching this place.

In another letter from Honolulu, he reported that the Hawaiians remembered the surgeon-naturalist Archibald Menzies as "the red-faced man, who cut off the limbs of men and gathered grass." Douglas, who was pressed into being a doctor at times, would probably have also fit this description—as would have many of the fervent naturalists who visited Hawai'i in this period.[3]

When Douglas died, the American government had yet to send any scientific explorations into the Pacific, despite successful voyages by other nations which had been costly both in human life and in money. American ships and citizens were in the Pacific in great numbers, but for the most part they were whalers, traders and missionaries. The respectability of American science was not enhanced by the lack of such voyages. The maritime prestige of America was in doubt as well, especially since the Navy's pride had been stung on several occasions by unchallenged seizures of American property in the Pacific. What was needed was a show of force. And there were enormous economic advantages still to be gained for whaling and trading in the area, especially if new lands or new routes to older trading destinations were discovered.

Some years before, a retired army captain from Cincinnati named John Cleves Symmes had had an idea. According to Symmes, the globe is not round at all but sort of like a doughnut, with big holes in the top and bottom. When birds migrate north, he reasoned, they reach these holes and fly down inside the earth's hollow center, where it's warm and pleasant, and "stocked with thrifty vegetables and animals."

Some people called it the "Holes in the Poles Theory." Others called it "Symmes Holes." As science it was fantastical, but it was not too crazy to prevent a petition drive from starting in Congress, and lobbyists were soon at work to mount an expedition at government expense to prove the theory. This revolutionary notion was going to show the world the kind of scientific genius that nineteenth-century America could produce.

By 1838, ten years after the authorizing legislation was passed for an expedition, though Symmes's believers had by then dwindled in number, the first American government scientific adventure into the Pacific and around the world was finally launched. It was the largest expedition mounted by any country up to that time.

The United States Exploring Expedition, as it was called, commanded by Charles Wilkes, set out in 1838 with six ships. Commercial and pragmatic on the one hand, it nevertheless carried nine scientists—or Scientifics, as they were called. Joseph Draton and Alfred T. Agate were the illustrators, Charles Pickering and Titian Peale were the naturalists, William Rich was the botanist and William Brackenridge was the horticulturist. James Dwight Dana was the geologist.

The orders given to Wilkes established the priorities he was to follow. They read in part, "Although the primary object of the Expedition is the promotion of the great interests of commerce and navigation, yet you will take occasions not incompatible with the great purposes of your undertaking, to extend the bounds of science, and promote the acquisition of knowledge." Wilkes himself was suspicious of the "clam diggers and bug catchers" he took along. During the expedition he managed to stir up animosity between the crew and the small band of Scientifics, and continued to stir up trouble over their collections when the expedition was completed.

The botanical specimens that were gathered in Hawai'i in 1840 and elsewhere were finally sorted and described by the preeminent American botanist of the time, Asa Gray, whose way of handling the collection transformed natural science in America into an academic profession, conducted by specialists in laboratories. The expedition's five-year voyage had yielded more than fifty thousand plants, insects and animals; they were classified by Gray and others using the latest European methods, and the work was eventually published in twenty-four volumes and atlases.

American citizens avidly followed newspaper accounts of the progress of the expedition. Among those interested was a young naturalist who would alter literary natural history in America as much as Asa Gray would alter botany, Henry David Thoreau. As Thoreau thought more and more during his lifetime about the interior and exterior worlds, Hawai'i and the South Pacific in particular became important metaphors for him.

In his early twenties in 1840, Thoreau was just out of college and still wondering what he should do with his life. One of his classmates, Horatio Hale, was on the Wilkes voyage as the expedition's expert in linguistics; as an undergraduate, Hale had already published a pamphlet on the Peboscot Indians.

Many of the scientists on the voyage were young, like Hale. And for more than one reason, then, Thoreau must have felt keenly his own position—at home, helping out with his family's pencil factory. After his early failure as a teacher, he seemed destined, in the opinions of many, to become, at best, a handyman.

But Thoreau had larger plans for himself, though they were as yet somewhat vague. That year, he began taking notes on the life of Sir Walter Raleigh, and worked on an essay titled "A Chapter on Bravery." In a youthful journal entry on March 21, 1840, thinking of Hale and of the Pacific expedition, he mused on his possibilities: "By another spring I may be a mail-carrier in Peru, or a South African planter, or a Siberian exile, or a Greenland whaler, or a settler on the Columbia River, or a Canton merchant, or a soldier in Florida, or a mackerel-fisher off Cape Sable, or a Robinson Crusoe in the Pacific, or a silent navigator of any sea." Or, he added, "go on a South Sea exploring expedition."

Even at age twenty-three, however, he was already concluding that it was the spirit and imagination, not the globe, that was
still uncharted and in need of strong-willed explorers. "Our limbs,
indeed, have room enough," he wrote, "but it is our souls that rust
in a corner. Let us migrate interiorly without intermission, and
pitch our tent each day nearer the western horizon."

Going to the west would come to represent for him the essence
of renewal and expansion—but always in this metaphorical sense. He
sifted the notion over and over in his writings, turning it upside-down
and back again, as he liked to do with most ideas. His first published
book, it turned out, would therefore be about an exploration, but on
a local waterway not an exotic one, down which he and his brother had
leisurely floated in 1839. The title, *A Week on the Concord and
Merrimack Rivers,* was surely meant on one level to delight his sense
of self-mocking humor, so much did its modesty contrast with the
titles of such popular and ambitious books of the day as *Adventures on
the Columbia River* or *Observations and Reflections Made in the Course
of a Journey through Rome, Italy, and Germany.*

Later, the opening paragraphs of *Walden* would turn again to
Hawai'i and the Pacific. In the third paragraph he remarks on the great
geographical distance between himself and the "Sandwich Islander,"
literally a distance in miles, but figuratively an expanse he felt neither
he nor his New England readers needed to cross in order to experience
life's essential phenomena. The reference is followed by another self-
mocking comment on his own particular style of adventurousness, "I
have travelled a good deal in Concord."

The concluding chapter of *Walden* returns to a concern with the
Pacific and is culled from that same journal entry of March 21, 1840.
Walden thus becomes framed by references to the far horizons,
reaching specifically to Hawai'i but then beyond to the farthest shore
imaginable—a shore that can never be explored in literal ships.
Thoreau cites the Pacific expeditions, in this final chapter, as examples
of how much easier—and how much more readily undertaken—are
voyages to explore the exterior world, compared with those into our
own interiors. His imperative to the reader is to "be a Columbus to
whole new continents and worlds within you, opening new channels,

not of trade, but of thought." Then he adds, referring to the Wilkes voyage, "what was the meaning of the South-Sea Exploring Expedition, with all its parade and expense, but an indirect recognition of the fact, that there are continents and seas in the moral world, to which every man is an isthmus or an inlet, yet unexplored by him, but that it is easier to sail many thousands of miles through cold and storm and cannibals, in a government ship, with five hundred men and boys to assist one, than it is to explore the private sea, the Atlantic and Pacific Ocean of one's own being alone."

Although Thoreau wrote in these kinds of metaphors, he was simultaneously a precise and dedicated field naturalist. He spent every hour possible taking notes in the forests and fields, climbing mountains, rafting and hiking in all seasons, often at night, often in the worst weather. He would spend hours standing in freezing water to record the way pouts lay their eggs, would lie for long periods on the snow to watch snow fleas and would climb the tallest trees to peek into a hawk's nest. It was this kind of life in the field that probably contributed to his early death, at age forty-four, from influenza and tuberculosis.

Thoreau's contribution to natural history was not insignificant, although his death came before he could synthesize the large quantity of data he had gathered. One of his last pieces of writing was "The Succession of Forest Trees," inspired by his reading of Darwin's *The Origin of Species*. It was part of a longer projected work—in four hundred draft pages when he died—to be called *The Dispersion of Seeds*. During his life he was elected a corresponding member of the Boston Society of Natural History and was appointed to Harvard's Committee for Examination in Natural History. At the time of his death, he was considered by most people to be, principally, a natural historian. Thoreau knew his own region so well that the children, it was said, "thought Mr. Thoreau had made Concord." They were certain that "if anything happened in the deep woods which only came about once in a hundred years, Henry Thoreau would be sure to be on the spot at the time and know the whole story."

I remember hiking some time ago up Mauna Loa in search of a small white flower that grows above seven thousand feet on the slopes there. Called hinahina, a common Hawaiian name for a number of local species, it has a five-petaled corolla and silvery leaves. Having never seen this particular variety in the wild on the island of Hawai'i, I looked intently for it as I hiked off the trail in the cold, subalpine air, across old, red lava laced with straggling kukae-nene, 'a'ali'i and pukiawe. At last I spotted a single white blossom and called to my companion. We hurried over and looked intently at the flower for a long time, happy to have come upon what to us was a small but rare find. At last we stood up, stretched our legs and looked around. To our surprise, we were standing in a whole field of them. Dumbfounded, we went back to the trail; they were everywhere, as if suddenly they had become the most common flower on the mountain.

Thoreau once said that objects are concealed from our vision not so much because they are out of range, but because they have never yet been fully in our eye and in our mind. "To see the scarlet oak," he says, "the scarlet oak must, in a sense, be in your eye when you go forth. We cannot see anything until we are possessed with the idea of it, and then we can hardly see anything else."

The early naturalists in the Pacific traveled at great risk to see and collect the diverse wonders they knew were in the uncharted vastness. Some brought back the very things they had expected to find—and little else. Others brought back simply everything of a category that they could gather. The task for decades afterward—for those who sorted through the vast collections, and for those who ventured into the Pacific for more—was to understand the diversity of life they now saw laid out before them. Though the plants and animals have been given names and lie under glass in museums or are pressed in specimen books, a great many of the things that came into their possession have still not been truly seen or understood.

I'm not sure how different we are from those early travelers, how little and how much we really know about the natural world, not only about what is exotic and uncatalogued, but about what is local and underfoot. If nature were truly in our eyes and imaginations, as Thoreau suggests, we would finally be possessed *by it,* instead of the other way around. We would comprehend the tragedy and error in the holocaust of species extinction that's been going on for decades.

Literary natural history, at its best, attempts to awaken us: to "put nature in our eyes," so that, for the first time, we see it whole and all at once. It attempts to have us be possessed by each of the parts—by even the smallest entities and creatures, and by their integrity and relationship to the whole. Writing of this sort prepares the reader's imagination to see particularly those plants, animals and phenomena that are, in many cases, impossible for most people to experience firsthand, those things that seem remote, exotic and of no apparent personal meaning to us. Most amazingly, such writing prepares our eyes to see even those plants and creatures nearby, the ones we thought we knew.

Through some combination of all our cognitive resources—metaphor and cold measurement, poetry and taxonomy—through literary natural history, in short, we begin to understand the natural world perhaps for the first time, both as a part of it and self-consciously outside of it. This way of seeing is the revelation in all great nature writing: the revelation that natural history, in its fullest sense, is also human history, that the parts and the whole are not separable.

NOTES

1 See E.D.H. Johnson's *The Poetry of Earth.* Also, *The Golden Age of Plant Hunters* by Kenneth Lemmon and *Natural History and the American Mind* by William Martin Smallwood. More recent works include *A Species of Eternity* by Joseph Kastner, *Speaking for Nature* by Paul Brooks and *Nature Writing and America* by Peter A. Fritzell.

2 E. Alison Kay has written an overview of the contributions to Hawaiian natural history of various explorers, residents, missionaries and scientists, in *A Natural History of the Hawaiian Islands: Selected Readings.*

3 In fact, Douglas was known to the Indians of the Northwest as "The Grass Man." E. Alison Kay also makes the point that, in describing Menzies, Douglas could have been describing himself.

Richard Nelson

Cultural anthropologist Richard Nelson, born in 1941, received his doctorate from the University of California, Santa Barbara, and subsequently devoted his life to studying the native peoples of Alaska. Richard Nelson has authored several important works of cultural anthropology, including *Hunters of the Northern Forest* (University of Chicago, 1973), which documents the cultural ecology of the Kutchin Indians near Fort Yukon, Alaska, and *Make Prayers to the Raven: A Koyukon View of the Northern Forest* (University of Chicago, 1983), which examines the effect of the boreal environment on the Koyukon Athabaskan Indians of Huslia, Alaska. Richard Nelson lives with his wife and son on an island in the Alaskan panhandle; he prefers to keep the exact location unknown in order to help preserve its natural values.

In this selection from *The Island Within* (North Point, 1989), which won the John Burroughs Medal for Nature Writing in 1990, Richard Nelson describes a mid-February outing to a remote part of the island. So lush is the vegetation in this perpetually wet region of the Pacific Northwest that Nelson compares the forest to a tropical rain forest: "Filaments of cloud hover along the slopes and wreathe the high peaks. Except for the whiteness above timberline, this might be a hidden defile in Borneo or New Guinea." Nelson sets up his tent camp and then—in one of the most exciting passages in *The Island Within*—dons a wet suit and begins to surf on the big waves generated by some recent North Pacific storm. The next morning Nelson takes a long hike through the forest of giant trees: "Nature is not merely created by God; nature *is* God. Whoever moves within the forest can partake directly of sacredness. ... I believe that a covenant of mutual regard and responsibility binds me together with the forest. ... I am never alone in this wild forest, this forest of elders, this forest of eyes."

The Forest of Eyes
(circa 1989)

A seal drifts in the reflection of Kluksa Mountain, watching the boat idle into Deadfall Bay. Our wake shimmers through the mirror, distorting images of the surrounding hills, the forested shore, and the sallow disk of sun anchored in a thin, racing overcast. Falling tide leaves a line like a bathtub ring around the bay's shore, with snow-covered rocks above the water's reach and shiny black ones below.

I shut down the outboard and let the skiff glide, matching stares with the curious seal and enjoying the silence after a long ride from home. As I paddle toward the rocks, each clunk and plash echoes through the hollows of the bay. Impatient Shungnak jumps ashore to sniff the area while I unload. My raingear is soaked from rough water in the strait, but everything else is dry. The forward two-thirds of the skiff is protected by a canvas dome stretched over a metal frame, like a streamlined covered wagon. Only the captain, who stands in the stern, is exposed to the full brunt of wind and spray.

A pleasant, excited anticipation warms my insides as I spot the old logging road that runs across the island. I hiked the road once before, and during the few hours I spent at Roller Bay I was struck by the peace and beauty of the place. Along one side of the bay was a series of rocky headlands, and I've yearned to explore the isolated beaches and crannies between them. I've also hoped to see how ocean swells break along the shore, to learn if they might nurture the passion for surfing that draws me to this island in a special way. There is also a darker question: in the nearby hills and valleys are sprawling clearcuts, and I've wanted to experience them more closely, to learn how logging has affected this part of the otherwise pristine island.

Once the bicycle and backpack are ashore, I heft three watermelon-sized rocks inside the boat and paddle out to deep water. Then I lay the rocks on a piece of heavy trawl net, pull it up around them to make a pouch, and lace the whole thing shut with one end of a coiled half-inch rope. After making sure the rope is long enough to reach the bottom and allowing for a twenty-foot tide range, I tie a loop in the free end and fasten a small float onto it. This done, I push the netted rocks overboard and tether the skiff's bow line onto the floating loop. It's taken only fifteen minutes to make a secure mooring buoy for the skiff, using materials picked up from the island's beaches.

As I paddle the punt back to shore, Shungnak enjoys a frolic in the snow. It's only an inch deep here, but I wonder about the hills farther inland. This mid-February afternoon will pass quickly, and if there's too much snow to ride the bicycle we might not get to Roller Bay before dark. I inspect the vintage three-speed bike, then hoist up my backpack, with a final lament about bringing too much stuff. But there would be a lot more complaining if I found good waves and hadn't been willing to carry the extra weight of wetsuit gear and a small belly-rider surfboard.

The first section of road follows the bay's edge, behind a strip of tall, leafless alders. When we're about halfway around, a bald eagle in dark, youthful plumage sails down to a fish carcass on the beach just ahead. He seems careless or unafraid—quite different from the timid, sharp-eyed elders—so I leash Shungnak to the bike, drop my pack, and try to sneak in for a closer look. Using a driftwood pile as a screen, I stalk within fifty feet of the bird, but he spots me peering out between the logs. He flaps out over the water, turns for another look, and then lands forty feet up in a beachside spruce.

There's nothing to lose now, so I walk very slowly toward the eagle, looking away and acting uninterested. He seems content to watch me, or perhaps doesn't care now that he's beyond my reach. Foolish bird: nearly all dead or wounded eagles found in this part of the world have bullets in them. Finally, I stand almost beneath him, gazing up at the eagle as he looks back down at me.

The bird's placid demeanor gives rise to an idea. A gray skeleton of a tree leans beneath his perch, making a ramp I can climb to get closer. His eyes fix on me as I ease to the leaning trunk's base; but he holds fast to the branch. I've never been this close to a wild, free eagle. I think of the ancient hunters, lying hidden in loosely covered pits with bait fastened above, waiting to grab the descending talons. But I seek no blood, no torn sacred feather. Closeness is my talisman, the sharing of eyes, scents twisted together in the same eddy of wind, the soft sound of a wheezing breath, quills ticking in the breeze, feet scuttling on dry bark, and the rush of air beneath a downswept wing.

I inch slowly ... slowly up the bare trunk, twist myself around the stubs of broken limbs, until I'm twenty feet from the bird and can't come closer. Nothing is left except to be here—two intense, predatory animals, given to great suddenness, for these moments brought within whatever unknowable circle surrounds us. Perhaps neither of us will ever be so near another of our respective kinds again. I don't need to believe that we communicate anything more than a shared interest and regard, as we blink across the distances that separate our minds.

When the eagle moves or teeters, I can see his feet clutch the branch more tightly, and the needled tips of his talons pierce more deeply through the brittle, flaking bark into the wood beneath. Two loose, downy feathers hang incongruously from his breast, out-of-place feathers that quiver in the gentle current of air. I think how strange it is that I expect an eagle to look groomed and perfect, like the ones in books.

The bird cranes his head down to watch me, so the plumage on his neck fluffs out. His head is narrow, pinched, tightly feathered; his eyes are silver-gold, astringent, and stare forward along the curved scythe of his beak. Burned into each eye is a constricted black pupil, like the tightly strung arrow of a crossbow aimed straight toward me. What does the eagle see when he looks at me, this bird who can spot a herring's flash in the water a quarter-mile away? I suppose every stub of whisker on my face, every mole and freckle, every eyelash, the pink flesh on the edge of my eyelid, the red network of vessels on the white of my eye, the radiating colors of my iris, his own reflection on my pupil, or beneath the reflection, his inverted image on my retina. I see only the eagle's eye, but wonder if he sees down inside mine. Or inside *me*, perhaps.

I take a few more steps, until I stand directly beneath him, where for the first time he can't see me. This is too much. He leans forward, opens his wings and leaps out over my head, still staring down. He strains heavily, like a swimmer stroking up for air. One of the loose feathers shakes free and floats down toward the thicket. I've always told Ethan that a falling eagle's feather, caught before it reaches the ground, might have special power. I wish I could run and catch this one; but the bird has shared power enough already.

As I watch the eagle rise above the bay, I let myself drift out beyond an edge, as though I were moving across the edge of sleep. I feel his quickened heartbeat in my temples, stare up through his eyes at the easy invitation of the sky, turn and look back at the figure of myself, cringed against the leaning snag below. I am filled with the same disdainful surge that releases him from his perch, feel the strain of air trapped in the hollows of his wings.

Fixed within the eagle, I see the bay slowly dilating below, and the long black line of the island's border, stretched out for ten miles against the gray waters of Haida Strait and ending in the distant finger of Tsandaku Point. The island is a variegated pattern of dark forest and snow-covered muskeg, splayed out beneath the slopes of Kluksa Mountain and neighboring Crescent Peak. As the eagle lifts on currents of air, his eye traces the ribbon of road to the island's far side, where it meets the bight of Roller Bay. I try to imagine his view of the other shore, to satisfy the hope that brings me here. But I see only myself, a fleck at the timber's edge, like an insect crawling through feathers of moss—an irrelevant flaw on the island's face.

The eagle sweeps away in great, lazy arcs, drifts against the corniced peaks, and soars up toward the smooth layer of cloud. From this height the island looks like an enormous, oblong cloth, pulled up at its center, curving symmetrically down to its timbered edges, its fringe of contorted rocks, wide bays, and crescent beaches, then plunging through the lace of whitewater and tortured reefs, to root itself beneath the sea.

At three thousand feet, the feathered sails flex and shake against a torrent of wind. Kluksa Mountain stands like a rock in a swift river; the wind whirls and eddies in its lee, rolls over its summit, and tumbles in breaking waves. I can feel the lash of gusts as the eagle planes above the mountain, gaze through his eyes at the fissured, snow-laden peak, and share the craving that draws him more deeply into the island's loneliness.

Nearly lost in the bottom edge of clouds, the bird has risen until his eyes take in the whole encircling horizon. He looks out over the island's whitened mass, beyond its western shore, where the Pacific lies out to the hard seam of sky. A banking turn brings him back toward the strait and a view of the mainland's mountain spine. Toward the north it rises to a frozen massif; toward the south it falls away and sinks like an otter's tail beneath the sea. For the eagle, the crest of land is a ridge to glide across, a spangle of streams that brings the feast of salmon each year, and gray tiers of ranges that fade into the interior beyond.

I am lost in a dream of eagles, balanced on the precipice of sky, peering into the waters below, waiting for the flicker of prey to be revealed. Prey? The thought awakens me. I have flown, however artificially, and have looked down over the island and the strait. But I can never know what the eagle sees with those blazing eyes, what are the shapes of mountains and shores amid the maze of detail that leaps into his brain.

There is the eagle's world, and there is mine, sealed beyond reach within our selves. But despite these insuperable differences, we are also one, caught in the same fixed gaze that contains us. We see the earth differently, but we see the same earth. We breathe the same air and feel the same wind, drink the same water and eat the same meat. We share common membership in the same community and are subject to the same absolutes. In this sense, the way we perceive what surrounds us is irrelevant: I have the eagle's eyes and the eagle has mine.

Shungnak prances and wags her tail when I return, then she sets a lively pace beside the bicycle. The road bends inland, crosses several forested hills, and gives way to swales with a mix of muskeg and open woods on either side. Recorded in the snow are many red squirrel crossings, the meanders of a few marten, and the place where a raven landed, hopped around without apparent purpose, then took off again. Tracks of large, solitary deer cross the road in a few places, and a mixed scuffle of four or five smaller ones follows it for half a mile. Like their human counterparts, adolescent deer seem to prefer going around in bunches. I'd hoped to see at least one or two deer along the way, but apparently they've all found resting places in the woods.

The road opens to a stretch of logged-over hills that look like a war zone, partly screened from view by alders pushing in from either side so they only leave a narrow pathway. In some places, we glide through a tunnel of silver trunks with laceworks of branches arching overhead—the beauty that shelters us from jarring ugliness. Along its whole length, the road is covered with one or two inches of snow, which helps to cushion the eroded gravel underneath. The snow makes pedaling uphill a real sweat, but on level stretches and downhill runs the bike seems to float on a bed of feathers. I think of Ethan's enthusiasm for bicycles, and how he would love to share this ride. But even if there were no school, he'd probably choose to stay behind with his friends.

Shungnak lolls her tongue, bites snow to refresh herself, and occasionally lags behind. I remember her as a young lead dog up north—the effortless way she danced at the head of the team, looking back at the other dogs to beg more speed out of them. She still has some of the boundless, rollicking, contagious energy that mushers love to see in their dogs, but at eleven years old, she's begun to ration it more carefully.

Atop the last rise, I can see Roller Bay and the open Pacific through a space between overlapping hills. My back aches from the heavy pack and my legs are tired, but then the road tilts into a mile-

long downhill, levels out, and dead-ends beside the grassy expanse
of Deer Meadow. A river wanders down the valley and enters the
ocean at Roller Bay. Usually the stream is only a few feet deep, but
with a strong high tide this evening, sea water has pushed up into
it, swelled over the banks, and turned much of the meadow into a
brackish swamp.

Shungnak sprawls on the snow to cool off, while I consider
the options. We're only a mile from the beach at Roller Bay. But
the trail crosses the flooded meadow, so we'd have to find a
different route on higher ground. Sunset glows through the
overcast and steep hills loom dark beside the valley. I'm drawn
toward the sound of surf beyond the distant line of forest, but it will
soon be night under those trees. We're not far from an abandoned
settler's cabin in a grove of spruce at the meadow's edge. My tired
body registers a vote to sleep there, and I take Shungnak's interest
in the fresh deer tracks headed that way as a vote of agreement.

Deer Meadow is well named, but it's also the favorite haunt
of a more formidable animal. During the salmon runs, this road is
so littered with bear droppings that it looks like a cow path; but in
midwinter, only the most eccentric bear would be away from its
hibernation den in the high country. This is the one season when
I can feel comfortable on the island without carrying a rifle and
keeping a close watch for trouble. Though I've never had a
frightening encounter with a brown bear, the possibility is real
enough. Every year there are close calls or worse; not long ago a
hunter was badly mauled on this island.

The deer tracks are as wet and fresh as Shungnak's, so I suspect
their maker is in the brush somewhere nearby. After a short hike we
reach the sagging, saturated cabin where we'll spend the night. It's a
simple frame of split logs, covered with cedar shakes. The roof
supports a fair growth of moss, matted grass, and sapling spruce,
giving it a distinctly organic touch. I peer through the gaping hole
once occupied by a door and part of a corner. The inside is a chaotic
mess of rusted cans, broken bottles, shredded blankets, and assorted
debris left over by trappers, hunters, and other itinerants like myself.
But it does have a roof of sorts, a tiny window with glass intact, a

wooden bunk along one wall, and a punctured barrel stove. The stove is an unexpected gift, though a little work is needed to make it functional.

Working by candlelight, I pile the rubble outside the door, then cut open a few cans for stove patches, and finally scrounge nails to hang a chunk of soggy cloth over the missing corner. It takes some patience to start a fire, which hisses indifferently in the stove, but eventually the place warms enough to seem almost cozy. I spread out my sleeping bag, eat voraciously, drink icy water, and then eat some more. Shungnak curls up in a corner while I lie down to rest. A breeze sifts in through cracks in the wall. I think of ways to patch the perforated roof, but only have enough energy to hope it doesn't rain.

Everything is quiet, except for distant fulminations from the shore. I can hardly wait for morning, when I'll hurry down to see the shape of those waves. But for now, I savor a contentment that comes only with exhaustion and in the most basic of circumstances. I wonder how much longer it will be until a storm gust or heavy snow collapses this old shack. And then the bears will take full possession of the meadow once again.

Candle out. Pitch dark. And I think if this were summer I would spend the whole night watching that flimsy rag door.

I'm awakened at dawn by the demented chattering of a red squirrel outside the cabin wall. Shungnak slips under the curtain door, chases the squirrel up a tree, and waits for it to come down the whole time I'm getting ready to go. The bulging pack feels like a sumo wrestler riding piggyback on my shoulders. But now that the tide's drained out it's easy walking along the trail. I can see the entire length of Deer Meadow, stretching flat and dead brown for three miles up the valley behind us, gradually narrowing between mountain walls. Filaments of cloud hover along the slopes and wreathe the high peaks. Except for the whiteness above timberline, this might be a hidden defile in Borneo or New Guinea. The overcast is jammed together like an ice floe and drifts on the same southeast wind that shivers through the trees. The ocean's sound has not diminished and the breeze will blow offshore—ideal conditions for surfing, if only the waves are right.

Our path cuts through a peninsula of forest and comes out on the riverbank. While we're taking a rest, a pair of red-breasted mergansers work toward us along the shore, diving for feed, unaware that they're being watched. Long bodies, narrow bills, and crested heads give them a rakish, streamlined appearance. The female is a fairly nondescript cinnamon and gray, but the male is striking and gaudy. His body is marked with an intricate, geometrical pattern of black and white spikes, chevrons, and fine hatchwork. A speckled, burnished glaze saturates his chest, like the color of old porcelain, and an ivory collar encircles his neck. Mounted atop this ornate body is a head that looks almost imaginary—high-browed, flaring back to a shaggy, double-pointed crest suffused with emerald iridescence like a hummingbird's back, and set off by a flaming red eye.

He looks like an exotic bird from the mangroves of Asia, not a common duck of these northern waters. Perhaps because I see mergansers so often, I'd forgotten to appreciate them. This is especially ironic in a place where few animals show the colorful extravagance so common in the latitudes of parrots, toucans, and birds of paradise. Of course, our animals have their own kind of loveliness, but there is a plain, businesslike, almost protestant flavor to it. In such a community, the merganser is all the more stunning. Chief Abraham, an old Koyukon hunter, once told me that in the Distant Time, when animals were people, Merganser's wife was known for her fancy sewing. She made her husband an elaborately decorated set of clothes, and when he was transformed into a bird his feathers took on the same color and pattern. Chief Abraham kept a merganser's stuffed skin inside his house so he could have the pleasure of looking at it, the way someone might admire a painting.

The muffled throb of surf becomes clearer and more rhythmic as we weave through the last stretch of forest. I hurry along the trail behind Shungnak, forgetting the weight of my pack, looking anxiously for streaks of light that mark the woods' edge. When we get close, Shungnak whisks off and disappears. I'm afraid she's following a deer scent, but I find her standing above the beach, taking in the view like a tourist.

The smooth crescent of black sand slopes gently toward lines of onrushing surf. At one end, the beach gives way to cliffs and cobbled coves, with mountains rising sheer above them. At the other is the rivermouth, channeled against a point of bare white rock that thrusts into the breakers. Beyond the rock is more beach and several headlands, along a shore that curves out for a mile and slopes down to a storm-battered point. The opening of Roller Bay is several miles wide and faces directly into the Pacific. Barren rocks and timbered islets stand off from either side, and there is one fair-sized island near the middle, covered with tall, flagged spruce. Those trees must be wedged into bedrock to survive the winds that thrash in from the sea beyond. In the peak of the highest one is a bald eagle, silhouetted against the tarnished clouds, gazing over its stormy domain.

Before getting on with the exploration I find a place to make camp. The beachside forest is an open, shaded gallery of tree trunks, like a park with cushiony moss instead of grass; all that's necessary is a flat place away from any dead trees that could guillotine the tent in a heavy wind. In case we get back near dark, I put up the tent, get everything set for cooking and sleeping, and find good water in a tiny creek nearby. Then I cram the surfing gear into a small pack and head off toward the beach.

Shungnak lopes out across the hard-packed sand, stopping to sniff at stranded jellyfish, razor clam shells, fragments of crab, and hawsers of bull kelp. My rubber boots are barely high enough to cross the river's mouth where it splays out over the beach, so there could be problems if we come back at a higher tide. We climb up onto a rock point and I sit for a while watching the surf. Each swell rises in a long, even wall, bends to the curvature of the beach, crests against the wind, and breaks almost simultaneously along its entire quarter-mile length.

Three harlequin ducks bob up in the froth behind each wave, then dive just before the next crashes on them. Occasionally, they ride partway up a wave's face and plunge into the vertical mass of water at the last instant before it breaks. I'm amazed by the boldness and timing of these birds, and wonder what food is rich or delicious enough to entice them into the impact zone. Beautiful as the waves are, I feel a twinge of selfish disappointment that the sudden, explosive way they break makes surfing impossible. But it's near low tide, and a rise of water level could change the surf considerably.

In the meantime, I wonder what lies beyond the next point. Shungnak scrambles across the rock and down onto another long beach, where she inscribes her tracks among those of deer and otter, the little prints of mink, and the odd scratchings of eagles. At its lower edge, the beach is covered with a sheen of water, but high up it darkens and dulls, then becomes dry sand with clumps of dead grass. They bring to mind one of the riddles that Koyukon people use to entertain themselves and test each other's eye for nature:

> *Wait, I see something: My end sweeps this way and that way and this way, all around me.*
> *Answer: Long tassels of winter grass, bent down so their tips have drawn little tracks around themselves in the breeze.*

At the end of the sand, we climb a headland covered with timber and laced with deer trails trodden down to bare dirt. I stick to the trails, knowing they're always the best routes along slopes and through tangles of brush or fallen trees. On the point's far side is another beach with pounding waves much like those at the harlequin place. Littering the strand are dozens of sand dollars, and down near the tide I find several still alive, covered with fine, stiff bristles that must rub off soon after they die. The bristles undulate like wind blowing in slow motion through a field of grass. These animals live half buried on edge in the sand offshore, but heavy surf must have gouged them up and deposited them here to die. I pitch them as far out as possible, with a warning that months could pass before another rescuer comes along. Then I put a dozen bleached, unbroken ones in my pack, thinking Ethan might enjoy giving them to friends.

Beyond the next point we find a magical little cove, nearly enclosed except for a narrow entrance, with an apron of white sand along its inner shore. The water grades from pearl to turquoise to vibrant tropical blue. A crystal stream rushes out from the forest, tumbles over white rocks and down across the beach. Tiny waves wash up and slip back, rolling pebbles and shells. At the far end, a deer stands in the grass, waits until we come close, then turns and struts into the woods. For a moment I wish I'd found this idyllic cove on some equatorial island, but then admonish myself to appreciate things as they are given. There are perfect places everywhere on earth, and a part of their perfection is in belonging exactly where they are. This thought is punctuated with a gift partway down the beach—a softball-sized net float made of green glass, lying like a pearl on the sand. I wonder if wind and current brought it all the way from Japan, or if it was lost from a fishing boat nearer this coast.

On our way back, we come across two ravens on the sand dollar beach, pulling ribbons of flesh from a dead lingcod awash in the surge. A seagull stands to one side, clucking incessantly, pointing its beak this way and that, waiting for a turn. Along this coast, there are always plenty of scavengers to welcome any death. Greedy and tugging, but ever watchful, the ravens wait until Shungnak bounces playfully toward them, then lift on a gust and circle above us. The wind has strengthened to a fair southeaster and a few drops of cold rain prickle against my face. There could be a blow tonight, but the skiff is well moored and we have a snug camp waiting.

Partway down the next beach, I notice something different in the pattern of the surf ahead. Straight off the jetty of bare rock, where the harlequins were feeding, rip currents have dredged a channel in the sand underwater, and waves breaking along either side of it look ideal for surfing. I run down the hard, wet beach, my heart pounding with excitement. Shungnak's happiness is in the running itself, as she darts back and forth in front of me. The closer we get, the better it looks.

I was thirty years old when I first encountered surfing, and I've pursued it intensely ever since, not only as a sport but as a way of engaging myself with a superbly beautiful part of the natural world. Places where swells break at the right angle and speed for surfing are a rarity, and searching for them amid the island's wildness and solitude has given me tremendous pleasure. Only a few times have I experienced a moment like this—standing on a remote shore, watching nearly perfect waves that may never have

been ridden before. And now I can reward myself for carrying this
heavy gear across the island. Up under the trees, sheltered from the
rain and wind, I shiver into my wetsuit, gloves, boots, and hood.
With the winter Pacific at forty-two degrees and the air a breezy
thirty-five, I could hardly touch this water without protection ...
and even this way it isn't easy. Shungnak finds a comfortable place
to lie down as I dash toward the water.

Carried out by the rip current, I push through a series of broken
waves and finally reach the spot where they first begin to peak. After
a few minutes a large swell approaches. Moving onto the sandbar, it
grows higher and steeper, and its face hollows against the offshore
wind. Then the crest pitches out to make a flawless, almond-shaped
tube, and exploding water flails down the length of the wave like a
zipper closing a cleft at the ocean's edge. I stroke toward the elevating
face of the next swell, turn around just when it begins to break, paddle
with all my strength, and feel it pick me up like a pebble in a cupped
hand. There is an electrifying sense of weightlessness and acceleration
as I drop toward the bottom and twist the board into a hard turn that
sets me skimming along parallel to the wave's crest, like a skier
traversing the slope of a liquid mountain. The reticulated wall of water
stretches out ahead of me, lifting and feathering, gleaming and
shattering, changing shape as it moves toward the shallows. I strain
forward to outrace the whitewater cascading at my heels, and feel like
a molecule hitching a ride on a meteor.

Suddenly the wave steepens, its crest throws out over my
body, and I careen beneath a translucent waterfall that pounds
down beside my shoulder, surrounded by the noise of erupting
whitewater, barely able to stay ahead of the collapsing tunnel. An
instant later I shoot out into the wind, turn straight up the wave's
face, and fling myself over it toward the open sea. Spindrift blown
from the wave spatters against my back. Surprised, ecstatic, hoot-
ing breathlessly, I thank the ocean and the island for this gift. And
I wonder, does the sea that bends down across half the earth's
surface care that I've flecked its edge and given back the token of
a grateful voice? Does it matter, this acknowledgment amid the
immensity and power and fecundity of an ocean? I can only trust

the rightness of what Koyukon elders teach—that no one is ever alone, unseen, or unheard, and that gratitude kindles the very heat of life.

Looking at the swells as I paddle back out almost equals the exhilaration of riding them. Breaking waves pour against the sandbar, leap and spin like fire as they roll shoreward, then climb the rocks and thunder against the sand. I could spend whole days watching them, and the last would be as hypnotic and fascinating as the first. Each wave is unique, and the surf breaking at every beach or reef has qualities found nowhere else, subtle differences that take much practice even to see. I've never watched breaking surf without also studying it, trying to understand what tricks of tide and reef and wind have shaped it. But still, I've only begun to learn. Perhaps there is too much difference between the human mind and the mind of water.

Or perhaps I haven't watched long enough. I think of Koyukon elders, who have spent their lifetimes studying every detail of their natural surroundings, and have combined this with knowledge passed down from generations of elders before them. The more people experience the repetitions of events in nature, the more they see in them and the more they know, but the more they realize the limitations of their understanding. I believe this is why Koyukon people are so humble and self-effacing about their knowledge. And I believe that Koyukon people's extraordinary relationship to their natural community has emerged through this careful watching of the *same* events in the *same* place, endlessly repeated over lifetimes and generations and millennia. There may be more to learn by climbing the same mountain a hundred times than by climbing a hundred different mountains.

For the next hour, I lose myself at play in the breaking waves, ignoring my numb hands and feet, paddling as hard as I can to delay the onset of shivering. At one point a bull sea lion breaks the surface nearby, snorts a few times, and dives. I think little of it, but then three sea lions appear, looming like an apparition in the translucent face of a swell as it begins to break—body surfing underwater. They disappear as the curtain of whitewater falls, and afterward I watch nervously, wondering what might happen next.

Although I'm somewhat prepared, my heart makes a terrific jump when a huge bull sea lion—easily ten feet long and weighing perhaps a ton—rolls up a dozen feet behind me, not the usual way but upside down, with his eyes underwater. I sit high on my board, staring into the blue-green murk, trying to make myself inconspicuous by some act of will, hoping the animal doesn't feel territorial, doesn't have protective urges about the two females, doesn't mistake my dangling legs for a plaything, doesn't feel vengeful because someone tried to shoot him for stealing fish from a net or line. Then I see his shape ghosting toward me. He hovers just under my feet, apparently checking me out, but showing no inclination to be playful or aggressive. After he leaves I consider going ashore, but then glimpse all three of them heading away, perhaps to surf in a less crowded place.

The swells become larger near high tide, and I feel uneasy about staying out alone. Then a series of ponderous waves mounds on the outer shoals. I paddle desperately and manage to escape the first, then plunge into the sheer wall of the second like a harlequin duck, and surface just as it breaks behind me. Looking up at the third, I realize my luck has run out, so I take a deep breath and dive. Caught at the point of impact, I'm pushed down, thrashed around in the frigid, swirling water, and finally released to the surface, gasping for breath. Afterward, I wonder how those little harlequins kept from being torn apart and having every feather plucked from their bodies.

Shortly, an even larger series of swells approaches, but I'm far enough out to catch the biggest one and prudent enough to make it my last. As I wade ashore, I watch the energy of the wave die, rushing to the top of the beach and slipping back down again. And I remember its power rising to a crescendo around and under me during the final moments of its life, after traversing a thousand miles of ocean from its birthplace in a far Pacific storm. The motion that so exalted me was given freely by the wave, as the wave was given motion by the wind, as the wind was given motion by the storm, as the storm was given motion by the whirl of the atmosphere and the turning of the earth itself. Then I remember the sea lions, cradled by the same ocean and pleasured by the same waves. All of us here, partaking of a single motion. Together and alive.

Shungnak's greeting barks and wags are especially welcome after I've surfed this winter place alone. She makes good company when we're on the island together, and she lets me focus my attention on the surroundings without the need for conversation. I always miss Nita and Ethan, and I enjoy the companionship of friends who often come along to explore or surf together. The social part of these experiences is a special pleasure, but they are very different from times when I come only with Shungnak. The desire for company is so strong that it's often tempting to let the solitude in nature slip away. But when I do this, I eventually feel out of balance; my mind clutters with work and personal concerns, and only a good immersion into the island can cleanse it. I come back from the wild places feeling renewed.

When we reach the rivermouth, Shungnak takes one look and realizes her predicament. The tide has risen, and six feet of water cover the place we waded across this morning. So we have two choices: hike several miles back to the shallows in Deer Meadow or swim across right here. Part of Shungnak's sled dog heritage is a strong aversion to water. She cowers in the woods while I put my packful of clothes on the surfboard, then watches dejectedly as I swim across the stream, pushing it ahead of me.

When I paddle back, she knows it's her turn but has no intention of coming along voluntarily. After some struggling and impatient words, I carry her into the water and plant her on the teetering surfboard. She stands straddle-legged, shivering and terrified, and almost capsizes the board several times despite my efforts to keep her calm. Halfway across, I wonder what someone would think who chanced to witness this strange behavior in such an improbable place. Finally we reach shallow water and the reluctant surf-dog slips off. She scrambles ashore, shakes herself, then dashes around on the dry sand, elated. She even sprints out to me again, splashing happily in the water she so dreaded a few minutes ago.

Numb and shaking, I strip to bare skin outside the tent, dry off as quickly as possible, and blissfully experience the genius of human clothing. A brilliant blue Stellar's jay perches in the branches nearby, rasping the chill air with calls, apparently drawn by the spectacle of a creature that takes off one skin and puts on another.

We lavish ourselves with the rich comfort of food and warmth inside the tent after nightfall. Rain drives down through the trees, as they tilt and hiss in a gusty southeaster. I'm truly relieved to be in this tight little pod rather than in the dubious protection of the Deer Meadow cabin. Intensifying surf sets the earth trembling beneath the tent. During the quiet between squalls, heavy droplets thump without rhythm from the high boughs. These two sounds epitomize the twin personalities of water—gentle or powerful, peaceful or tempestuous, life sustaining or life threatening.

The rain envelops me, like a lover breathing in my ear through the black night. My heart finds sanctuary in this love, who will never slip away and leave the dawns empty.

By morning there is scarcely any breeze, but the ocean still rumbles. I peer out in the early light, and through the gaps between tree trunks I can see enormous swells rising along the horizon, first gray, then darker, then black in their hollows, then suddenly white as they break with a force that reverberates through the timber and the shore. I know immediately that the surf is only for watching. It looks like a good day to hike through the forest toward the distant clearcuts.

After breakfast, we walk down the shore in the opposite direction from the one we took yesterday, where there is no river to cross. Cooler air has sunk in behind last night's weather front, and a blue rift has opened amid high escarpments of cloud. For a few minutes, sunshine glistens on the windrows of gray and amber drift logs. Beyond the shore of Roller Bay, Kluksa Mountain is bright with new snow. A huge cornice purls down a thousand feet of fluted ridge beneath its crest. Radiating outward on the lower slopes are corrugated hills patterned with forest and muskeg, descending toward points of black rock that vanish beneath the sea.

We come to a broad pond less than an inch deep, covered with rippled islets of sand floating in the reflection of our surroundings. Standing at its edge, I suddenly feel adrift in midair as I gaze down at the whole sweep of Kluksa Mountain plunging into the earth and reaching toward the subterranean clouds. Then I look up to see the mountain soaring skyward and the clouds hovering high above. I step across an abalone shell at the bottom of the pool, and walk on, feeling like a man who has just been given sight.

We follow the beach until it ends abruptly against a rockbound shore—cobbled coves separated by pillars and fists of stone, then impassable cliffs with timbered mountainsides above. After picking our way along the rocks just above the surge, we climb to a high, grassy overlook. The whole breadth of Roller Bay is laid out beneath us, like arms opened to embrace the sea. This side of the bay is scalloped into a sequence of three promontories: Black Point the closest in, then Ocean Point, and finally Ragged Point at the bay's outermost edge, five miles away. Towering waves sweep onto the reefs off Ragged Point, throwing off clouds of spindrift and roiling shoreward in bores of whitewater that must be huge to be visible from this distance. Closer at hand, a series of enormous swells moves toward us, ridges twenty feet high, extending across the mile between shores, building higher as the bight narrows and rises into shoals. Each swell bends like an enormous wing, as its middle slides ahead in deeper water and its tips drag behind in the shallows, careening across rocks and raking the cliffs on either side. There is a terrifying inexorability and slowness about these waves, sweeping in from the open sea, rising above the canyons of their own troughs, and making the island tremble with their explosions.

The entire bay is alive with leaping water, scrawled with thick streamers of spume, and stained by patches of half-decayed organic debris scoured up from the depths. An eagle looks down from its perch in a weathered snag on the cliff, then suddenly launches, planes out over the bay, and sets its eye on a glint amid the froth. A hundred yards from shore, its descent steepens, like the down-curved flight of an arrow. The eagle bends its head to look straight below, releases its grasp on the air, swings down its opened talons, and plunges bodily onto the water. For a moment it lies there, wings extended like pontoons. Then, with great effort and flailing, it strokes against the sea and rises, shaking streams from its feathers. A fish the size of a small cod swims helplessly in its grasp and stares uncomprehendingly at its lost element below.

The eagle labors back toward shore, water still trailing from its pinions. It circles at the timber's edge, drops down, then rises to the high bough it has chosen and grasps it with one foot, still holding its prey in the other. The slender treetop sways as the bird settles, shakes its head, ruffles the white feathers of its nape, and stares at the cold, shining fish.

I shrink away into the forest, mindful of the paradox that life sustains itself in the violence of that flensing beak, brought down beneath the closing shadow of wings.

Released from her boredom, Shungnak bounds ahead into the woods, weaving through faint webs of scent, exploring a rich world of odors that scarcely exists for me. We work back along the hillside, through tall timber with a fair undergrowth of blueberry and menziesia bushes. The gales of fall and winter are channeled along this exposed slope, yet the trees are not huddled or bent or gnarled. Apparently the straight-trunked forest creates its own wall and protects itself by shunting storms over its heights. But while the whole community stands, each tree must eventually succumb. A massive trunk blocks our way, sprawled across the ground, its fractured wood still bright and smelling of sap, its boughs green and supple. Because it looks so healthy, I surmise it was thrown down by a contrary gust, perhaps the only one to hit just this way in a hundred years, or five hundred. And I imagine the maelstrom that ripped through the forest as it fell, carrying two others with it and clouding the air with a mass of splintered debris.

Studies of coastal forests like this one reveal that exposure to wind is what most determines the age of trees. Whereas spruce trees in vulnerable stands live an average of two hundred years, those in sheltered, fertile areas like the Deer Meadow valley can live eight or nine hundred years. Yellow cedars, which are better able to resist wind, commonly survive for a thousand years. Small openings created by the fallen trees allow diversified plant communities to grow up, enriching the environment while the surrounding timber remains intact. The biomass in these forests—that is, the combined weight of their living material—is among the highest in the world, greater even than the biomass of tropical rain forests.

Farther on, two fallen giants with an uptorn mass of roots lean against a stone outcrop, half their length projecting over a cliff like bowsprits. They appear to have come down at least twenty or thirty years ago, perhaps even before I was born. Green algae coats the trunks, and the thick, branchless limbs are swaddled with patches of moss. Eventually these sodden hulks will snap and crash down the slope, then rot away to a lump in the forest floor. But they will not disappear until long after my every trace has vanished. Trees decay as slowly as they have lived and grown.

A sluggish stream runs along the base of the hill, with forest impinging closely on either side. We follow the bank looking for a place to cross. After a quarter-mile it opens to a long meadow bordered by alder patches and muskeg. I notice a few signs that plants have already begun to stir. Alder, salmonberry, and red-stemmed blueberry have swollen buds with tiny fissures of embryonic leaves. In the yard at home, some of our domesticated plants are much more adventuresome. The little, drooping snowdrops came up in mid-January and are now in full bloom. A few crocuses have put up blossoms, though most of them only show grassy bladelets. Daffodil sprouts are finger-high; and fleshy red domes show at the base of last year's crumpled rhubarb leaves.

The wild flowers stay dormant and hidden well after our yard is bright with blooming domesticates. Yet our carefully tended plants show no sign of spreading into the thicket beyond. Garden flowers can afford their springtime gambles and flashy moves only as long as we're around to hold back the competition. But someday the house will decay, the walled gardens will crumble, grass and sedge will strangle the flowers' roots, while cow parsnip and salmonberry rise above them. The garden plants have cast their lot with us; if we go, so will they.

As we wade across the stream, I notice the sky has darkened and gray haze has settled against the mountains. Shortly afterward, a mix of drizzle, sleet, and snow begins to fall. But when we slip back beneath the canopy of trees, there are no needling flakes, no icy droplets, and the chilling breeze is gone. I feel enveloped by the soft, wet hands of the forest. Moving in from the edge, I realize this is one of the purest stands of aged spruce and hemlocks I've found on the island. The forest unfolds like a lovely and complex symphony, heard for the first time. It has a dark, baritone richness, tinkled through with river sounds and chickadees. There are almost no shrubs or small trees, just an open maze of huge gray pillars. And everything is covered with a deep blanket of moss that mounds up over decaying stumps and fallen trunks like a shroud laid atop the furnishings in a great hall.

There must be few wetter places on earth. My rubber boots glisten each time I lift them from the swollen sponge underfoot. Stepping over a mossy windfall, I press my knees against it and instantly feel the water soak through. When I call Shungnak, the feathers of plushy moss deaden my voice, as if we were in a soundproof room.

The sense of *life* in this temperate jungle is as pervasive and palpable as its wetness. Even the air seems organic—rich and pungent like the moss itself. I breathe life into my lungs, feel life against my skin, move through a thick, primordial ooze of life, like a Paleozoic lungfish paddling up to gasp mouthfuls of air.

It seems that the rocks beneath this forest should lie under a thousand feet of soaked and decaying mulch. But the roots of a recently toppled spruce clutch small boulders torn up from only a foot or two below the moss. What has become of the trunks and boughs and branches that have fallen onto this earth for thousands of years? And the little showers of needles that have shaken down with every gust of wind for millennia? Digested by the forest itself, and dissolved into the tea-colored streams that run toward the island's shore. The thought makes me feel that I truly belong here—that I, too, hold membership in this community—because all of us share the same fate.

Looking carefully, I pick out the shapes of many fallen trees and their root masses. They are nearly hidden by robes of moss that reduce them to hillocks, and by the camouflage of trees that have grown up on top of them. Tendrils of living roots wind down through the lattice of older, decaying roots, straddle broken stumps, and wrap over prostrate trunks. Sometimes four or five large trees grow in a straight line, each supported by an elevated, empty cagework of roots. These roots once enclosed a fallen mother tree which has completely vanished. The whole impression is of a forest on contorted stilts, sheathed in moss, climbing up over its own decay, breathing and wet and alive.

Only a few raindrops and oversized snowflakes sift through the crown of trees as a squall passes over. I'm grateful for the shelter, and I sense a deeper kind of comfort here. These are living things I move among, immeasurably older and larger and more deeply affixed to their place on earth than I am, and imbued with vast experience of a kind entirely beyond my comprehension. I feel like a miniscule upstart in their presence, a supplicant awaiting the quiet counsel of venerable trees.

I've often thought of the forest as a living cathedral, but this might diminish what it truly is. If I have understood Koyukon teachings, the forest is not merely an expression or representation of sacredness, nor a place to invoke the sacred; the forest is sacredness itself. Nature is not merely created by God; nature *is* God. Whoever moves within the forest can partake directly of sacredness, experience sacredness with his entire body, breathe sacredness and contain it within himself, drink the sacred water as a living communion, bury his feet in sacredness, touch the living branch and feel the sacredness, open his eyes and witness the burning beauty of sacredness. And when he cuts a tree from the forest, he participates in a sacred interchange that brings separate lives together.

The dark boughs reach out above me and encircle me like arms. I feel the assurance of being recognized, as if something powerful and protective is aware of my presence, looks in another direction but always has me in the corner of its eye. I am cautious and self-protective here, as anywhere, yet I believe that a covenant of mutual regard and responsibility binds me together with the forest. We share in a common nurturing. Each of us serves as an amulet to protect the other from inordinate harm. I am never alone in this wild forest, this forest of elders, this forest of eyes.

Terry Tempest Williams

Terry Tempest Williams, a naturalist-in-residence at the Utah Museum of Natural History in Salt Lake City, is the author of three widely acclaimed nature books: *Pieces of White Shell: A Journey to Navajoland* (Scribner's, 1984), *Coyote's Canyon* (Peregrine Smith, 1989) and *Refuge: An Unnatural History of Family and Place* (Pantheon, 1991). One of the most promising of the younger generation of American nature writers, Williams emerged nationally with the publication of her most recent book, *Refuge,* which chronicles the loss of her mother to cancer and the slow death of a fragile wetland in northern Utah. Jim Harrison has written of *Refuge* that the book "is an almost unbearably intense and skillful essay on mortality, our own and that of the creature world. It is isolated from nearly all others of the genre by Ms. Williams's 'greatness of soul'—there is no other way to express the dense beauty and grace of this book." In these two essays from *Coyote's Canyon*—"Lion Eyes" and "The Bowl"— Williams offers us brief but intense glimpses and parables of the Utah desert. The power of the desert to inspire and to heal is evident in these evocative vignettes, as is the quiet intensity of Williams's prose.

Lion Eyes
(circa 1989)

It was going to be a long ride home for fifteen Navajo children. Dropping kids off five, ten, and twenty miles apart is no small task. We were committed for the night. The sun had just vanished behind Giant's Knuckles, causing those in the back of the pickup to huddle close.

"It gets cold in the desert," I said.

"It's winter," one of the children replied. They covered their mouths with their hands, giggling, as we continued to bump along the dirt roads surrounding Montezuma Creek. What did the driver and I know? We were Anglos.

We had been down by the river for the afternoon. A thin veneer of ice had coalesced along its edge, and the children, bending down, would break off pieces and hold them between their thumbs and forefingers. Before the ice would melt, some brought the thin sheet to their eyes as a lens, while others placed it in their mouths and sucked on the river. Still others winged the ice sheets across the cobbles, watching, listening to them shatter like glass.

Life on the river's edge was explored through whirligig beetles, water skaters, and caddis fly larvae under stones. Canada geese flew above the channel, landing for brief intervals, then continuing on their way. The children followed tracks, expecting to meet a pack of stray dogs hiding in the tamarisks. Our shadows grew longer with the last light of day reflecting on river rapids and willows.

The hours by the river were all spent. Now, in the back of the pickup, the children told tales of days when a horse could enter a hogan and leave as a man; of skinwalkers disguised as coyotes who stalk the reservation with bones in their hands, scratching white crosses on the doors of ill-fated households. They spoke of white owls, ghostly flashes of light that could turn the blood of mice into milk.

Just then, my friend hit the brakes and those of us in the back fell forward.

"What was that?" The driver leaned his head out the window so we could hear him. "Did you see that?"

"What?" we all asked.

"A mountain lion! It streaked across the road. I'll swear it was all tail!"

The children whispered among themselves, "Mountain Lion ... "

We filed out of the truck. My friend and I walked a few feet ahead. We found the tracks. A rosette. Five-toed pads, clawless, imprinted on the sand in spite of the cold.

"No question," I said. "Lion. I wonder where she is now?"

Looking into the darkness, I could only imagine the desert cat staring back at us. I looked over at the children; most of them were leaning against the truck as headlights approached.

"What's going on?" a local Navajo asked as he rolled down the window of his pickup with his motor idling.

My friend recognized him as the uncle of one of the children. "We think we saw a mountain lion," he said.

"Where? How long ago?"

The other man in the cab of the truck asked if we were sure.

"Pretty sure," I said. "Look at these tracks."

The men got out of their vehicle and shined their flashlights on the ground until they picked up the prints. One of the men knelt down and touched them.

"This is not good," the uncle said. "They kill our sheep." He looked into the night and then back at us. "What color of eyes did it have?"

My friend and I looked at each other. The Navajo elder began reciting the color of animals' eyes at night.

"Deer's eyes are blue. Coyote's eyes are red." His nephew interrupted him. "Green—the lion's eyes were green."

The two men said they would be back with their guns and sons tomorrow.

We returned to the truck, the driver with a handful of kids up front and the rest in the back around me as we nestled together under blankets. The children became unusually quiet, speaking in low, serious voices about why mountain lions are considered dangerous.

"It's more than just killing sheep," one child explained. "Mountain Lion is a god, one of the supernaturals that has power over us."

Each child gave away little bits of knowledge concerning the lion: that it chirps like a bird to fool you; that parts of its body are used for medicine; that in the old days, hunters used the sinew of lion for their bows. The children grew more and more anxious as fear seized their voices like two hands around their throats. They were hushed.

We traveled through the starlit desert in silence, except for the hum of the motor and four wheels flying over the washboard.

In time, from the rear of the pickup, came a slow, deliberate chant. Navajo words—gentle, deep meanderings of music born out of healing. I could not tell who had initiated the song, but one by one each child entered the melody. Over and over they sang the same monotonous notes, dreamlike at first, until gradually the cadence quickened. The children's mood began to lighten, and they swayed back and forth. What had begun as a cautious, fearful tone emerged as a joyous one. Their elders had taught them well. They had sung themselves back to hózhó, where the world is balanced and whole.

After the last child had been taken home, my friend and I were left with each other, but the echo of the children's chant remained. With many miles to go, we rolled down the windows in the cab of the truck, letting the chilled air blow through. Mountain Lion, whose eyes I did not see, lay on the mesa, her whiskers retrieving each note carried by the wind.

The Bowl
(circa 1989)

There was a woman who left the city, left her husband, and her children, left everything behind to retrieve her soul. She came to the desert after seeing her gaunt face in the mirror, the pallor that comes when everything is going out and nothing is coming in. She had noticed for the first time the furrows under her eyes that had been eroded by tears. She did not know the woman in the mirror. She took off her apron, folded it neatly in the drawer, left a note for her family, and closed the door behind her. She knew that her life and the lives of those she loved depended on it.

The woman returned to the place of her childhood, where she last remembered her true nature. She returned to the intimacy of a small canyon that for years had loomed large in her imagination, and there she set up camp. The walls were as she had recalled them, tall and streaked from rim to floor. The rock appeared as draped fabric as she placed her hand flat against its face. The wall was cold; the sun had not yet reached the wash. She began wading the shallow stream that ran down the center of the canyon, and chose not to be encumbered by anything. She shed her clothing, took out her hairpins, and squeezed the last lemon she had over her body. Running her hands over her breasts and throat and behind her neck, the woman shivered at her own bravery. This is how it should be, she thought. She was free and frightened and beautiful.

For days, the woman wandered in and out of the slickrock maze. She drank from springs and ate the purple fruit of prickly pears. Her needs were met simply. Because she could not see herself, she was unaware of the changes—how her skin became taut and tan, the way in which her hair relaxed and curled itself. She even seemed to walk differently as her toes spread and gripped the sand.

All along the wash, clay balls had been thrown by a raging river. The woman picked one up, pulled off the pebbles until she had a mound of supple clay. She kneaded it as she walked, rubbed the clay between the palms of her hands, and watched it lengthen. She finally sat down on the moist sand and, with her fingers, continued moving up the string of clay. And then she began to coil it, around and around, pinching shut each rotation. She created a bowl.

The woman found other clay balls and put them inside the bowl. She had an idea of making dolls for her children, small clay figurines that she would let dry in the sun. Once again, she stopped walking and sat in the sand to work. She split each clay ball in two, which meant she had six small pieces to mold out of three balls she had found. One by one, tiny shapes took form. A girl with open arms above her head; three boys—one standing, one sitting, and one lying down (he was growing, she mused); and then a man and a woman facing each other. She had re-created her family. With the few scraps left over she made desert animals: a lizard, a small bird, and a miniature coyote sitting on his haunches. The woman smiled as she looked over her menagerie. She clapped her hands to remove the dried clay and half expected to see them dance. Instead, it began to rain.

Within minutes, the wash began to swell. The woman put the clay creatures into the bowl and sought higher ground up a side canyon, where she found shelter under a large overhang. She was prepared to watch if a flash flood came. And it did. The clear water turned muddy as it began to rise, carrying with it the force of wild horses running with a thunderstorm behind them. The small stream, now a river, rose higher still, gouging into the sandy banks, hurling rocks, roots, and trees downstream. The woman wondered about the animals as she heard stirrings in the grasses and surmised they must be seeking refuge in the side canyons as she was— watching as she was. She pulled her legs in and wrapped her arms around her shins, resting her cheekbones against her knees. She closed her eyes and concentrated on the sound of water bursting through the silence of the canyon.

The roar of the flood gradually softened until it was replaced by birdsong. Swifts and swallows plucked the water for insects as frogs announced their return. The woman raised her head. With the bowl in both hands, she tried to get up, but slipped down the hillside, scraping the backs of her thighs on rabbitbrush and sage. She finally reached the wash with the bowl and its contents intact. And then she found herself with another problem: she sank up to her knees in the wet, red clay, only to find that the more she tried to pull her foot free, the deeper she sank with the other. Finally, letting go of her struggle, she put the bowl and her family aside, and wallowed in it. She fell sideways and rolled onto her stomach, then over onto her back. She was covered in slimy, wet clay, and it was delicious. She stretched her hands above her head, flexed her calves, and pointed her toes. The woman laughed hysterically until she became aware of her own echo.

Her body contracted.

She must get control of herself, she thought; what would her husband think? What kind of example was she setting for her children? And then she remembered—she was alone. She sat up and stared at the coiled bowl full of clay people. The woman took out the figurines and planted them in the wash. She placed the animals around them.

"They're on their own," she said out loud. And she walked back to the spring where she had drunk, filled up her bowl with water, and bathed.

The next morning, when the woman awoke, she noticed that the cottonwood branches swaying above her head had sprouted leaves.

She could go home now.

John A. Murray

This essay from a work-in-progress on Denali National Park describes the summer solstice as it is experienced in the subarctic. At the latitude of the park, the sun does not set until after 1:00 A.M.; the sun then rises shortly after 3:00 A.M. For the intervening two hours there is sufficient light to read a book. The essay discusses how the longest day of the year has been celebrated at other times and in other cultures. "Summer Solstice" makes parallel references to Shakespeare's summer solstice play, *A Midsummer Night's Dream,* and in the process reexamines the Elizabethan worldview *vis-à-vis* nature. The fabled "white nights" of summer in the far north make the solstice a particularly enjoyable event. No one should consider their experiences of the North American wilderness to be complete without having first traveled to the latitudes where there is no darkness to the summer night.

Summer Solstice
(circa 1992)

Dispatch, I say, and find the forester.
                    —A *Midsummer Night's Dream*

I

Halfway up the hill above Wonder Lake I stop and lean against my aspen walking stick, the one I found beside a beaver pond on the Chena River two summers ago. From this vantage, looking south, the heart of the Alaska Range is visible. Sixty miles of perpetually snowclad mountains, disappearing at either extreme into the country of yesterday and tomorrow. Toward the west, beyond Mount Foraker, is Rainy Pass, where the dogsledders will race this winter on their way from Anchorage to Nome. On the other side of the horizon, past Mount Eielson, is the Yanert Glacier country, where hunters pursue those agile white rams with the wide sweeping horns like hammered gold. Denali presides over it all, a massive peak as old as the rivers and deeply scarred, with a scattering of clouds downwind like a school of arctic grayling holding in the pool behind a boulder. Within a few days the mountain will attract darker, heavier clouds and the summer thunderstorms will begin. There will be lightning strikes and forest fires and the highlands will be shrouded in smoke for a month before the first of the fall rains. But for now, for the solstice, there is light and warmth on the country. These are the days I hold close when the snow brings the moose down into the valley. The breeze wanders off for a moment and the mosquitoes rise up from the moss like a swarm of freshly hatched devils.

I press on, climbing steadily through low tangled blueberry bushes and dense thickets of dwarf birch, stopping occasionally to admire the open eye of a wild dogwood blossom or to touch the sticky tendrils of a sundew—the carnivorous plant—growing in a moist bucket of ground far from the nearest bog. Always the bugs appear, driving anything with the ability to move and the will to survive either upward, into the windy heights, or downward, into the sheltering water. And always the plants become smaller as I leave the lowlands behind, a moment ago past my thighs, now just barely to my knees. Somewhere on the slope above me, out of sight at the moment, is a bald spot the four elements have been wearing on the withers of this mammoth-backed ridge since before the last Ice Age. I will sit on that weathered piece of lichen-covered turf and watch the last red light of the longest day go off the tallest peak north of the Peruvian Andes. In the pack I carry a quart of water, the essential notebook and pencil and a worn copy of *A Midsummer Night's Dream*. I have not opened that celebration of the summer solstice since Professor Squier's class in the crowded lecture hall of Old Main twenty years ago. Even in paradise you need a good book, one with lines like

> *I know a bank where the wild thyme blows*
> *Where oxlips and the nodding violet grows*
> *Quite over-canopied with luscious woodbine,*
> *With sweet musk-roses, and with eglantine,*
> *There sleeps Titania sometime of the night*
> *Lulled in these flowers with dances and delights.*

The grade steepens near the top and I scramble up a slide of talus, scratching and clawing like a hoary marmot in the shadow of a golden eagle as I lose one yard for every three gained. But finally

I reach the crest and flop over. There is a good breeze here, and no mosquitoes, and I am glad. In the outliers the absence of mosquitoes assumes a significance completely out of proportion with the size of the animal's bite. All across the one thousand or so acres directly in view small groups of caribou, their coats half shed from the annual molt, stand or sit or look to be passed out on the lingering banks of snow. Their presence recommends the place, and so I take off the pack, spread my old Marine Corps poncho on the ground, and sit on the softest hard spot I can find. Down below, on the shores of Wonder Lake, a natural impoundment shaped like a four-mile-long silver salmon, the summer heat and bugs have driven several bull moose into the shallows, where they stand with only their velvet antlers, huge floppy ears and dark bewildered eyes visible. The birds, of course, love the mosquitoes. They fly from as far away as Africa, South America and Antarctica each spring just to enjoy the bountiful polar feast. Their global flight—especially the golden plovers from the South Pole—is a miracle of nature that will not be equaled by the human race until we can travel to a star in the Ursa Major constellation and back, annually. It is seven o'clock in the evening and at this latitude—just north of the sixty-third parallel—the sun will not leave the mountain until around one o'clock in the morning. That gives me the entire evening to study Denali, sketch it crudely in the notebook, and simply look at it, something that was young when my ancestors were scampering tree shrews, something that will still be young when our hubris is known only by the small curious bones protruding from the river cutbanks.

Ansel Adams, the concert pianist turned landscape photographer, climbed this same hill on the solstice of 1947. That was a good year. Albert Camus published *The Plague,* the Dead Sea Scrolls were discovered in Wak Qumran and Colonel Chuck Yaeger broke the sound barrier. Also, my parents were married in Philadelphia, and my existence—preordained since Creation according to the Calvinists—was brought that much closer. How Ansel Adams got his enormous 8 x 10 view camera, with heavy tripod, bulky lenses, changing bags and miscellaneous accessories up this ridge I do not know. But somehow he did, and over the course of his stay the broken-nosed Bierdstadt exposed two well-known negatives. The popular calendar photograph—what I call the "classical" image of Denali—captures the mountain in the hard clear light of early morning. There are no clouds and the snow-covered heights—icefalls, avalanche slides, buckled snow banks, deep crevasses, great hanging glaciers—are dramatically illuminated, while the foreground of forest and lake is so darkened by shadow as to be black. The scene is the very definition of geometry and order. By contrast, the other Adams picture—what I call the "romantic" view of the mountain—depicts Denali aswath in dream-like clouds, with a half-moon setting on the alpine ridge just to the east. This print summons up all the grandeur of the romantic as it blurs the boundary between earth and atmosphere and reveals as much of the mountain as it conceals.

I prefer the cloudy version of Denali for the same reason I would choose any of Gauguin's Tahitian paintings over the cold, idealized perfection of Praxiteles's sculpture of Aphrodite. For one thing, the stark polished stone of the Greek leaves nothing to the imagination; the contemplation of beauty is as much an act of the imagination as it is an activity of the senses. For another, the emotionless repose of Aphrodite is more sublime than sensuous, more refined marble than moving revelation. That Ansel Adams showed both sides of the mountain, and of the human perception of beauty, is a tribute to his vision. As I cast my eyes about the sky I am pleasantly surprised to see, by happy coincidence, that the half-moon is again in the heavens over Denali. In six hours, the residence of Apollo will, from the looks of it, set in very nearly the same place as it did forty-four summers ago:

> Snout: *Doth the moon shine that night we play our play?*
> Bottom: *A calendar! a calendar! Look in the almanac. Find out the moonshine, find out the moonshine.*
> Quince: *Yes, it doth shine that night.*

I take the clear skies, bright moon and steady breeze to be propitious signs.

Stare too long at the mountain and you find yourself shrink-
ing into the realm of Cobweb, Moth and Mustard Seed. Not
wishing to join the atoms, I shift my perspective to the world at my
feet, which by comparison with the Alaska Range makes me a
lumbering giant, standing astride continents. There are, first of all,
rocks everywhere. Most are pebble- or pocket-sized, but a few
range upward to the size of a cafeteria-sized cooking pot. I identify
in the alpine rubble yard right around my neighborhood quartzite,
granite, marble, schist and slate. These are the basic rocks. There
are also samples of serpentine, chert, biotite, feldspar, copper and
pyrite. Pyrite is fool's gold. Dynamite is required to see the real
gold. The schist is the oldest rock, and has been around since the
blue-green algae and single-celled protozoa first trafficked in the
tides of the moon. To touch one of these glistening dark beauties
is to touch time itself. The larger rocks lay in a vaguely patterned
disorder, as if ages ago a squad of drunk soldiers with a Roman
catapult used the hill for target practice and the crude artillery shells
lay pretty much where they landed, half-driven into the ground,
the targets long lost, and the gunners too. This patterned ground—
filled-in rock circles, open polygons and meandering streams—is
caused by the way freezing and thawing mold the tundra and the
permafrost. The singing voles and burrowing parka squirrels know
all about the permafrost. Beneath the country rocks, and stretching
away in every direction, are the vast luxurious beds of green
sphagnum moss and gray reindeer lichen over which the caribou
lightly spring with their widely splayed hooves and long limber
legs. The rest of us stumble, curse and fall at regular intervals. The
reindeer lichen, also a primary food of the caribou, comprises
miniature hollow branches that would make perfectly sized antlers
for a caribou about the size of a scarab beetle. One of the theories
as to why the caribou have departed the park—these hills recently
had thousands—is that the lichens absorbed Strontium 90 from
Soviet nuclear tests and the caribou then consumed the deadly
isotope. Even here, five river valleys west of the nearest paved road
and five hundred miles east of the Bering Sea, you cannot escape
the tentacles of the Hydra.

Flowers abound. Red shooting star, Siberian phlox, mountain heather, arctic lupine, Kamchatka rhododendron, dwarf fireweed, alpine marigold. To my left a flourishing patch of bluebells is aflutter with a flock of freshly hatched hair-streaks. As I watch the light gray moths drain the pollen from the blossoms, a rosy finch flies out of nowhere and eats every last one of them. This happens only five feet away, but occurs too quickly for me to do anything about it. The finch then disappears, trailing a cheerful song. Over yonder is a dense bed of red-flowered moss campion surrounded by yellow monkey-flower, Iceland poppy and arctic meadowrue. Not one of the lilliputian plants attains a height greater than my ankle. Perfect habitat for the Elizabethan fairy. As near as I can tell, the wildflower arrangements on the tundra are wholly random, as if at some distant time a group of children dispersed seeds and bulbs from overflowing baskets as they sang and danced across the hills. The flowers grow wherever they take root in a kind of gardener's chaos. How unlike the elaborate formal gardens of the Elizabethans, for whom the wilderness was an uncontrolled riot and for whom, by contrast, every planted bed had to observe a mathematical relationship of degree and proportion to the whole. So concerned were those nervous monarchists with order that they often shaped their gardens, and their familiar wood-beamed and white-plastered houses, in the form of the letter *E* to honor their beloved red-haired queen. Those fanatic Tudors lived in a fragile cosmos in which everything—from the heavenly spheres to the humblest grain of sand—had its assigned place in the "great chain of being." In a few years, the whole doomed system would come tumbling down. Somewhat like this century before Einstein.

Not far from my roost is a cluster of blue harebells, a flower I have not seen since leaving the Rockies. Many years ago, while I was shoeing a particularly obnoxious strawberry roan in the heat of a July afternoon, a very special blue-eyed girl—one on whom I'd had my eyes all summer—suddenly walked up and gave me a blue harebell for no reason other than to be sweet, and thus opened the corral gates on a wonderful summer romance. I was nineteen and she was eighteen and we were working at a guest ranch near Yellowstone. Apparently someone had taught her Oberon's secret:

> Oberon: *Fetch me that flow'r; the herb I showed thee once.*
> *The juice of it, on sleeping eyelids laid,*
> *Will make a man or woman madly dote*
> *Upon the next live creature that it sees.*
> *Fetch me this herb, and be thou here again.*
> *Ere the Leviathan can swim a league.*
>
> Puck: *I'll put a girdle round the earth*
> *In forty minutes.*

Where is she now? Perhaps she thought of me just then. Who knows.

One thing is certain, as my stomach growls on this solstice fast, a man need not go hungry very long in these Kantishna Hills. From my hermitage I can spot, among other things, a vast pink nebula of alpine bistort. Beneath each one of those pink flower spikes is a thick, twisted root that can be either stewed or roasted. Grizzly bears love bistort and learn from their mothers while still cubs where all the choice beds are located. On the hike up here I passed a good many patches of wild sweetpea, also known as Eskimo potato or bear root. These roots can be eaten raw, like carrots, or boiled in a soup like onions or potatoes. Again, the local bears know where all these outdoor markets are found. Not quite flowering yet are the saxifrage, or bearflowers. Their leaves make a nutritious salad, high in protein now in June before the plants channel their energy into making flowers and seeds. Follow a bear through this country, as I'm sure the Beringeans did, and you could quickly learn what is safe and good to eat. After all, the only difference between a bear and a man is a couple of hundred pounds and a permanent fur coat. In fact, after the solstice fast, I should adjust my diet to approximate that of the local bears. I'll probably live a longer and happier life.

The most spectacular bounty of these hills are the fall berries—blueberry, crowberry, soapberry, low-bush cranberry and raspberry. On that bald knob where Wonder Lake turns into Moose Creek my father and I picked about a pint of blueberries each last August. In the process, our lips, tongues, faces, hands and shirts turned blue. At this time of year all the blueberries have to offer are tiny pink inverted bells, tolling the fairies to the season of fertility. Sometime after Bastille Day they will begin to show the world the first of their blue fruit. Down the hill a few yards in a solitary patch of dwarf alpine willow is the scapula of a caribou calf. Sunbleached it is, and picked clean by the scavenging insects that make their living, like undertakers and gravediggers, from the dead. The bone resembles a small musical instrument, a triangularly shaped lyre, deprived of its strings. Made for a child, perhaps, or something smaller. In a museum the flat shoulder bone would be given a specimen number and placed in a drawer over sterile cotton, but here it has been cleaned of valuable leftovers and thrown back into the seething cauldron of life. Part of the caribou, through the medium of soil, is now included in those green willow leaves, which, as every Eskimo and Athabaskan knows, make a potent medicinal tea. The reason? Willow leaves contain salicylic acid, the same active ingredient as commercial aspirin. A man could live quite well here at Wonder Lake, with all the necessities of life, were he so inclined.

> *Titania:*   *Be kind and courteous to this gentleman.*
> *Feed him with apricots and dewberries,*
> *With purple grapes, green figs, and mulberries,*
> *The honeybags steal from the humblebees,*
> *And for night tapers crop their waxen thighs*
> *And light them at the fiery glowworm's eye.*
> *Nod to him, elves, and do him courtesies.*

II

Nine o'clock and the mountain is still standing. Resembles an enormous axehead left out in the snow overnight, recently sharpened, shining brightly against the sky, with the near corner chipped, as if the blade struck some *thing* harder. What would that be? Evil? Injustice? Mortality? Suddenly, as if to proclaim the season is not right for such interrogatories, the songbirds rise to a raucous chorus. Five minutes ago, the hills were virtually silent, but now the land is suddenly transformed and uplifted by a thousand beaks opening and closing, warbling, echoing and trilling. Why do they sing just now? Are they defending territory? Is it love? Or does the chorus arise simply from the joy at having lived another day on this uncertain earth? Not much cerebral cortex in those little bird brains, but still you wonder. Lapland longspurs make a delightful, tinkling sound like wind chimes in the window on a summer weekend. And then there are the squeaky cries of the longtailed jaegers, like the happy creak of a hanging swing on a comfortable back porch. I like the song of the white-crowned sparrow best. It sounds like a child's flute practicing "Old Sam Peabody!" over and over. And there are others, the horned lark, with its sad mellifluous lament that makes me homesick for the meadowlark prairies of eastern Colorado, and the redpolls, and northern wheaters and arctic warblers. Shakespeare knew his birds:

> *The woodsel cock so black of hue,*
> *With orange-tawny bill,*
> *The throstle with his note so true,*
> *The wren with little quill—*
> *The finch, the sparrow, and the lark,*
> *The plain-song cuckoo grey,*
> *Whose note full many a man doth mark,*
> *And dares not answer nay.*

Heard together, these evening melodies sound like Elizabethan madrigals, those amorous contrapuntal tunes with the interweaving vocal harmonies. The Elizabethans loved music, and the influence of their madrigals is still evident—the harmonies of the Fab Four go right back to those early ballads. But who needs Lennon and McCartney, much as I love them, or madrigals for that matter, when you have an arctic warbler and a Lapland longspur to provide the evening's entertainment? All we poor humans can do is try our best to imitate the original songwriters.

This is the slow hour—between nine and ten—when it seems the sun will never set. The mountain does not change perceptibly and remains an imposing monolith, like a frozen wall beyond which none can travel or an ivory carving so enormously perfect no craftsman could ever hope to equal its artistry. This blinding white heap of matter becomes at times so formidable you would rather walk away from it. This is the hour, like first intermission, when many people who swear they will sit for the entire show begin to pace back and forth and look at their watches and make idle excuses to hike back to the comforts and distractions of base camp. Time to open the book. The first thing I notice about this old paperback edition of *A Midsummer Night's Dream* is that it was made from acid-based paper and after twenty years, the pages are falling apart in my hands. In archival vaults I have examined books that were made before the French Revolution—even before the Glorious Revolution—that are still perfectly intact. This book, published when grown men were still playing golf on the moon, is about to disintegrate into thin, baseless air. The next thing I notice is my scribbling, my marginalia, my juvenalia. I was eighteen when I took Professor Squier's course in the Comedies and Romances of Shakespeare, and reading my notes and doodles after nearly twenty years provides an interesting perspective. Here is a note from my girlfriend that semester, written in the margin beside Theseus's famous speech that begins:

> *Lovers and madmen have such seething brains,*
> *Such shaping fantasies, that apprehend*
> *More than cool reason ever comprehends.*
> *The lunatic, the lover, and the poet*
> *Are of imagination all compact.*

She wrote "I love you, John. Remember that," and drew an arrowed heart with our initials inside. I remember that day. We were sitting side by side, as usual, in the last row of the lecture hall, and after she wrote the inscription we held hands and the professor ... well, the professor ignored us. He knew neither of us would ever amount to anything. I still have a lock of her blond hair in a book of Sanskrit poetry somewhere. Where is she today? I honestly do not know, but I hope she is well.

Shakespeare, I note here in my jottings—my how the Murray script has remained illegible over the years—wrote the play in part to celebrate the summer solstice, although the first scenes technically occur in May. Shakespeare always confused things. No matter. The first performance of the play was at a wedding in either 1594 or 1595. Shakespeare was thirty in 1594, and this play represented, according to my notes, his first mature effort, the first time he worked with such a complex structure, synthesized so many diverse sources and willingly suspended credibility so effectively. Had he written only this play, the professor said, Shakespeare would be immortal. Says here a little further on that in antiquity the Greeks held the Olympics on the summer solstice to celebrate the mythical marriage of the moon and the sun. I like that concept. Maybe that is why I prefer the Ansel Adams photograph with the moon in it; you really do need the moon to work its romantic magic on the solstice. And of course *Midsummer* is a play filled with moonlight. Here is some more interesting information. The Elizabethans called the summer solstice St. John's Day, in honor of St. John the Baptist. John was the man, as I remember from Sunday School, who baptized Jesus. John was also the fellow who wandered up and down the Jordan River exhorting sinners to repent. (I read recently that the last free-flowing tributary of the Jordan River is about to be dammed.) John the Baptist was later beheaded on command of Herod, probably at the request of Herod's daughter Salome, who was known to dance without her clothes on, and whom Oscar Wilde used in a play to make himself famous. Why would the Elizabethans name the solstice—which they called Midsummer's Day, despite the fact that the solstice marks the *beginning* of summer—for St. John? I don't know. Have to answer that question when I get back to the twentieth century.

What else? Here on the inside cover of the book—I was often too poor to afford notebooks in those days—I jotted down that on Midsummer's Eve bonfires were built all over Europe, from Spain to Sweden, from Ukraine to Ireland. Old pagan ritual, it seems, to scare away the wizards and witches and to help rekindle the sun as it returned from the northern apex. This fire-building was also found among the Arabs of North Africa, which is puzzling in that the Islamic calendar is lunar. No one knows quite what they did at Stonehenge, but the light of the solstice sunrise illuminates a prominent stone that the Druids probably used for an impressive ritual, like a human sacrifice. In ancient Egypt, the summer solstice fell during the week when the Nile began to flood, after the seasonal rains upstream in the mountains of Abyssinia. This event marked the beginning of the sacred Egyptian year. Ramses II built his great temple at Abu Simbel on the west bank of the Nile so that the light of the summer solstice would strike a sculpture of him and his wife every year, thus ensuring their eternal life. That's a nice thought at first, eternal life, but is not so attractive after you think about it for a while. My paternal grandparents visited Ramses' temple once. Nana told me later that the middle valley was incredibly hot and that eighty-year-old granddaddy almost died from the amoebic dysentery he contracted there.

I skim completely through *Midsummer,* reacquainting myself with its myths and mischief, mysteries and marvels. The play, of course, is about love, the love between Oberon and Titania, the King and Queen of Fairies, and the love between Hermia and Lysander, two mortals like you and me. The Elizabethans believed that plants achieved their greatest magical powers on the summer solstice. Hence Oberon summons Puck, a minor fairy, to give Titania the juice of a wild pansy, which causes her to fall in love with the first thing she sees. As anyone who lives within walking distance of a university theater knows, Titania then falls in love with Nick Bottom, a roguish sort of man who, if he lived today, would have a velvet Elvis hanging in his trailer, drive a broken-down pickup truck painted three or four different colors and enjoy All-Star wrestling at the arena on weekends. A somewhat similar entanglement awaits the human lovers, and leads to further dramatic conflicts that bounce around for a while until all are happily resolved. "My Oberon," Titania exclaims at the end, "What visions have I seen!/Methought I was enamored of an ass." Shakespeare was right. Love does make fools of us. All of us. Even if, especially if, we ignore it. "Lord, what fools these mortals be!" observes Puck. But what a delightful foolishness it is. The world could use a lot more, even if, as the bard acknowledged, "The course of true love never did run smooth."

We could also, it seems to me, use a lot more of the Elizabethan worldview in our time. We live in such a dreadfully serious age. Their humor could deflate and democratize us all. We are specialists, they were universalists. They were sensuous, we are puritanical. They were extravagant, we are fastidious. They had high ideals of beauty, we settle for the mundane. They had a zest for life, we save for retirement. They learned from the classics, we are at the mercy of every new fad and wind up graduating computer illiterates. They led a slow-paced life that valued family and community, we live in a fast-paced, disposable culture in which the ephemeral is too often confused with the permanent. They lived with fairies, wizards, witches, ghosts, goblins and wood spirits. We live with Linnean taxonomy, tweezers and chloroform. Their world of nature was closer to the world of nature we experienced as children. We need to recover, if only partially, this older, saner view. Our relations to nature are so purposive and industrious, always seeking greater knowledge that can be translated into seductive new technologies and powers. This point of view quite often sets us apart from nature. There is certainly no universal panacea, and I would never want to resurrect the sentimental viewpoint, but I would argue for the personal, aesthetic experience of the Elizabethans over the objective and ratiocinative outlook of the modern age. We could, each of us, stand to get down on all fours occasionally and say, with Bottom:

> Let me play the lion, too. I will roar that I will do any man's heart good to hear me. I will roar that I will make the Duke say, "Let him roar again; let him roar again."

In fact, the world would probably be a much more peaceful place if we did, laughing at ourselves and at the beasts within us.

What is that awful racket coming from the backside of the hill? Sounds like a raven squawking. I take out my binoculars and scan the contours of the valley, where the head of a nameless arctic grayling stream dissolves into an amphitheater of wet grass springs and thick green alder hells. What's that? A bit of motion near that beaver pond just below. Looks like a wolverine, only smaller. It's a ... grizzly bear cub. I focus on the cub and then see two more cubs, scrambling from the patch of willows. And here comes the mother, emerging wearily from the bog of a nursery where they spent the day. Apparently the family has been napping in the cool wet shade, waiting for the insufferable heat to finally pass. Not too comfortable sunbathing when you're wearing a fur coat six inches thick. The mother is a beautiful animal, with sunbleached fur that is dark underneath and shimmers as she moves, vibrating as the wind on a forested mountainside causes the trees to shake ever so slightly. To her cubs, she is a mountain, the center of the universe, and they move around her accordingly. She stands motionless, still groggy from her dreams, and the cubs nose her belly, probing for those six mammaries full of milk. She swats the most persistent cub and the other two then gang up on that one as if to say "See, you made her mad. Now we won't get fed because of you." There is a great fold hanging from her chin—the "roach"—as if, recently taken from the kiln, she sagged slightly while cooling. This weighty feature tells me she is an older bear, as does the substantial heft to her shoulders, belly and hindquarters.

The Athabaskans call the grizzly *bik-ints-itldaadla,* a superstitious circumlocution meaning, literally, "Keep out of its way." Here I don't have much to worry about. The family is downhill and will remain there. Nothing to eat on this dry ridgetop. At least not until blueberry season. She moves off across the drainage, away from me, with the three cubs hungrily circling her like satellites around a sun. This is the bear mating season and she has chosen a safe minor drainage in which to hide, far from the major watercourses where the big males roam in search of females. The boars will kill the cubs as soon as they find them, and then wait a few days until the sow comes into heat again. Some sort of evolutionary advantage there. Male African lions do the same thing. Other than bears, she has no real enemies in this world, besides man, and since this is a national park, she is relatively free of the dangers and distractions Shakespeare wrote about:

I was with Hercules and Cadmus once
When in a wood of Crete they bay'd the bear
With hounds of Sparta. Never did I hear
Such gallant chiding; for besides the groves,
The skies, the fountains, every region near
Seem'd all one mutual cry. I never heard
So musical a discord, such sweet thunder.

By Shakespeare's time, the brown bears—genetically the same as a grizzly bear—were no longer found in England, although wolves still roamed Wales and Scotland, where they would not last much longer. Greece still has plenty of brown bears, much to the disgrace of Western Europe. I watch the bear until she passes out of sight, topping a distant ridge into a fresh drainage.

Not long after, to my everlasting surprise, a horse-drawn hay wagon rolls up the old dirt road from Moose Creek and discharges a dozen or so solstice celebrants on the shores of Wonder Lake. My god they are noisy. First the ritual fireworks are set off. Then someone turns on a cassette recorder. No Elizabethan lutes, triangles or dulcimers here. These folks are playing a rap song, M. C. Hammer's "Can't Touch This!" I focus my binoculars on the party and it appears they are enjoying themselves quite a bit more than I am. Now might be a good time to come down off the mountain and rejoin the human race. What's this? A young man in a wet suit is paddling a windsurfing board into the shallows. I guess he has volunteered to be the human sacrifice. He paddles about as far into the lake as you could cast a little gold Mepps spinner, stands up warily, steadies himself, turns to wave to a girl shouting something from the shore and then promptly falls over backward into the water, which is about ten degrees colder than a pitcher of water placed overnight in your refrigerator. Now *that* was a scream. Despite his agonies, everyone is getting into the water now, splashing each other and screaming in miserable delight. It's not too long before the happy, newly baptized revelers throw themselves into the bed of the wagon and the Belgian draft horses wearily lug their shivering human cargo back to the hot tubs at the wilderness lodge. At last peace returns to the land. Through all this, the mountain has

remained impassive, disinterested. That quality—disinterested-
ness—is what most distinguishes Shakespeare from the rest of the
guild. Shakespeare passed no judgments *per se*, he simply let people
speak and act for themselves. We are left to make our own decisions
about heartless Regan and haughty Macbeth and hapless Hamlet.
The Romantic poet John Keats—often cited as the most
"Shakespearean" poet since Shakespeare—used the phrase "nega-
tive capability" to describe this trait. The impersonal poet, he
wrote, "has no self—it is every thing and nothing—It has no
character ... It has as much delight in conceiving an Iago as an
Imogen." That is the way Denali looks tonight, cold and aloof, but
wholly attentive to what transpires in the thousands of square miles
it surveys, uplifts and empowers. I sense no judgments, only
comprehending awareness.

III

For all these many hours—it is nearly eleven now—the
mountain has not significantly changed. Although the shadows
between the North and South peaks have lengthened somewhat,
darkening the intervening abyss, and the foreground has gradually
receded into twilight, Denali has remained fully illuminated by the
sun, which is setting far toward the north. (The June sun sets in the
north near the poles because of the way the earth wobbles on its
axis.) Frankly, for the first four hours I was primarily distracted by
my immediate surroundings, but now, as the sunset approaches,
the mountain commands my full attention. As the angle of the
setting sun brings out more relief and more of the fine features of
the mountain, you begin to notice details. With my binoculars I
slowly ascend the precipitous scarred heights, traverse the cracked
icy ramparts, peer over the deadly cornices. I study closely where
glacial slabs have been shaken loose by earthquakes and where
huge avalanches have buried ancient snowfields and where the
inexorable forces of time and gravity have ripped entire chunks out
of the mountain. There is a canyon into which an entire Midwestern city could disappear and not far away is a wall of rock that would
dwarf the tallest building ever built by man. A lifetime could be

spent just studying the features of this mountain. Entire volumes could be written on just one rock formation, just one glacier, just one colony of red-colored algae living in the upper layer of a snowbank. Finally I have to put the binoculars aside and rub my eyes, as sore as those of an astronomer from squinting through the glass. Time to look at the whole mountain.

Because of the increasing obscurity of the lowlands, Denali at this hour begins to resemble a colossal island, with the green foothills towering over the dim lower terrain in the same way the steep headlands of an island plunge dramatically into the gray sea. The same clouds I described to you in the first five minutes of my stay here have now sunk with absorbed moisture and float off the headlands like enormous ships riding at quiet anchorage. From this hill I gaze up at the mountain as a man in a tiny boat might look up at a vast island from the momentary height of a passing wave, wondering where it is safe to put in and what sort of people live there and what language they speak. This is one piece of geography I will never explore. Denali is just too damned dangerous. Since 1913, when Reverend Hudson Stuck first climbed the South Peak—all his three-man party carried from their eleven-thousand-foot base camp was a thermos of coffee and some chocolate donuts—over sixty climbers have perished on the slopes. I think of the young man in Dave Roberts's book *The Mountain of My Fear*, who fell four thousand feet to his death in some rocky chasm where he remains buried to this day, and of the four Japanese climbers several years ago who were swept away by a sudden wind, one by one, and who tumbled a thousand feet into oblivion. No, I won't be climbing Denali in the near or distant future. Not with a son to raise. I climbed mountains earlier in my life, obscure walkups you've never heard of like Longs Peak and Pole Creek Mountain and Mount Audubon in Colorado, Elkhorn in Wyoming and Mogollon Baldy in New Mexico. Even the tallest of those five peaks—Longs—is only 14,255 feet high. That wouldn't reach Denali's brisket. No, I am content to sit here thirty miles away on this anonymous hill and just look at Denali, scaling those prodigious ridges with my number two pencil and drawing paper.

The light leaves my hill by degrees, slowly at first and then faster, like the light of a trail fire going out. As soon as the light is gone, the air becomes cool. The breeze now carries on it the clean, washed smell of snow and brings to mind memories of winter, of cross-country skis pushing trail through the birch groves and spruce grouse exploding from powder drifts and pulsing green northern lights overhead on the last run before turning home. It would be nice to build a fire, if there was any wood to burn. There isn't. So I put on my sweater, the torn red reindeer sweater that has kept me warm on so many hikes. The country is very still now. I can hear the quack, quack of the wood ducks and the wind in the willow patches and the lap of the water against the smooth stony shores of Wonder Lake. There is the buzz of an errant bumblebee at my feet and the hum of a stubborn mosquito, which I reflexively flatten on my drawing of Denali, forever staining the paper with the unmistakable color of my own blood. An enormous lake trout leaps from the middle of Wonder Lake and makes a resounding splash. Nearby a flock of trumpeter swans, unable to fly during the molt, paddle near some cattails with their young in tow. Each pair pretty much mates for life, like golden eagles, or subarctic wolves, or red foxes or rock ptarmigan. We all hope for that. A loon calls from somewhere on the lake, a wild haunting tremolo that sounds like the very essence of the lake made audible. The water goes still for a moment and Denali is reflected in the lake, without a ripple, as if there is a tear in the earth and I am glimpsing a hidden world beneath. Whoever believes that heaven is beyond the stars has never witnessed such a view.

At such a moment it is natural to consider your good fortune at being in such a place, to recall all those people trapped in cities, chained to work they hate, and to remember the family and friends you'd like to have beside you. I think, too, of those who cannot, will not ever be here, like Lynn Castle, who lost his life yesterday while flying his plane just north of the Yanert Glacier, or Billy Campbell, who died in his plane with his nephew Dominick along the Chena River last June. I consider how very lucky I am to be here, alive and in good health, with my family and friends in good health, and the planet in relative peace at the moment, and I say a prayer of thanks. Suddenly I notice, am truly aware of for the first time all evening, Mount Foraker, a 17,400-foot peak about ten or twelve miles to the west of Denali. Foraker, which sits at the head of the Foraker River, marks the gateway to the western reaches of the Alaska Range. Anywhere else in North America, Foraker would be honored with its own national park, but here the mountain is just a footnote to Denali. Beyond Foraker is a country few have traversed. I do not know one person who has been there, who has seen, from the ground, Herron River, and the Swift Fork River, and Heart Mountain, and the Tonzona River and Mystic Pass. All those places I've studied on the map. Many have flown over it, and some dogsled near that territory in the winter, but who has walked there in the summer, and seen what kind of land it is? Who can tell me about the caribou there, and the wolves, and how Denali looks at sunrise when viewed from the west, instead of the east and the north? Over an intervening ridge, I study what little of the wilderness beyond is visible. I know I must go there now. I make a promise to myself. Every day is precious. Especially the one you are living today. This moment.

Midnight now:

The iron tongue of midnight hath told twelve.
Lovers, to bed; 'tis almost fairy time.

It is the new day, but the sun has not yet gone down on the old day. The first yellow of the sunset has illuminated the North Face of Denali, the immense Wickersham Wall, named for Judge Wickersham, the exact significance of whose life I have no recollection. The mountain would be almost impossible to photograph now, with the intense light of the sun irradiating its every crevasse. Nineteen minutes into the new day, the light turns tangerine—the same color of the tangerines I sold from my stand in front of the house when I was a boy—and then the light shifts to orange, a natural citrus orange like those you pick right off the branch in southern California. The atmosphere is scattering all those weaker blue, green and yellow wavelengths now, and only the high-energy oranges and reds are getting through. The top of Denali may be orange, but near the base a line of faint red is working its way upward. How remarkable it is to see the electromagnetic spectrum displayed on a mountain that is nearly four miles high. Hard to believe that nine minutes ago this light was not light at all but plasma, the fourth state of matter, burning ferociously on the surface of the sun. Here is the elementary energy from which all matter and life and culture arise, from which civilizations are made and into which they are returned. Here is the infinite made visible, exploding red giants and drifting interstellar clouds and hot new stars, colliding particles and congealing worlds and brave new life in the warm intertidal pools where the waves come crashing down. Here is the beginning and the end.

The moon, at last, is very near the east ridge of Denali and is sinking fast through the clouds, like the freshly laid egg of a trumpeter swan in the thick white feathers of a nest in the reeds. I watch the moon until it is gone—how fast it vanishes (how fast the earth turns). The mountains on the moon, I think, are not so lovely as this mountain. At twelve-thirty the land and lake are very quiet, like parents holding their breaths as they wait for a fussy baby to fall asleep. The breeze is still and there is not a sound. Only the top third of Denali is light and the orange has a drop of red stirred into it. Beneath the orange is a band of pink and then a bar of red. Six minutes later a pink ray flushes across the summit—the color of a spawning salmon as it dies in the shallows—that gradually deepens to red. By ten minutes to one only the very top of Denali is red—the venerated summit where successful climbers pose for pictures a few minutes before descending—and that red is fading fast. Twelve minutes later, at two minutes after one in the morning, the light is totally gone from the mountain. Suddenly I feel very tired:

> *Are you sure*
> *That we are awake? It seems to me*
> *That yet we sleep, we dream.*

A boreal owl calls to me from the edge of the high spruce forest, and I turn to gather my day pack and walking stick. The grade is steep and I grasp the alpine willow branches tightly with my free hand to avoid slipping down the slope, as a child still learning to walk holds his mother's hand. I stop halfway for one last look. Just when I was certain the spectacle could not be surpassed, something unexpected has occurred. In the afterglow, with the heavens fading through all the hues of pink and purple and blue and the lowlands sinking deeper into shadow, the mountain has become even more resplendent. The snowy bulk is luminous with the soft colors of the arctic evening, all those lavenders and lilacs, violets and blues, and resembles a giant piece of fluorite glowing beneath a fluorescent lamp. I am not worthy of such beauty. Consider this. Each night I read to my infant son before he goes to sleep. For a long time, as I read him stories of bears and bumblebees, birch trees and butterflies, he is wide awake and there is that lively twinkle in his eyes and that quick smile each time he sees me smile. And then gradually his eyelids become heavy and his head nods and he falls asleep. I turn at the nursery door and, just before the lights go off, see that he is even more beautiful now, at rest, than when awake, with his face relaxed, his eyes closed, his little hands at rest over his heart, asleep in gentle dreams. The mountain is most beautiful when it dreams.

> Puck: *If we shadows have offended*
> *Think but this, and all is mended,*
> *That you have slumbered here*
> *While these visions did appear.*
> *And this weak and idle theme*
> *No more unyielding but a dream.*